Arthur G. Donahue

High School Graduation
Age 17   June 1930

Battle-tested RAF Pilot Officers
Age 27   November, 1940

Combat Veteran, Flt.Lt, DFC
Age 29   August, 1942

A LIFE NOT LONG BUT WIDE:

Memoirs of a Yankee in the Royal Air Force

By

Flight Lieutenant Arthur G. Donahue, DFC, RAF

and

Colonel Kenneth L. Weber, USAF (Ret.)

Published by

Mach 25 Press

1911 Southern Hills Drive

Borden, IN 47106. USA

www.mach25press.com

ISBN: 978-0-9819136-1-2

Library of Congress Control Number: 2010935533

Printed in USA

DEDICATION

To the memory of Robert F. Donahue, Art's older brother, confidant, and literary agent. Bob's life story in musical theater and in the development of east-coast broadcast radio easily justify his own biography. Bob highlighted the closeness of the Donahue family and the demands of maintaining a large dairy farm. He gave me complete access to Art's voluminous correspondence, RAF personnel file, his log book, and newspaper clippings that covered his brother's accomplishments. Bob became my dear friend and I was able to provide him with a complete manuscript before his death.

CONTENTS

Preface

CHAPTER	PAGE
1. Minnesota Farm Boy	1
2. Pawns on the Chessboard	11
3. Narrow Squeak—No Game	25
4. Baptism by Fire	37
5. Barnstorming	49
6. Time Out	63
7. Convalescence	77
8. Eagle Squadron	91
9. Back to Work	103
10. Interlude	117
11. Ferry Pilot	129
12. Channel Watch	141
13. Toward the Unknown	153
14. Fortunes of War	169
15. Long Road to Singapore	179
16. At the Front	189
17. Shade-tree Mechanic	205
18. Into the Fight	215

CHAPTER	PAGE
19. Last Flight from Singapore	227
20. Out of the Frying Pan	245
21. Into the Fire	251
22. Last Flight from Sumatra	263
23. Million-Dollar Wound	277
24. Passage to India	285
25. Respite	293
26. Once More Again to England	303
27. Goodbye to All That	311
28. Epilogue	317
Order of Battle	
British Aircraft	334
German Aircraft	335
Japanese Aircraft	337

PREFACE

This is the story of an obscure American aviator who, at the age of twenty-seven, volunteered to fly with Britain's Royal Air Force (RAF) in what he and Winston Churchill agreed was a battle to save Christian civilization. In the cockpit of a Spitfire fighter, Arthur Gerald Donahue became the first of only seven American volunteers to experience combat in what was to become known as the Battle of Britain. He went on to live the fantasy of thousands of young men and boys, and in the midst of war, write and have published two bestselling books—*Tally Ho! Yankee in a Spitfire* and *Last Flight from Singapore.*

I was one of those who vicariously accompanied Art as he destroyed Messerschmitt fighters, parachuted from a burning cockpit, and later threw his Hawker Hurricane into mass formations of Japanese aircraft attacking Singapore and Sumatra.

As a teenager I not only experienced the thrill of adventure, but also encountered the emotions, challenges, and sacrifices that shape a person's development. My guide was a modest, unassuming spirit with a genius-level IQ who made friends easily and seemed to touch, and be touched by, everyone he met and everything he saw.

My subsequent career as a military aviator had certain parallels with Art's. When I re-read his books as an adult, I felt that I was again seeing events through his eyes. As a result, Art's spirit and I have teamed to tell his story in the first person using many passages from his letters and books. I've labored under one constraint which proved never to be a hindrance: the admonition of John A. Campbell, Art's friend and squadron mate, that no one had license to write "anything bad about Art Donahue."

I thank those of Art's friends, associates, and admirers who helped over the last twenty years in the creation of this story. Each supported my original supposition that Art Donahue is a unique personality who should never be forgotten.

Mr. Lyle A. Harrison, currently of La Crescent, Minnesota, is the person most responsible for keeping Arthur Gerald Donahue's memory alive since 1983. Having established the Donahue Memorial Education Fund, he has worked tirelessly to see that the student body of St. Charles' public high school know and appreciate the accomplishments of its most famous graduate. His goal is to fund scholarships for deserving students who best exemplify the character traits and selfless devotion to the ideals of liberty and freedom for which Art Donahue gave his life.

On a personal level, I must acknowledge Lyle's guidance when I first began to delve into Art's background. He put me in touch with Bob Donahue, guided my research in St. Charles, and introduced me to many of Art's schoolmates and associates. Lyle is one of the few persons I can describe as being dedicated to assisting others. Among his many projects, he has donated Art Donahue books and memorabilia to the air museum at Oshkosh, Wisconsin, the St. Charles, Minnesota library, and the St. Charles High School. I owe him a debt that cannot be repaid.

I must also acknowledge the invaluable encouragement, guidance, and assistance given me by my wife of 58 years, Mary Katherine, and daughter, Sharon Kay, my project manager who was responsible for all formatting, and production matters. My daughter, Maria Worthington, designed marketing initiatives. All are passionate about resurrecting the story of this most heroic American.

Los Angeles artist, Dwayne Vance, produced the cover illustration and a subsequent fine art print of Donahue's beloved "Message from Minnesota" departing on the morning's "dawn patrol" reconnaissance.

KLW
Borden, Indiana, USA

Fear not: for I have redeemed thee,

I have called thee by thy name; thou art mine,

When thou passest through the waters,

I will be with thee . . .

Isaiah 43:1, 2

Chapter One

Minnesota Farm Boy

I never considered myself a prophet, but once I told my brother that I suspected my life might not be long, but it would be wide. My name is Arthur Gerald Donahue, but most people know me as "Art." Prophet or not, I've always known good from evil. That's the reason I found myself at five hundred feet in a Spitfire fighter near Ostende, Belgium, just after first light on September eleventh, 1942, trolling with my undercarriage and flaps hanging and the hairs on the back of my neck telling me that a German night fighter was jockeying to intercept me.

If my scheme worked, I'd soon have a go at the Hun who'd shadowed "Bud" Young's most recent dawn patrol. We in the RAF—Royal Air Force—had a quaint policy: the leader belonged at the "sharp end," the point of action. Since I was acting commander of Number 91 Squadron, I'd retraced Bud's flight path, laying a trap for the assassin rather than performing the usual shipping reconnaissance. With eyes scanning the ragged cloud base above me, I expected at any moment to see my quarry materialize. I knew I held the high cards: I was the experienced veteran, I knew the enemy's intentions, and I knew he was mine.

Like an actor on cue, the mottled-gray Junkers 88C popped out of the cloud curtain, its massive twin Jumo engines hugging a nose cone bristling with antennas feeding my image back to a *Lichtenstein* airborne radar. *Time to go to work,* I thought as I eased the throttle open, manipulated the undercarriage lever upward into its notch, and then flipped the disk on the instrument panel that raised the flaps. Turning and accelerating, I closed with my antagonist. *Gunsight on; arming ring to "fire." He's wise to me, sees my turn, starts to dive away. Too late my friend. Here's a little message from Minnesota!*

The two 20mm Hispano cannon and four Browning machine guns sounded terribly capable. I saw my explosive bullets converge on his left engine: sparks flew, flame erupted. Nudging my right rudder pedal, I forced the stream of lead into the greenhouse where pilot and rear gunner hunched. Orange tracers leapt out at me. I felt a single impact up front somewhere near the glycol tank.

But I'm getting ahead of myself. My story really began in St. Charles, Minnesota, where my family operated a 200-acre farm and dairy. Dad bore the brunt of the field labor, while Mother took care of everything else. When brother Bob and I were little, our youngest sister, Ora, looked after us while Dorothea and Blanche did chores which included driving the horse-drawn dairy wagon on the route each weekday before school.

Later, Bob, who was six years older than I, had to do a man's work from the time he turned twelve or thirteen.

2

During winter his day began about 5:30, so that he could feed the livestock, help milk twenty-five to thirty cows, eat breakfast, change clothes, and get to school by half-past eight. Afterwards, chores or field work, supper, feeding, and evening milking rounded out the day. During summer, field chores from eight in the morning until dusk augmented the usual routine. I followed in his footsteps, but new equipment and milking machines powered by a gasoline engine allowed me time to edit the school newspaper, act with the drama club, sing bass in the quartet, and hone my skills on the debate team.

The St. Charles public school system educated me to transcribe accurately what I saw, and the exploits of daredevil pilots made me want to see it all. At the age of fourteen, I especially gloried in the triumph of Charles Lindbergh, a fellow Minnesotan whose youthful chores, feeding and milking a dairy herd and tending Duroc Jersey hogs, paralleled my own. His solo flight to Paris in 1927 inspired a decade of record-breaking feats, technical innovations, and legislative acts that ignited an explosive growth in aviation. Sometime during all of the excitement, the flying bug not only bit me but also burrowed deep beneath my skin never to be excised.

Because of that bite, life really began for me not on my birth date of the nineteenth of March 1913 but rather on Friday, the twenty-seventh of September 1931, when Max Conrad and I lifted off the airfield at Winona, Minnesota, in his big cabin plane. We entered the clouds at twenty-five hundred feet and broke out between layers at six thousand. Three layers were above us, but they were scattering, and the sun shone through on those below. I felt like a ground-hog that had poked his head out of the hole he'd occupied

3

for eighteen years, saw the serene beauty of the sky, and was instantly transformed into an eagle.

I realize now that I was fortunate to have had a kind-hearted, sympathetic soul to teach me flying. I don't ever remember Max yelling at me, or tricking me, or shaking my emerging confidence. One of my high school classmates, Glen Alleman, said he thought I almost worshiped Max Conrad. No "almost" about it.

All of us who trained under Max at Winona felt the same way. He'd take on boys who wanted to learn to fly, and he'd teach us regardless of whether we had the money. If others, like me, were penniless, he'd give us jobs around the airport, use us as line boys or mechanics, and ultimately employ us as barnstormers and fully qualified charter pilots. We never forgot him. When a fire destroyed his uninsured hangar and all but one of his airplanes in January 1942, his wife put out the word among his former students, many of whom were airline captains or otherwise successful pilots. Their contributions made up the $125,000 needed to refinance the flying school. After the Second World War, Max stepped into the national limelight as "The Flying Grandfather" who delivered Piper single and twin-engine light planes throughout the world. He deserved his own book, and Sally Buegeleisen gave it to him when she wrote *Into the Wind,* which Random House published in 1973.

Max allowed me to sleep in his hangar and paid for my meals in a boarding house across the street in exchange for my opening the hangar each morning, helping to overhaul engines, and running the gas station. A month after my arrival, having just over five hours of instruction, I became the ninety-sixth student soloed by Max Conrad.

About this same time, he brought a battered Remington over from his Rochester branch since I'd told him I could type. Immediately I started doing all the company's mail in addition to my own letters home, public relations pieces for *The Winona Republican Herald* telling about the increasing amount of traffic at the airport, and submissions to publications such as *Western Flying Magazine*. None of my creative writing efforts were ever accepted, but it wasn't from my lack of trying.

On the seventeenth of December 1931, the twenty-eighth anniversary of the Wright Brothers' first flight, I took both my written and flight tests seeking to become a private pilot. A veteran of the First World War, F. H. Longeway, was my inspector and he tried to intimidate me with a gruff demeanor and contradictory instructions for my flight test, which he would observe from the ground.

"Go to a thousand feet," he said, "get right over the field, and do three shallow figure eights and three steep ones. But now don't go up and do half a dozen eights." I concluded that he meant for me to do one or two of each kind to show that I knew how to do them and then imagine the rest instead of wasting time.

"Well, that was all right, young fellow," he said as he filled out the "Letter of Authority" that would allow me to operate until the formal license could be mailed from Washington. The next day or two I got my first chance at stunt flying, including tailspins. I was lucky because Max subsequently eliminated intentional spins from his training program after a student almost augered into the ground. The instruction was invaluable especially when I transitioned so quickly from cabin monoplanes and trainers into front-line fighters.

5

In a letter home explaining the principles of recovering from a spin, complete with a diagram of an airfoil, I emphasized that practically no danger existed if one "just keeps his head and makes reason triumph over instinct." Had I stayed in commercial aviation, that might have been enough to stake a career upon. But in war I realized that frequently there wasn't any reason, and oftentimes instinct made the difference.

After their senior class picnic, Art's friends financed his first flight with Max Conrad. (Left to right) Frank M. Butler, Lyle F. Patterson, Arthur G. Donahue, Mert E. Hemming, John N. Pike, Kenneth G. Smith, and Frank B. Harcey. Photo courtesy of Lyle F. Patterson.

Art, his Mother, and niece Mary Saul. August, 1934.

Art Donahue at left, unidentified friend (possibly co-owner of aircraft), 5-year old nephew Robert "Bobby" Donahue, Jr. and Art's brother Bob. Art frequently flew passenger hops from this field adjacent to the family farm. In August, 1934, Art gave Bob and Bobby their first flight. Bob didn't care for it, but Bobby later made aviation his career.

7

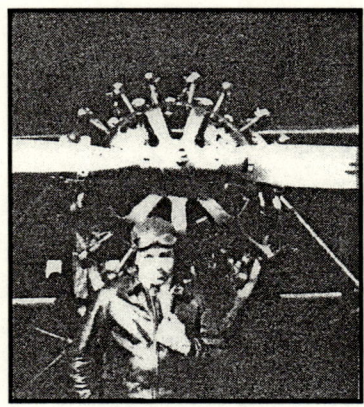

Art wearing his new leather flying jacket bought in Chicago at a discounted price of $7.85. February 7, 1934.

Art's barnstorming Parks P-1, designed and built at Parks Air College in 1929.

Art as Instructor-Pilot. Photo most probably taken at Municipal Airport in Laredo, Texas. Mid-1940.

Chapter Two

Pawns on the Chessboard

As war clouds brewed over Europe, instinct caused me to throw in with a shadowy group organized by Colonel Charles Sweeny, an American soldier of fortune, about whom I'd heard while instructing in Laredo, Texas, during the spring of 1940. Sweeny, operating on the jagged edge of neutrality laws and presidential proclamations, seemingly offered a chance at a Royal Air Force commission and a fighter's cockpit. Since my year-long attempt to join our Army Air Corps had come to naught because I lacked two years of college, he offered my only hope of doing what my heart and mind told me was my destiny.

I arranged for an interview with the Sweeny people in Chicago, quit my job, and went home to St. Charles for a week with my folks. Once there I spent much of my time guiding the corn cultivator back and forth contemplating my move from low-powered, fixed-geared, fabric-covered puddle-jumpers to Spitfire fighters with thousand-horse-power engines, retractable wheels, wing flaps, and

Browning machine guns. How to prepare my family for what could well be the consequence of my folly also weighed on my mind.

On Monday, the twenty-fourth of June, two days after France surrendered to the Germans thereby leaving the British without an ally, I interviewed in Chicago, became a "Sweeny Candidate," and got the go-ahead for step two, a meeting with Royal Canadian Air Force people in Windsor, Ontario. Two other fellows and I drove to Detroit, arriving on the twenty-sixth in time to cross the border to take our physicals. Shock waves from France's capitulation still reverberated through the building, and it was a somber board of officers who interviewed us. Wasting no time in idle chit-chat, they cleared two of us to proceed to Ottawa for step three. Lacking the three-hundred hours of flying experience which now seemed the minimum for potential fighter pilots, Bob Jackson was recommended only for instructor duties in Canada.

In Ottawa on the first of July, I submitted to a flight check in a twin-engine "Hudson" bomber made in the USA, outfitted in RAF livery, and loaded with everything but bombs. A derivative of Amelia Earhart's ill-starred Lockheed 10-E "Electra," it was one of two hundred the British had purchased from the United States, each at a cost of seventeen thousand pounds—roughly eighty-five thousand dollars. At the same time, they had ordered two hundred North American single-engine "Texan" trainers, which they subsequently christened "Harvards."

Hitler's seizing of Austria in 1938 had caused the British immediately to dispatch a purchasing committee to the States to see what was available for quick delivery. Hard times had decimated our aircraft industry, but those

12

companies remaining clearly heard opportunity knocking. They also knew the cupboard was bare. In forty-eight hours, however, engineers at Lockheed's Burbank plant cobbled together a full-scale mock-up of a reconnaissance bomber based on their Super Electra. Impressed, the British ordered the first increment of an eventual production run of two thousand. I was to see more of the venerable Hudson during a life-or-death struggle with an enemy I didn't even know existed in midsummer 1940.

Although I'd never flown anything nearly as sophisticated as the sleek bomber, I must have put on a pretty good show because right after landing an officer outlined the deal. In exchange for my services for the war's duration, they'd commission me in the RAF's Volunteer Reserve, provide first-class passage to Liverpool, train me on Spitfires, and post me to a front-line squadron. In light of the obstacles I'd experienced petitioning my own army, I found the lack of red tape astonishing. I'd shown I had the goods: eighteen hundred and twenty flying hours, an Air Transport Rating, and an engine mechanic's license. They said in effect, "All right. We'll buy. Sign here and you can start delivering."

I assumed I'd lose my citizenship even though I had only to swear to obey superior officers, not to give allegiance to the King. But any price was okay with me if I could be one of those whose skill and devotion Prime Minister Winston Churchill expected would defend "the cause of civilization itself."

Unbeknownst to me the British Air Council had decided to form an all-American "Eagle" Squadron within the RAF if Sweeny provided twenty-five pilots and a like number of alternates. I was to be one of their first boys, but

I'd join a regular squadron until the Eagle structure was in place.

My handlers told me I'd sail from Montreal on the seventh of July wearing civilian clothes and posing as a technician who'd assemble and test American-made aircraft shipped from Canada. That's the tale I wrote to my family along with great assurances that I'd have nothing to do with active hostilities. I collected British money for expenses aboard ship, a ticket for the morning train to Montreal, and a sealed envelope to be opened once the *SS Duchess of Atholl* weighed anchor. The plan unfolded as advertised: the envelope contained my commission, enormously beautiful icebergs punctuated our voyage, and seven days later an RAF officer drove me from dockside to the station where I boarded the midnight train to London.

After more paperwork at the Air Ministry, I had two days to procure my uniform, learn to salute, and orient myself before reporting on the eighteenth to the Fifth OTU—Operational Training Unit—at Aston Down, Chalford, Gloucestershire. Traveling by train during daylight for the first time, I found the landscape surprisingly like that of southern Minnesota—rolling country, very green, with lots of small pastures and a great deal of woodland. At my school I met many Polish pilots and a few Belgians who were also undergoing training. Most of them had fought the Hun already. They were cheerful, happy-go-lucky fellows except when the subject of Nazis came up.

The airdrome itself contrasted sharply with those I was familiar with. At home we did everything possible to make an airport easy to find. We placed bright markings on hangars, laid out conspicuous runways, and painted big arrows pointing toward the field on the tops of buildings for the convenience of transient pilots. Aston Down, on the other hand, didn't welcome uninvited guests, and everything had been done to hide the airdrome. Hangars, shops, offices, and even vehicles and roads were painted in wavy combinations of dull greens, grays, browns, and black, so designed that seen at altitude the airdrome merged with the countryside.

The day following my arrival, I flew three flights in two different types of trainers: ten minutes with an instructor and twenty minutes solo in a US-built Harvard followed by an hour in a Miles "Modified Master," one of a number of two-seat trainers converted to a single-seat configuration and fitted with six Browning machine guns as a last-ditch invasion fighter. Before I left the States, I had never flown anything that cruised faster than a hundred and ten miles per hour. The Master cruised at one hundred eighty; had flying characteristics similar to the Hurricane and Spitfire, and I thought it more wonderful than anything I'd ever imagined. I practiced on it for a few days and then was told I might go on to flying Spitfires.

That was the very height of my hopes! Supermarine Spitfires were considered to be the masters of all the world's fighters, and the pilots assigned to fly them considered themselves the luckiest of aviators. The "Spit," as we affectionately called her, was the outgrowth of designer Reginald J. Mitchell's fantastically capable racing seaplanes which allowed England to retire the Schneider Trophy from international competition in 1931. The Spitfire Mark I was a single-seat, low-wing monoplane fitted with a twelve-cylinder Rolls-Royce "Merlin" engine (named for the pigeon hawk, not King Arthur's magician) of a thousand sixty horsepower with an "emergency boost"

15

giving nearly fourteen hundred horsepower for actual combat. Cruising at two hundred eighty miles per hour, the machine did three hundred sixty-four flat-out. The speed differential between it and the forty-horsepower kites I had instructed in for the previous year and a half was such that no connection seemed to exist between the fighter and my former flying experience.

Each Spitfire had eight machine guns mounted in the wings which the pilot fired by depressing a single button on the top of his control stick. Dull green and brown camouflage paint enveloped the aircraft except for the national insignia, the white identification letters which flanked it on the fuselage sides, and the entire underside which was gray. Its wings were wide and tapered in such a way that they resembled those of a giant moth.

The only detriment to my complete happiness was knowing I'd set up my folks for tragedy if something untoward happened. Like my father, I had prided myself upon being a dutiful son. Yet, as I explained in a letter home after my cover was blown, the chance to play my part in the course of history and the opportunity to help resist the invasion on which I believed the whole future of the United States probably depended outweighed whatever sacrifice the risk entailed.

Shortly after arriving at the OTU, I met Squadron Leader Aeneas Ranald Donald MacDonell, the Hereditary Twenty-second Chief of Glengarry and a veteran fighter pilot who needed only the briefest introduction to the Spitfire before dashing off to command Number 64 Squadron. He was slender, with fine wavy hair, a mustache, and piercing blue eyes. I seldom remember the color of a person's eyes, but I couldn't forget his. He fairly radiated strength of character and will power. As we were close to the same age, shared an interest in piano accordions, and yearned for a crack at the barbarians, we seemed instantly bound by mutual respect—even the first vestiges of friendship. When it came time to request assignment, my flying mate (Peter Kennard-Davis) and I chose 64 Squadron and its impressive commander.

Speaking of friendships, I must enlighten you about Peter. He was a big dark-haired husky fellow. We took to each other as soon as we met. He had been in the Navy at sixteen, and at twenty he was bronzed and hardened and looked and acted several years older. We made a pact that, if we survived, he'd return to the United States with me. Peter became one of my closest friends even though we'd met scarcely a fortnight previously. We were of differing nationalities; I was seven years older; he was tall and dark whereas I was short (five feet two inches) and blond. Nevertheless, we had the same motive; we had tamed, if by no means mastered, the world's premier fighter aircraft; and we both realized that our chances of living out our old age in America were problematical.

Kenley Airdrome, home station for 64 Squadron, was a first-class facility ideally located some ten miles south-southeast of London. It boasted two concrete runways and twelve dispersal pens, each capable of protecting three aircraft. Britannia's situation at this time was absolutely critical. She stood alone against Hitler who, in two astounding years, had annexed Austria, occupied Czechoslovakia, successfully invaded Poland, Norway, and Denmark, and overrun the Netherlands, Belgium, Luxembourg, and France. Only a month previous to my arrival in Liverpool, a make-shift fleet of 848 vessels, plying between the French port of Dunkirk and England, had snatched some 338,000 encircled British and allied soldiers from the merciless bombing and strafing of the German *Luftwaffe*.

The press of time, lack of sufficient sea transport, and constant air attack had forced the evacuees to abandon all of their heavy equipment and stores, so that afterward the British army faced the threat of invasion almost devoid of artillery and vehicles. Only the English Channel, the Royal Navy, and forty-seven Royal Air Force Hurricane and Spitfire fighter squadrons stood in the way of Nazi domination of both Europe and the British Isles.

Although I had never done any previous military flying, I believed I could adapt if I were allowed time to overcome the handicap of being a novice matched against experts. In welcoming us to 64 Squadron, Donald MacDonell said we Spitfire pilots would most often engage escorting German fighters, leaving the bombers to our Hurricanes—highly maneuverable machines looking somewhat like humpbacked Spitfires. Armed with eight machine guns and capable of sustaining an unusual degree of battle damage without faltering, the Hurricane suffered from a speed deficiency some thirty-six miles per hour slower than our mutual nemesis, the sleek Messerschmitt single-seat fighter designated Me 109.

MacDonell allowed as how each of our squadrons could anticipate facing odds averaging ten to one but stressed the Spitfire's edge in turn radius over the 109, which matched or exceeded our top speed at 19,000 feet and was more heavily armed with twin 20mm Oerlikon cannon and two 7.9mm machine guns versus our eight .303-inch (7.7mm) Brownings. Our guns were rifle-caliber weapons inefficient against enemy aircraft with armor protection and self-sealing fuel tanks. Winding up his summary of aircraft characteristics, he warned us of the 109's fuel-injected Daimler-Benz engine that didn't momentarily cut out when the pilot pulled negative Gs as did the carburetor-aspirated Merlin engines installed in early model Hurricanes and Spitfires.

Absorbing novice aviators into his unit gave Squadron Leader MacDonell a formidable task not demanded of his German counterparts whose replacements during the battle were fully qualified. Apprentice RAF fighter pilots (such as Lewis Isaac, Peter, and myself) possessing no battle experience joined front-line squadrons directly from training units. Most had in the neighborhood of three hundred total hours in the air and something over twenty hours of fighter indoctrination. My twenty hours and fifty minutes in the Spitfire was enhanced by more than eighteen hundred hours of flying experience. So I, unlike most replacements, had "air sense"—proficiency in instrument flying, familiarity with all types of weather, and a keen awareness of direction and timing. I lacked, as did they, gunnery proficiency, knowledge of fighter tactics, and a killer's instinct.

We were the pawns used to fill the chessboard. We guaranteed that the *Luftwaffe* encountered full-strength fighter squadrons regardless of the state of readiness of individual pilots. MacDonell knew this. Trying to assure the survival of his "sprongs," he gave us as much experience of attack and evasion as possible in order that we could live through our first ten or so sorties and learn survival. In my case he may have given me more than ordinary attention. If he did so, it was unconscious. But as I've said, a bond existed between us: something that develops between men only in periods of high anxiety where the odds for survival are minimal. It's a trust that eases, and sometimes transcends, the warrior's pain.

Sixty-four Squadron itself seemed to have been made for me. Its motto, *Tenax Propositi* (Firm of Purpose), was from Horace and summed up my feelings about the adventure that lay ahead. Knowing that the squadron badge featured the scarab (a sacred beetle in ancient Egyptian religious practices, a lucky charm for centuries, and a symbol of eternal life) caused me to entertain a secret feeling that all would be well and, if it wasn't, I would still be transported to Valhalla.

The squadron was an old-line, Royal Flying Corps unit formed in 1916 before the Royal Air Force became a separate service. It had flown DeHavilland ground attack aircraft and S.E. 5a fighters in France before deactivation in 1919. Reformed in 1936 as a two-seater fighter squadron stationed in Egypt, it returned to Britain in August of that same year.

In May 1940, scarcely a month after being equipped with Spitfires, it had been thrown into the battle to protect the Dunkirk evacuation. There, for the first time, German crews had to fight a modern, determined air force. Both the *Luftwaffe* and the RAF suffered grievous losses. Over the nine-day period, the Huns lost some two hundred aircraft and more than three hundred air crew members. Fighter Command alone—not including Bomber Command and Coastal Command—lost ninety-eight Hurricanes and Spitfires along with eighty pilots. These were machines and men critically needed to meet the anticipated invasion of Britain.

Sixty-four's commander and two other pilots had died in one swirling dogfight and, by the end of the operation, the squadron had seen half its complement killed or wounded. Subtracting from Fighter Command's assigned strength its Dunkirk casualties and those previously suffered attempting to bolster the French—a total of 435 experienced pilots—one realized that the remaining pool of 1,094 pilots was 362 below the number authorized. Moreover the ranks of topnotch squadron and flight commanders had suffered disproportionately, so that a crop of new leaders had immediately to assert itself.

Assessing his most recent replacements, MacDonell was particularly concerned that my short stature would prevent my seeing the entire battle panorama from my cockpit. Nevertheless, he took me literally "under his wing" by assigning me to fly tucked in just beneath his left-hand mainplane as the third member of his three-ship section.

Regarding our daily schedule, the C.O. (Commanding Officer) told us the squadron's aircraft would depart Kenley airdrome either early each morning or around mid-afternoon for our advance base at Hawkinge, located just inland from Dover. There we'd be "on readiness," prepared for take-off within five minutes of warning. Moving to the intricacies of combat tactics, he briefed our techniques in matter-of-fact tones that initiated us into the detached, impersonal, and unemotional attitude that fighter pilots quickly develop toward the taking—and losing—of human life.

Despite having been battered by a battle-hardened, more flexible *Luftwaffe* during the initial German blitzkrieg and subsequent Dunkirk evacuation, Fighter Command still insisted that its pilots fly in uniforms complete with collars and ties that chafed the neck and restricted the head's constant scanning for the enemy. Moreover squadrons were expected to adhere to an awkward formation composed of four groupings of three-ship, triangular-shaped "vics" flying line astern. The Germans derisively called this air-show arrangement a "bunch of bananas." Holding position in such a tight formation required a pilot's constant attention, leaving only the leader relatively free to search for prey or scan for attacking fighters. In six or twelve-ship formations, most often a single plane trailed the others acting as watchdog. As one might surmise, this "weaver" was usually one of the most recent, least experienced replacements, and his life expectancy was often short.

The Germans, on the other hand, flew in the "finger-four," a grouping of two pairs of fighters generally abeam of each other much as the tips of the fingers appear on one's outstretched hand. This arrangement could fight as a unit or split into two independent pairs, the leaders of which would always have a wingman to protect their rear. The *Luftwaffe* had perfected this arrangement during the Spanish Civil War, and it's still the formation preferred by the world's air forces.

Whereas the Germans had devised tactics and sharpened their combat skills fighting on the victorious fascist side in Spain between 1936 and 1939, Air Chief Marshal Hugh Dowding, Air Officer Commanding Fighter Command, used that time to perfect the warning and control system he believed would save Britain. The Germans also had radar devices to locate and track aircraft, but their tacticians lacked Dowding's vision, which linked attack warning with a command and control network that alerted, launched, and positioned fighters for interception.

Dowding was an intelligent, scientifically oriented decision maker who had fought to achieve a viable air defense scheme. By appointing a kindred soul, Air Vice-Marshal Keith Park to command his critically important Eleven Group, he picked an officer who used his fighters sparingly in order to break up bomber formations before committing the balance of his force against the disrupted attackers.

Dowding's opponent, *Reichmarshal* Hermann Goering, *Luftwaffe* Commander-In-Chief and decorated fighter ace of the First World War, was a rabid Nazi whom Hitler had also named Deputy *Fuehrer* and Air Minister. A complex personality with a penchant for grandiose uniforms and rich food—along with a drug habit resulting from treatment for a gunshot wound received during a confrontation with police in Munich—Goering exhibited unpredictable mood swings ranging from genial to dictatorial. Having promised Hitler that his air force alone could subdue England, he initially and correctly targeted Fighter Command's airdromes and the tall transmitting and receiving towers that constituted its radar eyes.

Chapter Three

Narrow Squeak—No Game

I remember especially the first time I took off with the squadron to fly down to Hawkinge for the morning readiness. August 5, 1940, two days after my arrival in 64 Squadron was indeed to be etched deeply in memory. When I arrived at my aircraft, I found a mechanic already in the cockpit working the engine's primer and another standing beside the "trolley-ack," the battery cart used for starting. The man inside engaged the starter to bring the big Merlin coughing to life, stabilized its idle, and climbed out to allow me to squeeze into the cockpit. Then he leaned inside to give me a hand fastening my parachute straps, securing the seat belt and shoulder harness, and connecting my headset and oxygen leads.

After checking the engine instruments, giving particular attention to the coolant temperature, I pulled on my helmet, cinched its chin strap, and snapped the attached oxygen mask across my face. Then I slipped my fingers into my gloves, signaled away the chocks, released the brakes, and taxied out to swing to the left and rear of where MacDonell had paused. He exchanged thumbs-up signals with Percy on his right and with me; then I saw a faint puff of smoke streaking back from his exhaust stacks, and though I could scarcely hear the engine because of my padded helmet, I saw his idling propeller become invisible and his machine begin to move. I opened my throttle and felt the tremendous surge of power. At the same time, I punched a button that energized my radio receiver and another that started a time-recording attachment on the clock in my instrument panel. I remember wondering how I'd do all of that during a scramble and still get airborne in two to three minutes!

As I dashed across the rough sod, the tailplane rose of itself into the take-off attitude, and soon I felt an indescribable lightness on the undercarriage as my Spitfire lifted off. Switching hands on the control column's spade-shaped grip, I reached down with my right hand to begin the ticklish business of raising the wheels while attempting to maintain position on my leader. First I disengaged the landing gear lever from the "down" position, then moved it to the "up" detent, and finally began manually cycling the hydraulic pump handle. A quick tap on the brake lever mounted on the control column stopped the wheels' rotation before they tucked themselves into their wells.

Sliding into formation on the C.O., I throttled back, set the propeller control lever for the climb, and concentrated on holding tightly to the leader while remembering his instructions: "If you see a Hun, stay in position until I call the 'Tally-Ho!' Then you can break formation and pick your targets."

In the argot of the time, all this was bloody disconcerting to a flyer who had been taught to do even his barnstorming in a slow and methodical way. It was nothing like the time I leisurely taxied out to the east end of Dad's south pasture after having given my brother his first airplane ride. Must have been 1934, Bob's first trip back since leaving to seek his fortune. I remember heading into the wind for a quick magneto check even as random thoughts coalesced into a deep feeling that I might be cutting it too close. *Just a short hop,* I thought. *Less than twenty-five minutes to Winona. Weather's good. Plenty of daylight left. Lots of fields to take a biplane if the engine quits.* But Max was in my head reminding me that transport pilots didn't take chances. So I taxied back toward the barn to bum some extra gas from the tank supplying our milking machine's fuel.

That was peacetime. This was war; and I trembled with excitement, trying to realize I wasn't dreaming. What a thrill finally to be aloft with a fighter squadron! We circled the airdrome majestically and then swept eastward toward our advance base on the seacoast. Flying in sparkling clear air, I wondered if we should be able to see across the channel. If so I would be seeing not only France but also enemy-occupied territory for the first time.

After seven or eight minutes of steady climbing, our sector controller called directing us to patrol Dover at "angels ten"—ten thousand feet. Another call extended our climb to "angels twenty-five" and advised "bandits approaching from the north."

Immediately the C.O. commanded, "Freema aircraft, full throttle!" For the first time, I pushed in the emergency throttle lever. My engine fairly screamed with new power, and I felt my plane leaping ahead like a high-spirited horse responding to the spur. I pulled the guard off my firing button. For the first time in my life, I was preparing to kill! The button was painted red, and it looked strangely grim now that it was uncovered. I turned its safety ring from the position marked "Safe" to the position which read "Fire." Then I switched on the electric gunsight.

Level at twenty-five thousand, back in the normal throttle range, and sucking oxygen piped through my mask, I snatched a quick look at the rear vision mirror above my windscreen and saw what looked like a blazing torch falling in the sky. For an instant I didn't realize that the first shots of battle had been fired. Whipping my eyes back to the leader and correcting a bit to maintain formation, I heard MacDonell transmit the Tally-Ho as he simultaneously rolled into a screaming dive. I followed, pushing everything forward—propeller control, throttle lever, emergency throttle—homing on a gaggle of Messerschmitts later revealed to be two *staffeln* (squadrons) of Me 109s of *Jagdgeschwader* (Fighter Group) 54.

Wind shrieked past my canopy, twelve-cylinders pounded inside the bellowing Merlin, and the airspeed needle moved steadily around its dial and past the four-hundred-miles-an-hour mark. My machine grew rigid with controls so stiff that I couldn't move the stick more than a quarter of an inch in any direction. Sweating to balance my pull-out against the effects of gravity which threatened to draw a misty grey curtain in front of my eyes, I bucked through a 109's prop wash and locked onto my prey. Casting furtive glances in my mirror, I drew almost within ramming distance. My secret feeling that airplanes with black crosses on their wings and sides couldn't exist in reality vanished as every detail of rivet pattern, exhaust smudge, and gaudy decoration burned itself into my memory.

Wedged into firing position, I centered the enemy in my sight and squeezed off a one-second burst—about a hundred and sixty bullets. The sound came muffled by my helmet; but it was venomous, and I could feel the Spitfire shudder and slow from the recoil as the eight Brownings snarled and barked. My plane bounced sideways as it encountered turbulence, and I lost sight of him for a second. He must have gone into a diving turn just then; for when I spotted him again, he was far below. Rolling over I went down after him realizing that, for the first time, I'd tried to take the life of another man. I caught him just over Cape *Gris Nez*, and that was how I first entered France! I followed him in the turn, cutting it shorter than he could and crowding in on him.

Powp! It sounded exactly as if someone had blown up a big paper sack and burst it behind my ears; it shook the plane and was followed by a noise like hail on a tin roof. I put all the strength I could muster on the controls to whip my machine into a turn in the opposite direction. My assailant had already flashed by below and ahead, and I now saw him wheeling to come back, his black crosses vivid on top of his wings as he appeared spread-eagled in a vertical turn. For the first time another man had tried to take my life! The three of us scrambled about in a terrible melee, climbing, diving, rolling and pirouetting in screaming vertical turns to get at each other. I finally managed to separate one of them from the other and settled into a beautiful firing position.

Then I got a heart-breaking shock: my gunsight wasn't working! The precious image in orange light wasn't to be seen on the bulletproof windscreen in front of me. Just then a set of four snaky white fingers reached across my right wing from behind and stretched far ahead. I panicked and rolled into a turn so violent that my machine shuddered and flipped over into a spin—at more than two hundred miles an hour! It must have made me look like an amateur, but it temporally shook off my attacker.

The melee continued. I was terribly hot and tired and sweaty, and conscious of that more than of being scared. I wished I could rest. The bright sun beat down through the transparent hatch over my cockpit. My clothes were heavy, and I was hampered by my parachute straps as I twisted trying to see above, below, behind, and to the sides to keep track of my playmates.

During those next few minutes, I must have blacked out at least twenty times in turns. I remember starting to spin at least once more. I wanted to flee but couldn't get my directions straight. My compass couldn't help me unless I'd give it a chance to settle down. Finally I noticed across the water a ribbon of white lining the horizon, and I remembered reading years before in my geography book about the "white cliffs of Dover." I turned out across the sea and homeward. It was an ignominious way to end a fight which had begun with such promise, but I thought it was the wisest.

Thus was I introduced to combat flying. On final approach to Hawkinge, my poor Spitfire emitted a high-pitched moan as wind whistled through a hole in the fuselage just two feet aft of my seat. As I positioned the aircraft for landing, the elevator trim wheel spun uselessly.

I wondered what other control cables were frayed to the point of snapping, but I put the thought out of my mind and concentrated on breaking my glide just over the field boundary and easing her onto the turf just as I used to baby Max's fragile Spartan.

On landing I taxied to one end of the field where I saw the squadron's planes being re-serviced. All except Isaac had returned. Two of the boys remembered seeing what looked like a Spitfire going down in flames in the distance behind the squadron at the start of the battle, and that caused me to think about the "torch" I'd glimpsed in my mirror. Sergeant Lewis R. Isaac, who'd joined the squadron just a day or two before Peter and me, had been our "weaver."

Everyone was concerned about Isaac, but as yet we had no confirmation, so they and a number of journalists including two from America—Quentin Reynolds representing *Collier's Weekly* and *Liberty's* Robert Lowe—crowded around to hear my story and examine my machine. An exploding cannon shell had blown a large hole in the left side of the fuselage in the lower part of the red, white, and blue roundel our enemies called "the peacock's eye." Had the hole been a foot higher, it would have been a bull's eye!

Control cables running close to the shell's impact were in bad shape. Those for the elevator and rudder were nearly severed, and the trimming cables dangled loosely. A twisted battery connection explained the failure of my electric gunsight and perhaps had spared the life of my opponent. Countless small perforations mutilated the opposite side of the fuselage and bits of light shrapnel littered its bottom.

31

The newspaper men and correspondents fired questions in volleys as numerous and almost as intimidating as the tracers from my recent adversaries. Squadron Leader MacDonell later recalled my saying: "I sure hit the goddamn bastard!" But I don't normally talk that way. The next day I was to learn that the gentlemen of the press had extolled me as the first of only seven American fighter pilots who would experience combat in what everyone was calling "the Battle of Britain."

Subsequently back home *Collier's* published a Quentin Reynolds dispatch enumerating the squadron's activities during our patrol, for which he substituted the more exciting term "scramble." He mentioned me by name, described a hole in the fuselage of my plane "you could stick your fist through," and quoted me as having said, "It was fun while it lasted." He went on melodramatically to profile a fictitious "lad named Douglas—very tall and very slim, and he had a baby face" who, after showing the author his Spitfire's cockpit, scrambled to intercept bombers. "*Fifteen minutes later*," he concluded, "*the boy was dead.*"

Drama enough existed in the unvarnished facts to which Reynolds only alluded when he mentioned that "Isaacs failed to return" from our patrol. At the beginning of our blistering dogfight, hard-eyed, battle-tested German veterans had jumped fledgling fighter pilot Sergeant Lewis Reginald *Isaac*, a twenty-four-year-old Welshman with a thin, intense face and pencil mustache, sending him flaming into the channel. His body was never recovered.

As my damaged machine was declared "unserviceable" and in need of a new fuselage, I knew my day's work was over. Leaving the others behind, I sought out my friend Peter, and we lay on the grass and basked in the warm sunshine. Taking out the pocket notebook I'd purchased just three months previously in Manitowoc, Wisconsin, I summarized the engagement with the notation "narrow squeak. No game."

Some time later I roused myself to begin picking out with a small knife a bit of shrapnel embedded in my boot. Lost in thought I was surprised when Peter asked if I would call his girl and "tell her the story" if anything happened to him. I offered the memorandum book which I always carried, opening it to a blank page so that he could write the girl's name and telephone number in it.

Because of the damage to my Spitfire, I couldn't fly back to our home airfield with the rest of the squadron when our shift was over at noon. One of my mates, Sergeant Pilot John Whelan, offered to come back for me in the unit's "hack" aircraft, a little two-seat, open-cockpit Miles M.14 "Magister." Like its bigger brother, the Master that I'd so enjoyed at OTU, the Magister was a low-wing monoplane constructed of wood with plywood covering. Designed as an elementary trainer and first flown in 1937, it suffered a series of crashes caused by its inability to recover from a tailspin. A rudder modification cured the problem and the little "kite" became as docile as a well mannered setter.

We lifted off from Hawkinge's grass strip in mid-afternoon and set course for Kenley. As John was flying, I was free to enjoy the scenery. Instead, I found myself replaying the morning's activities that had resulted in the sacrifice of Isaac. Who among us, I wondered, would be next?

Isaac's loss was more than a personal blow to those of us in the squadron. Experienced pilots, not machines, were the critical factor in the Battle of Britain equation. Each week as the battle progressed, fighter strength diminished by ten percent, and the OTUs—soon to be reduced to giving only one week of training per class— couldn't provide enough replacements for pilots who were killed or wounded.

Aircraft inventories, however, were fat. Lord Beaverbrook, the Canadian-born newspaper magnate appointed Minister for Air Production by Churchill in May, had slashed red tape and motivated his workers, so that our numerical losses sustained helping the French on the continent were made up before the cross-channel fighting started. Each squadron had twenty aircraft assigned along with two spares in reserve, and factories worked day and night assembling fighters at an unprecedented rate: 972 in the two months of July and August compared with 141 the previous February. Additionally a thriving industry collected and revitalized damaged aircraft. Members of "the Beaver's" Central Repair Organization would scoop up mangled carcasses, refurbish them with salvaged parts, and hustle them back to duty quick as you please. Their handiwork would constitute some thirty-five percent of all fighters involved in the Battle of Britain. In four days, for example, my forlorn Spitfire returned ready again to suffer more embarrassing damage while in my charge.

In retrospect it's easy to list tactical errors, equipment deficiencies, and the like in order to come up with a pat analysis of the battle. But in the event, and at my level, only elemental things mattered: height advantage, the sun's position, fuel remaining, and who occupied your rearview mirror. Our chief handicaps were flying outmoded formations, being constantly outnumbered and rarely enjoying a height advantage because of the short time between radar detection and enemy over flight. Whereas the Huns could cross the channel in five minutes, it took those of us who scrambled at least a quarter of an hour of hard climbing to reach the enemy's altitude.

The Germans, however, were fighting over hostile territory where a parachute was a ticket to a prison compound or a dunking in the channel with only a fifty-percent chance of rescue; their fighters had scant fuel for extended combat over Britain—only ten minutes or so when they ventured as far west as London; and their bombers' targeting was often based on faulty intelligence. As to why Goering didn't use auxiliary fuel tanks to extend his fighters' time over target as had been done frequently in Spain, one can only cite his belief that a quick German victory would follow a short, intense conflict.

Both sides' disadvantages seemed to balance out. But a number of us paid the price of Dowding's failing immediately to adopt German fighter formations. Most of my trouble came from behind when I was busy hammering an adversary. Having a wingman, or more likely flying the wing of an experienced pilot, would have polished my skills and lessened my chances of being mouse trapped.

Don't get me wrong. At this time I was no authority. During my early sorties, I often thought the eagle had turned back into a groundhog. So much was new; so much was scary.

Chapter Four

Baptism by Fire

AMERICAN IN ACTION a subhead screamed in *The London Times'* page-four article headed AIR FIGHTS OVER THE CHANNEL the day after my first combat. "One of the Spitfire pilots," it divulged, "was a 27-year-old American, who, seven weeks ago was showing young Americans how to fly on the Laredo airfield in Texas." Then it sketched my recent history: "reported for duty with his squadron only on Sunday, having joined up in Ottawa," and gave details of the action: "chased two of the Messerschmitts and hit one, and was himself attacked by the other enemy fighter." That did it. The cat was out of the bag. I knew the papers in the States would pick up the story and my folks would soon learn what the "kid brother" was up to.

I was right. *The New York Times* ran the story in its sixth of August edition proclaiming the "short, fair-haired American . . . landed safely, but the fuselage of his Spitfire plane was peppered with bullet holes." They added a couple of quotations attributed to me which, for all I know, may have been true as I had been so exhilarated when I landed that I don't remember what I said to the visiting journalists. Trailing the *Times'* article was an eleven-line squib from Laredo in which my former flying school boss, "Buck" Leighton, provided my name. Other papers throughout the country picked up the story. *The Los Angeles Herald & Examiner*, for example, gave it two columns on the front page.

My brother, manager of radio station WLLH (We Lie Like Hell joked the staff) in Lowell, Massachusetts, had already picked the story off the Associated Press wire and spread the news among my folks. The publicity pre-empted my letter home which gave essentially the same story but attributed it to a "friend" who was flying with the RAF.

What really irritated—even embarrassed—me was that the newspapers played me up as if I'd done something special. At the time the RAF discouraged public identification of any particular pilot so as not to detract from the team effort. Yet I was singled out and my modest contribution inflated. I realize now that the actions of an American volunteer during such a crossroads of British history held great propaganda value for those who wished to see the United States allied with Britain. But the reporters weren't getting the facts right, and that confirmed my resolve to write the fighter pilots' story and, thereby, set the record straight.

So I bought a portable typewriter and started pounding out a draft for a magazine article in addition to a steady stream of letters to the folks. Writing proved to be good therapy, although it required discipline to break out of the daily post-flight malaise that we all felt in varying degrees. In my case I didn't want to sleep, but I didn't want to move either, or talk, or fly, or anything else—just relax. It's a feeling that pervaded me after a fight or a nerve-racking patrol—a sensation of being drained completely. I wanted to surrender to relaxation, sitting or lying inert and absorbing whatever is missing back into my system.

Along with this lethargy, I experienced a heavy case of old-fashioned homesickness. Letters from home or from friends in Laredo acted like a tonic, but they were slow arriving because initially they had to be routed through Ottawa. Later, turn-around time was about three weeks: ten days out and ten back. The most pleasing note during this time was one telling me how the family felt about my volunteering. Their reactions reflected sentiments of my own that I had hated to uncover until I was sure my folks shared them.

Since only light activity took place during the next two days, Peter and I had a chance to learn about the RAF's air defense network by visiting the Sector "B" Operations Room located on our station in a brick building protected only by a six-foot bank of earth which surrounded it. Fighter Command was composed of four Groups, numbered Ten through Thirteen. The first three Groups were further divided into Sectors, each having an Operations Room to direct the air action within its own area of responsibility. Kenley's, for example, managed one of seven sectors in the southeastern part of Britain for which Eleven Group was responsible. Being situated under the *Luftwaffe's* main corridors of attack, Eleven Group bore the brunt of the Battle, reinforced by Ten and Twelve Groups when in danger of being overwhelmed.

In the Operations Room, members of the Women's Auxiliary Air Force, better known as "WAAFs," displayed in-coming information on blackboards and upon a large map table which dominated the room. According to the latest radar or visual sightings, those women moved wooden blocks across the map to represent the progress of friendly and enemy formations. From a gallery overlooking the activity, RAF controllers could see the complete picture and radio instructions to position our fighters to meet the enemy. Afterwards Peter and I departed with feelings of great admiration for the men and women who carried out their critical tasks while located above ground in a flimsy hut situated on an airdrome targeted for destruction.

Three days after our first combat—the eighth of August—six of us waded into some thirty Me 109 fighters. This time they belonged to *Jagdgeschwader* 51 (JG-51), commanded by Major Werner Molders, a renowned ace who was to amass a hundred fifteen "kills" before his death in 1941. Both sides sparred for several minutes, the fight quickly spreading over a wide territory. Something about the shape of Messerschmitts reminded me of rats sailing about on little narrow, stiff-looking, square-tipped wings. I think it was because of the shape of the machine's nose and the way its radiator was tucked up under its propeller spinner like the forefeet of a rat running close to the floor. I got shots at several of our playmates, just firing whenever I saw something with black crosses in front of me and not having time to see the result.

Computer buffs involved in flight simulator programs can vicariously experience a bit of what I describe, can even participate in the Battle of Britain—on either side! They can see the same flashing shapes, hear the drumming of gunfire, and feel something of the bewilderment that accompanies a real dogfight. What's missing is the fear, the heat, the blazing sun bleaching one's vision, and gravity's thumb crushing one's brain into hues of red, gray, and—finally—black.

Then a 109 got on my tail and gave me a burst just as I saw him. I laid into a vertical turn, and as he followed, I hauled my Spitfire around as tight as I could. He broke into a dive, twisting about wildly to upset my aim as I opened fire. I pressed my firing button three or four times for bursts of about a second each, and then he quit twisting. I was able to hold the sight dead on him while I held the firing button in for a good three-second burst.

I didn't think he needed any more, for I knew of only one reason for him to stop twisting. He disappeared into the clouds below, diving straight down, and although he might have gotten home, he certainly wasn't headed there right then. The powder smoke from my guns smelled strong, and I felt good.

Elsewhere in the melee of wheeling aircraft, and unbeknown to me, Peter's machine was hit, and he baled out wounded. After landing I learned Peter was "still adrift"—overdue. I thought at once of our conversation, but I determined to be optimistic once we got word that he was in hospital. After all, he was strong: strong and young. I assured my mates that he would make it and immediately dispatched a letter to Royal Victoria Hospital, Dover, telling him to keep his chin up and that I'd visit him as soon as I could break away. His youth and physical condition were cause for optimism, but he was hurt much worse than I suspected. His sister Pamela, who opened my letter and read it to him, later wrote that he was in great pain but managed a grin as she read. I had also made the telephone call to his girl, which enabled Sheila Murray to join him at his bedside.

Until Peter's misfortune I had not been particularly introspective although I had by nature always rooted for the underdog. My empathy for the cause, combined with feelings of acute embarrassment that only a handful of Americans were standing with the British, had helped motivate me to volunteer. The overblown publicity attending my first combat, followed by the tragic death of my friend, caused me to confront my feelings of fear, fatigue, and loss, and reaffirm my intent to commit them to paper.

But I was a fighter pilot, so I continued to mouth the line that fighting and losses were my job. I knew, however, that my job now included telling the stories of the Kennard-Davises and the MacDonells and even the ordinary Donahues so that my readers might share and, perhaps in a token way, understand the magnitude of the task we had taken upon ourselves.

The following day, Friday, our squadron again flew over from Kenley to take up afternoon stand-by duties at Hawkinge. Two patrols produced no action. In the landing circuit after the second, I neglected to lower my wheels and was jolted out of my complacency as my Spitfire settled on her underside amid a cloud of choking dust and the unnerving sound of her propeller flailing the ground. I expected to receive a formal "dressing down," but MacDonell accepted the damage philosophically.

What was the cause? Fatigue? Reversion to previous habits when all my aircraft had fixed landing gear? Or was my conscious mind hovering over Royal

Victoria Hospital in Dover? Who can say? Ironically the aircraft, coded SH-B, was the very same that had required a new fuselage after my combat initiation. In this case the mechanics ("fitters" who maintained the engine and "riggers" who cared for the aircraft's systems and controls) had only to change the engine, fit a new prop, and rework the sheet metal. For what it was worth, the squadron still had the services of a combat pilot who possessed the sum total of twenty-seven hours and forty minutes of Spitfire time.

The next morning we weren't scheduled to do readiness, and MacDonell used the opportunity to give me forty-five minutes of formation flying practice. In reality I suppose it was a check ride, but I believe it was more a chance for me to get my confidence back before the big push we could all see coming.

I had a late breakfast, brunch you'd call it, took stock of the events of the week in relation to myself, and decided it hadn't been bad. I certainly wasn't sorry I had come. Although I was still pretty scared while on patrol, I felt that, given a little more time to get used to it, I'd be all right. I'd been through two good engagements and felt quite sure that I'd already accomplished a little for the flag I was fighting under.

Afterward in the squadron office, the adjutant handed me a telegram he'd just received. Peter had a relapse that morning and died. I kept trying to tell myself that this was good for me, that it would give me the hardening that I needed; and somehow that seemed to help me control my pounding heart and wild emotions. Gradually the waves of feeling grew less intense, and I felt cleaned and chastened, and toughened a little too, perhaps.

Peter was taken earlier than the average survival time of eighty-seven hours calculated for Battle of Britain pilots. He now lies with his grandparents in a family grave beside St. Cyprian's Avenue in the London Necropolis Cemetery at Brookwood. Should you happen to visit, you may wish to place not one but two red roses on his grave, for I'm sure a part of my spirit lies with him.

Sunday, the eleventh of August, dawned clear with high cirrus clouds. Max and I would always go to church before our Sunday air shows back in Winona. But getting to Mass on this particular day was impossible because of other blood sacrifices being made to the ambitions of a hate-crazed, power-maddened dictator who wanted to take the place of God. Instead the squadron flew to Hawkinge for the dawn readiness, and it was an unforgettably beautiful flight.

It was just getting light when we took off, and the countryside was dim below us. Wicked blue flames flared back from the exhausts of the engines as I looked at the planes in formation about me. We seemed to hover motionless except for the slight upward or downward drift of one machine or another in relation to the rest, which seemed to lend a pulsating life to the whole formation as the dark carpet of the earth below steadily slid backward beneath us. The sun, just rising very red and big and beautiful, cast weird lights over the tops of our camouflaged wings. We were like a herd of giant beasts in some strange new kind of world.

My oxygen apparatus broke down during our first patrol, thereby restricting me from flying above fifteen thousand feet for the rest of the day. I flew two patrols in this manner, each time being forced to leave the squadron formation when they were ordered to patrol at higher altitudes. Hesitant to return to our airdrome, I trailed the squadron reasoning that any developing air battle might drift down into my envelope.

Descending to land after the second of these unproductive sorties, I noticed an overtaking aircraft in my rearview mirror. Thinking it was another Spit, I was amazed to see that his tracers were reaching out across the space between us! I didn't think any of his bullets had hit my machine until I noticed that my air speed indicator wasn't working. On landing I found that a bullet had gone through my wing, cutting the air speed indicator pressure tube and causing the instrument to fail.

Monday, the twelfth of August and the day of Peter's funeral, was to be a memorable day for me. We had one patrol in the latter part of the afternoon without making an interception, and while we were on the ground getting refueled, Operations phoned to say a "450 plus" raid was forming over the French coast. I guess we were all feeling a little subdued when we scrambled a few minutes later. We knew that if we intercepted the monster raid, we'd be fortunate to have more than one other squadron—a total of twenty-four aircraft—in the initial clash.

Climbing out we happened upon a comparatively small formation of enemy fighters, perhaps twenty or thirty. After the "Tally-Ho," which had become ritual in order to advise the sector controller that his charges had gone into action, we got all mixed together. I attacked three aircraft that appeared to be the new Heinkel 113 fighters intelligence had been telling us about. I found out later that the Heinkel 113 was a hoax; the Germans produced only twelve and never deployed them. Their propaganda photographs, however, convinced many of us that the aircraft was in widespread use.

So my "Heinkels" were actually Messerschmitts. Anyway they chased me down into the clouds; and when I broke out, they were no where to be found. What I did observe to the southeast was more airplanes than I had ever seen at one time in my life. It was the "450 plus" raid coming across. Farther southeast, not far off the French coast, the bombers were coming. I mistook them at first for an enormous black cloud.

I had gone just a little way, when in front of me flashed a "Heinkel 113" again. I whipped into a turn, shoved the throttle into emergency boost, and closed into firing position when the familiar sound of exploding cannon shells wracked my eardrums. My plane shook, shrapnel rattled, and white tracers streamed by. For all my care, I had been surprised from behind by a second Hun! I pushed ahead on the stick, but it flopped all the way forward to the instrument panel—elevator cables gone! I pumped my feet wildly back and forth on the rudder pedals. No response—rudder cables gone too!

I could smell powder smoke, hot and strong, but it didn't make me feel tough this time. It was from the cannon shells and incendiary bullets that had hit my machine. Smoke curled up beside me. My heart pounded, my mouth tasted salty, and I wondered if this was the end of the line. I jerked open the hatch over my cockpit, so that I could get away in a hurry if things didn't work out. A salvo from a third plane enveloped me. I remember seeing the instrument panel breaking up and holes dotting the gas tank in front of me.

Surprisingly I wasn't scared any more. A light glowed in the bottom of the fuselage, somewhere up in front. Then a red tongue of flame licked out inquiringly from under the gas tank in front of my feet, curled up the side of it, and became a hot little bonfire. I remembered my parachute, jerked the locking pin that secured my seat straps, and started to climb out just as the whole cockpit became a furnace.

There was a moment of searing heat just as I was getting my head and shoulders out, then the slipstream jerked and dragged my body the rest of the way with terrible roughness and flung it down the side of the fuselage and away all in a fraction of a second. Then I was falling and reaching for my rip-cord and pulling it. Long seconds of suspense ended with a heavy pull that stopped my fall, so that I hung quite safe if not entirely sound.

I ached all over, but the pain appeared to be mostly from bruises I received from being dragged out of the cockpit so quickly. My right trouser leg was torn and burned completely off, exposing a leg bruised and skinned in a dozen places with a sizable burn around my ankle where the skin hung loosely.

I could find no bullet wounds—bruises and burns only. Then I realized my right hand and the right side of my face were burned too. I sighed and said aloud, feeling that the occasion demanded some recognition, "Well, Art, this is what you asked for. How do you like it?"

Chapter Five

Barnstorming

Floating down in my parachute, my mind drifted back to the beginning, back as always to Minnesota. As a boy in St. Charles, the thought of becoming an aviator had claimed my attention, but I didn't know what path to follow, or whether I could be spared to leave the farm. With Dad's blessing, Bob had left in 1927 when he was twenty, and that got me to thinking. The more I thought, the more convinced I became that aviation would be my ticket to the world I'd read about in Dad's handsomely illustrated collection of John A. Stoddard's travel lectures.

Although I was deeply involved in various school activities, my conversation always reverted to the latest flying anecdote. Plenty was happening to talk about, especially after Lindbergh flew the Atlantic. But I wasn't all talk; I went so far as to construct in our hayloft a mock-up of an airplane's cockpit complete with moveable joy stick and rudder pedals. When my classmates, Clayton Miller and Frank Butler, would come over to shoot baskets at the hoop I'd nailed on the barn, I'd demonstrate my "trainer" and explain the principles of flight. Because we were the youngest members of the class, Frank and I seemed to be special pals. So he was one of the few to whom I showed my rejection slips and confided my goal of also becoming a writer. I remember telling him, "I'll make it some day."

All my classmates knew I wanted to fly, so they took up a collection on the day of our senior class picnic, and then six of them drove me east to Winona, a town of twenty-five thousand located beside the Mississippi. There they paid for my ride with the resident pilot, and that was the way I met Max Conrad.

Born in Winona, Max was twenty-seven (ten years older than I), stood just over six feet tall, neither smoked nor drank, and had the physique of a champion athlete. From a relatively well-to-do family nicely established in the retail fur business, he nevertheless lacked career motivation and had drifted from school to school for six years. He started at Marquette, moved to The University of Colorado, spent a year pulling back-to-back, six-hour shifts at the Cadillac and Plymouth factories in Detroit, enrolled at Berkeley where he ran track and tried out for the Olympics. He finally ended up at Minnesota where he changed his major to aeronautical engineering after Lindbergh's triumph.

Growing restless under the academic grind, he again quit school, borrowed five hundred dollars from a Winona bank, and went to Chicago to become a pilot. Lessons in 1928 were expensive: the cost of two hours in the air equaled an average worker's weekly salary. Making matters worse the Chicago instructor wanted forty dollars an hour, double what Max had budgeted.

A South Bend flyer, Steven Darius, offered him a package of eleven hours for $250. Darius, an ambitious and highly qualified instructor, was later to have his moment of glory. An immigrant from Lithuania, he had returned to Europe with the Forty-second Division during the First World War. Subsequently he learned to fly and remained to fight as a pilot for his motherland's independence. In 1927 he joined the throng at *Le Bourget* to witness Charles Lindbergh's arrival.

Returning to the States, Darius worked as a flight instructor and charter pilot. Inspired by Lindbergh's Atlantic crossing, he began to plan a 4,466-mile, non-stop flight from the United States to Kaunas, the provisional capital of Lithuania. He and a compatriot, Stanley Girenas, pooled their resources to buy the single-engine Bellanca Pacemaker monoplane that Darius had been flying for the previous three years. Knowing that the Bellanca required extensive rebuilding in order to outfit it for an ocean crossing, they embarked upon a successful campaign among Lithuanian-American communities to finance the project.

Darius and Girenas engaged Emil M. "Matty" Laird, a respected designer and builder, to do the work. Laird had opened his own aircraft manufacturing company in Chicago in 1919, moved it to Wichita, and then returned to establish himself in a building near the Chicago Municipal Airport. Extending each wing four feet, beefing up the landing gear, adding extra fuel tanks, and installing a new, supercharged Wright J6-9E engine produced an aircraft with a cruising speed of 121 miles per hour, a service ceiling of twenty thousand feet, and the endurance to complete the anticipated forty-hour flight with a healthy fuel reserve.

Launching after dawn on the fifteenth of July, 1933, from Floyd Bennett Field in New York, Darius and Girenas droned silently on course as they, like Lindbergh, lacked a radio transmitter. Nearing the end of their journey, darkness and deteriorating weather forced the pair to attempt a landing near a village some 120 miles northeast of Berlin. Under the flickering light of a parachute flare, they descended into treetops, crashed, and were killed just 422 miles short of their destination.

But at the time of their meeting, neither Max nor Darius could imagine the hazards each would encounter during long-distance, overwater flights in the future. For his part Max was happy with his deal, but frustrating weather-induced delays caused him to leave after having flown only three and a half hours in Darius' Pheasant trainer. He finished his formal training in Denver's clear air for fifteen dollars per hour. In something over five months, he had accumulated almost sixteen hours of instruction, realized he'd found his calling, and talked his father into signing a note enabling him to buy an airplane.

His choice from among the wares of sixteen aircraft manufacturers clustered in Wichita was a "Swallow" biplane designed and built by Matty Laird. It carried a pilot in the rear cockpit and two passengers together up front. Max got it for $3,588 plus an extra hundred dollars for a turn and bank instrument. The Swallow came equipped with a Curtiss OX-5 engine that provided a 75-mile-per-hour cruising speed. Having been in production for eight years, the airplane had a solid reputation and was a good choice.

Returning to Winona in May 1928 as the area's only rated pilot, Max started flying charters, giving instruction, and selling sightseeing hops. Inside of a week he had accumulated fifty hours, but he'd also cracked up the Swallow so badly that it took all summer to repair. Not deterred he acquired a replacement biplane and continued his frenetic pace thereby racking up fifty hours of cross-country experience in order to apply for an "Industrial" rating, which a pilot could obtain by writing to Washington attesting to having done so. This allowed him to conduct interstate flights. After quickly gaining three-hundred hours of experience, he applied for his transport rating which required him to pass a written examination and a flight check.

Because only three or four traveling inspectors served the country's nearly four thousand aviators in 1929, a pilot could get a two-month temporary license upon application and the rating could be renewed up to three times while awaiting an inspector's visit.

The second year of operation, 1929, saw two crashes: a landing accident which demolished the repaired Swallow and a stock market crash which demolished almost everything else. Max mourned the first and ignored the possibility of the second's occurring. He saw only opportunity at Winona, and he worked to exploit it. His quest for a Swallow replacement took him to Tulsa, home of the Spartan Aircraft Company. After a stint as a factory test pilot for five dollars an hour, he returned to Winona with two brand-new Spartan biplanes and the regional distributorship.

I didn't know any of this background at the time; all I knew was that an honest-to-goodness pilot and a beautiful, year-old, red and white biplane with a modern Siemens-Halske engine stood eager to give me my first "dollar-ride." With my friend, Clayton Miller, I scrambled into the front seat and tried to wipe the grin off my face.

I remember a pretty bumpy take-off, lots of engine noise, and a strong slipstream threatening to blow off my cap that I'd turned backwards like Lincoln Beachey. We circled for what seemed like thirty seconds, mostly with me hanging over the left side taking pictures, and then we were on the final approach.

"What do you think?" Clayton shouted as we hopped down from our perch.

"Wonderful," I yelled back. "How about taking up a collection for another ride!"

Max seemed almost as excited as I was and didn't appear in any hurry to break away. It wasn't as if he stayed around to work the crowd for more business; he just seemed proud to talk to someone who loved flying as much as he did. I asked him about the airport and what a fellow would have to do maybe to work off some flying time.

He showed me the hangar he'd built on a concrete slab and pointed out the lights and rotating beacon the government had provided after he laid out the runway. From what I could see, the Conrad Flying Service operated something like an informal club with fellows hanging around doing odd jobs in exchange for flying time. Two of them lived in the hangar, pumped gas for automobiles and airplanes, and waited on tables in the restaurant. In just three years, Max had accumulated seven biplanes, a truck, and tools and machinery that allowed him to work on aircraft and overhaul engines. In addition he was the distributor for the Spartan as well as the star of a weekly air show featuring acrobatics and parachute jumps along with the real business of selling hops at two dollars a person to local citizens.

I didn't want to leave even when my friends started yelling from the Ford. I knew right then that, unlike my new hero, I wasn't going to drift even for a moment. I wanted to be an aviator, to have some adventures and see some places, to be somebody known outside of St. Charles, and maybe even to make my home town proud of me.

It took over a year, until the twenty-fourth of September, 1931 to be exact, before Max side-slipped the Spartan into Dad's field, picked me up, and whisked me back to Winona. Actually things worked out rather well at home since we had stopped bottling our own brand of milk and my brother and three sisters already had gone. Our two-hundred-acre enterprise was down to something more manageable by Dad and some part-time help. We now had an automobile and a reliable source of staples at the grocery in town, so we didn't have to be as self-sufficient as previously. Beginning my training at the end of September also meant that most of the harvest was in, and I could more easily be spared.

Nevertheless, I left with a heavy heart, glad to sit in the front cockpit alone with my thoughts. I wrote a postcard home the morning after my arrival and a five-and-a-half-page letter three days later telling the folks of my first lesson with Max in his Ryan cabin plane, of my first cross-country flight to Eau Claire with Max curled up in the passenger seat for ten minutes on the way so as to show his confidence in my ability to hold a steady course, and of my first stunt flight with Gerald Kohner.

In addition to me, Max had three other serious students (including a woman doctor who took instruction whenever Max visited our Rochester branch) and about twenty people who took lessons whenever they could manage the cost. Max had set up our Rochester satellite as an opportunity for his younger brother, Art, whom he had taught to fly three years previously. Having earned an Air Transport Rating, Art was well qualified as an aviator; but he wasn't a hustler like Max. Consequently the Rochester operation was never a money maker.

After getting my private pilot's license, I immediately started working toward my limited commercial ticket which would allow me to carry passengers for hire within a certain area. Five of us were pursuing that goal. In addition I was studying for my mechanic's license which I figured would give me the edge in a tough labor market. When Max saw that I was in the profession for the long haul, he started confiding more in me and obviously grooming me for something better. He even filled in some of the details that I didn't know concerning the stability of the company.

At the time I arrived, Conrad Flying Service was just beginning to emerge from some pretty rough times caused by slip-shod bookkeeping—if not downright criminal embezzlement—by previous members of the "club." Old bills had gone unpaid, and cash was missing from the till. Two months before my arrival, Art Conrad and four passengers had been killed in the crash of one of Max's two Ryan "Brougham" cabin airplanes. It happened on the twenty-first of July, 1931; the day Max married Betty Biesanz. Lawsuits developed, creditors attached his airplanes, and students stopped flying based on the rumor that Art had been stunting.

Investigation proved, however, that someone had installed a new propeller improperly, so that vibration caused it to fracture and sling a portion into the left wing, breaking the spar and causing the structure to fold. One of the victims was a sixteen-year-old fishing guide without a dollar's worth of insurance. Max sent his life savings to the boy's family.

Shortly before my arrival, Gerald Kohner had taken over the books, and the company started showing a profit. Max had clear title to the airplanes; and his hangar, even though mortgaged, was hardly in jeopardy since his mother held the note! Things seemed to be falling into place, and Max began thinking of expanding the business to Riverside, California, so that he could establish passenger service to the west coast. On occasion he spoke of setting up a service facility in South Bend, Indiana, where he had business connections.

Max's plans seemed a bit grandiose in light of what was happening in the country during 1931. Drought parched the Sunbelt states causing starvation conditions in Arkansas. Unemployment in cities throughout the country affected one in six persons. Detroit was the hardest hit with a quarter of a million people out of work, a hundred and fifty families being evicted each day, and people starving to death at the rate of one every seven hours. In September and October, seven hundred banks failed.

But Max was riding high! To finance the purchase of a used Ford TriMotor transport needed to inaugurate his air route to California, he charmed thirty Winona businessmen into putting up a hundred dollars each. The route never panned out, so we used the Ford for charter work, passenger hops, stunting at county fairs, dropping parachutists, and multi-engine pilot training. Two years after its purchase, the engine mounted in the nose caught fire on the ground and flames spread to the main structure. We sold for parts what little we salvaged. We had no insurance.

In early June 1932, after passing the written and flight tests for a limited commercial license on the first attempt—an "almost unprecedented feat" I was told—I received from Max a tremendously ego-boosting letter outlining his plans for me. Nothing materialized immediately, as I had to build my time and experience, but I intimated in my letters to Mother and Dad that I had hopes of drawing a "small salary" sometime in the fall. Until then I hopped passengers for the privilege of getting free flying time and, later, for the time plus fifteen cents a head as my share of the profits.

Really needing to make the air shows pay off, we concentrated on selling hops to the people attracted by our acrobatics and Max's parachuting. During the winter of 1933, we flew off frozen Lake Winona charging fifty cents a head for a circle over the town. One Sunday we used three airplanes to fly seventy-one passengers. On the side Max hawked punch boards, our precursor to POWERBALL, charging five cents a punch for each of the four-hundred "chances" and offering four $2.50 hops as prizes.

For the uninitiated, punch boards were approximately the length and width of a piece of typing paper and about an inch thick. The individual chances were tightly rolled pieces of paper that one literally punched out of the board's honeycomb grid with a small metal key. Unrolling the paper allowed the player instantly to know if he was a winner. Max made a profit of five dollars on each board.

One Sunday when I was selling tickets for hops, I ran onto a girl, Bernice Ferguson, who went to St. Charles High. She and the fellow with her bought tickets knowing they'd have to wait for those ahead of them to be served. As I helped a couple of passengers into Gerald's orange and black plane, I mentioned that I had sold a ride to a schoolmate and her friend. He told me I could fly them, as it would be good advertising back home.

When it was their turn, darkness was upon us. I had never flown alone at night, much less landed. Taking off to the west, I kept straight ahead until I judged we were about five hundred feet (I couldn't make out the altimeter). Then I turned north across the west end of the city. When I was pretty well to the river, I turned eastward. Gerald took off a few seconds after I did, and as his plane was faster than mine, he passed us over the business section. It seemed like a page out of one of those magazines specializing in tales of the future. The pattern of brilliant lights underneath, the roar of the motor, and the ghostlike outline of Gerald's plane flitting by didn't seem real at all.

I was a little anxious about getting down, as I didn't know what it would be like at night. I could make out the snow-covered lake, so I glided down until I could see little rifts in the snow streaking by. Judging my altitude from the speed they seemed to travel, I managed to make an almost perfect landing.

I realize now that I've always had a mystical feeling about flying, something beyond the beauty; it has to do more with time and space and establishing contact. I remember once early in my stay with Max that Bud Munsing, the night mail pilot between the Twin Cities and Chicago flew over. I could see the lights of his Waco biplane far above and hear the roar of his motor, which sounded eerie way up there in the clear, still night. I flashed on the light under the wind sock at the end of the hangar, and then flashed it on and off a few times. A second later his lights flashed off and on several times in answer. It all seemed weird and hard to realize as being real.

Sometime later, while studying hard for the Air Transport Rating test, I perceived that in this profession many things go on that are hard to explain. A few nights before, one of the Northwest Airways mail pilots passed over heading down the river; at one hundred and thirty or forty miles per hour, he was just a trio of tiny lights streaking through the sky. Bad weather along his route forced him to come back and stay awhile with us at the airport. As we sat on the cot talking, I tried to realize that the person who sat beside me, close enough to touch, was the same person whom I had just watched streaking through the night sky far above at two hundred fifty feet or so per second.

Writing in *The Spirit of St. Louis* years after the Paris flight, Lindbergh mused over how, during a flight of long duration after periods of crisis and danger, the mind and body could become disunited. Furthermore he'd experienced moments "when existence appeared

60

independent even of the mind," periods when he became "an awareness spreading out through space, over the earth and into the heavens. . . ." At these times he believed that physical desire and immediate surroundings "became submerged in the apprehension of universal values." He believed, as I came to believe, that pilots lived on a higher plane than earthbound skeptics, "one that was richer because of its very association with the element of danger they dreaded." He resolved that if he could fly for ten years before losing his life in a crash, "it would be a worthwhile trade for an ordinary lifetime."

But most of the time the mysticism was far overshadowed by the hard work and, sometimes, the anxiety (if not fear) that I might not make it in aviation after all. At this time I was nineteen years old, the depression showed few signs of easing, and in my letters I frequently had to thank Dad for the "five" he had sent to tide me over. A big motivator to my wanting to make money was the preservation of the farm in St. Charles. So I was all for it when Max proposed my going out from Winona each weekend to barnstorm in surrounding towns. He promised me a significant amount of the profits and told me to select a place to establish a satellite operation for the winter. Even though we had closed the Rochester base after Art Conrad's death, to me that site again looked promising.

Earning my Air Transport Rating in September of 1932, making me the youngest person so rated in the northwest, was another ego boost and looked like my ticket to success for sure. Two months later Max announced that he had bought the equipment of the Ryan Aircraft Factory which was one of the largest in the United States and maker of Lindbergh's *Spirit of St. Louis*. Ryan was in receivership, so we got forty thousand dollars worth of material, tools, and parts for a fraction of their value. Max intended to become the sole source of factory-built parts for a brand of airplane that had a world-wide reputation and to complete the manufacture of one or two aircraft that were in the final stages of assembly. Toward this goal we built a large workshop in the hangar, one with enough room to allow us to construct a complete wing or run in a whole fuselage so we could work where it was warm. I had no idea that this experience would prove absolutely critical to my survival later in a climate in which keeping warm was the least of my concerns!

In late March 1933, just after turning twenty, I became the manager of the Winona airport! Rather than being cowered by the responsibility, I felt as if a great storm had suddenly subsided. I had survived all the rivalry and jealousy and cheating that's bound to confront one when he's trying to work up in an organization of this sort. I knew I'd find it pretty hard sometimes to give orders to the other fellows, and that I might find their friendship for me cooling a little. But I realized that if I could manage to substitute part of their friendship for respect, I would have made my first big accomplishment in my new job. Most comforting was my belief that I had won Max's confidence completely, something that no one else ever had done, and I thought that achieving this position meant conquering the last obstacle standing between me and a fairly secure future.

Chapter Six

Time Out

Dropping heavily into a field of oats, I realized that any remaining thoughts of a "fairly secure future" needed re-evaluation. I spilled the wind from my parachute and struggled to my feet as a group of soldiers approached with rifles at the ready. Peeling off my flying helmet, I stood so that they could see the remnants of my uniform. They started to escort me to their quarters, but when I was halfway there, my left knee began to give out, and they carried me the rest of the way.

They administered first aid, and the young man who worked on me gave me a shock. "You've got a couple of pretty nasty burns there on your leg and your hand," he said. "The one on your face isn't so bad, but the other two ought to take a month to heal. Then you'll get a spot of 'sick leave' of course. Yes, I'd make it all of six weeks before you're fit again."

I'd expected they'd bandage up my hand and leg, give me forty-eight hours off, and tell me to be careful for a day or two—that is, if they were worth bandaging at all! I guess my mind was still back on the farm where a few scrapes and burns was no ticket to ducking the morning milking. But an army doctor in a hospital near Canterbury confirmed the prognosis as he prepared to cut away the skin from the burned areas. Afterward they spread tannic acid over my burns until a tough black scab had formed. My nurses told me that it was a new type of treatment that didn't leave permanent scars. Later I found that tannic acid hardens on contact with open flesh. Had my burns been more severe, the application would have only complicated my recovery.

Someone has said that a wound, something that doesn't smash bone or do catastrophic damage, is good for a soldier. It makes him more confident of his ability to cope. I don't know about that, but I do know fire is the most feared consequence a pilot imagines. Many, particularly the new chaps, took elaborate precautions such as wearing a long-sleeved tunic and trousers, pulling on leather gauntlets over silk-fingered gloves, and flying always with goggles lowered. Veterans, however, frequently thought that gloves impeded their "feel" of the control pressures and that goggles compromised their peripheral vision. Those flying in desert or tropical climates usually had come to terms with their destiny and determined to fly in as comfortable a garb as possible.

Some of those who, like me, saw their cockpits transformed into blast furnaces suffered horrible burns. A four or five-second delay in baling out spelled hospitalization. Eight to nine seconds sentenced a pilot to a burn ward for the war's duration. After ten seconds flyers trapped by jammed hatches were overcome by flames and heat. Those managing to escape not infrequently found that flames had already torched their parachutes, so that they fell like misfired roman candles.

In a number of cases, pilots who cheated death or permanent incapacitation found themselves unable to justify their good fortune in light of the ill luck of so many others. I'm reminded of James Brindley Nicolson who was in the process of abandoning his shattered cockpit when he dropped back behind the controls upon seeing his attacker foolishly crossing directly in front of his flaming Hurricane. Only after blasting the twin-engine Me 110 fighter out of the sky did he propel himself "over the side." Almost completely blind, badly burned, and dangling in his parachute, he took a full pattern of buckshot fired by a defense volunteer as he neared the ground. Subsequently medical workers picked seventy pieces of metal from his body, tended his burns, and estimated he had at most a day to live. They also ministered to the over-anxious home guard who had been assaulted by an irate bystander.

Amazingly the twenty-three-year-old Flight Lieutenant rallied, regained his sight within two weeks, and responded well to extensive plastic surgery. On the twenty-fifth of November, King George VI pinned on his chest the only Victoria Cross awarded during the Battle of Britain. Believing his selection to have been politically motivated in order to lionize a fighter pilot, Nicolson considered himself undeserving. With that in mind, he returned to flying duties and pushed himself mercilessly in order to "earn" the award. Having done that so many times over, he died flying as a volunteer observer aboard a United States "Liberator" bomber that crashed in the Far East shortly before the war's end.

Richard Hillary—a movie-star handsome, Oxford-educated Spitfire pilot whose autobiographical novel, *The Last Enemy,* was published in June 1942 and quickly sold 135,000 copies—walked away from his first crash landing on the afternoon of August 29 and joined a garden party. Five days later Hauptmann Bode, flying his first sortie with II/JG 26, flamed Hillary's Spitfire at 10:04 a.m. and Flying Officer Stewart-Clark's four minutes later, forcing both men to bale out. Flying without gloves or goggles, Hillary suffered horrible burns on his hands and face before he escaped the flames. Men of the Margate lifeboat, a service organized over a hundred years previously by an ancestor, fished Hillary out of the North Sea and delivered him to the first-aid station where attendants coated his burns with tannic acid. He spent three months at the Royal Masonic Hospital before being accepted as one of Dr. Archibald McIndoe's "guinea pigs" at Queen Victoria Hospital, East Grinstead.

Archie McIndoe emerged as one of the legendary heroes of the war. A plastic surgeon in civilian life, he'd established a Burns Unit at the East Grinstead hospital which eventually contained over a hundred young men, mostly fighter pilots. It was Flying Officer Geoffrey Page, shot down in the same location and within minutes of Hillary, who christened McIndoe's patients "The Guinea Pigs Club" because of their benefactor's innovative and experimental procedures.

McIndoe sought first to neutralize the effects of the previous treatment, which toughened the burned flesh into a leather-like consistency and caused fingers to curl into useless claws, and then surgically correct the horrific damage caused by the flames. Simultaneously he reoriented his staff to foster the patients' mental rehabilitation by loosening ward discipline and introducing his clients into local society which had been prepared to accept their appearance.

Page had survived a fighter pilot's worse nightmare—the explosion of the reserve fuel tank which was mounted behind the engine on a level with his chest. Having forgone wearing his goggles and gloves, he saw and felt his fingers melting before he disconnected and propelled himself out of the cockpit.

Hillary's quirky personality—an intellectual approach to life, fascination with death, and desire to return to the cockpit—intrigued McIndoe who quickly realized that Hillary's sharp tongue had alienated all of his fellows except Geoffrey Page, whose goal was also to return to operational flying. Feeling that both flyers had done enough, McIndoe at first refused to support their pleas, Later, however, he applied his unprecedented skill in reconstructive and plastic surgery to mold faces and rebuild operative hands for Hillary and Page.

Returning to flying duties—his biographer theorized "to justify himself before the steady gaze of his dead companions of the 1940 battles"—Hillary died in a needless training accident. On the evening of the seventh of January 1943, just prior to completing operational training in an obsolescent twin-engine Bristol Blenheim modified as a night-fighter, he launched into reported icing conditions in order to complete his quota of night flying. Sometime later, while holding on a radio beacon, his machine spiraled into the ground killing both pilot and observer. This tragedy was compounded by the fact that McIndoe, having examined Hillary's eyelid, had written his commanding officer two weeks earlier recommending that he be grounded as it "might save him from a very serious accident."

His story inspired a two-part Masterpiece Theater television program some fifty years later, its producer substituting a happy ending rather than risking the displeasure of those who might have objected to such a depressing resolution after a battle so hard fought.

Page's return to flying was more fortuitous. In August of 1942, he led his Spitfire squadron on a low-level sweep over France. By Christmas, despite great pain in his hands and one eyelid, he was an acting wing commander flying the American-built Mustang fighter. Having been awarded the Distinguished Service Order and posted to the United States as an assistant air attaché, he met and married the daughter of the British-born screen actor Nigel Bruce. Page remained in aviation after the war, living in Switzerland where he represented various aircraft companies.

The subject of death or disfigurement by fire is a repugnant one. But as I learned on my first engagement, air combat isn't a game. In view of the continuing onslaught, my burns had quite possibly saved my life.

That is not to say that my wounds were without discomfort. I had second-degree burns on three fingers and the back of my right hand and around my right ankle, and a light burn on the side of my face. I'd been flying in low-quarter shoes and dress gloves rather than protective boots and leather gauntlets which would have covered my wrists and lower forearms. Helmet and oxygen mask had provided reasonably good cover even though I hadn't lowered my goggles. My right hand and wrist gave me the most trouble, as my forearm, hand and fingers swelled after a day or so and became terribly tender. Even the blood circulation made my fingers throb, and the only way I could keep the pain under control was to have my hand propped up high and hold it perfectly still. If I allowed my arm to rest down level, the increased blood pressure made the pain unbearable. The slightest quick movement caused an agony of aching, as did any quickening of the pulse—caused, for instance, by the sight of a good-looking nurse.

This incident, as do many such wartime experiences, had its humorous aftermath. John A. "Red" Campbell, an American from Chula Vista, California, who became one of my best friends when we served together in 258 Squadron, told me that he first saw me leaning against a mantelpiece in the officers' mess supporting a drink in my right hand by thrusting my thumb into a button hole in my blouse. My right foot was cocked at a vertical angle to the floor and held slightly behind my left leg. He said I was the most arrogant-looking so and so he had ever seen. Actually, I was merely adopting a pose that offered some degree of respite to my throbbing ankle!

The drink was most probably beer as I had somewhat relaxed my behavior of complete abstinence. Max Conrad had reinforced my natural inclination by never drinking or smoking, and he attributed his athletic prowess in large measure to taking care of his body. I thought often of Max as I endured the trauma resulting from my burns. Max had suffered more—much, much more.

Around the Winona airport, I'd heard whispers about his having been involved in some sort of accident, and I'd seen mental lapses and a general disregard for the administrative side of the business that suggested some kind of lingering effects. I wasn't prepared for the truth. It seems that during an afternoon of hopping passengers, a young woman—herself a pilot—dismounted from the front cockpit by moving forward and slipping off the leading edge of the wing. The engine was idling, of course, and the large wooden propeller was flicking invisibly. Max lunged for the girl just as she stepped into the propeller's arc. She was killed instantly; he received a terrible gash that exposed his brain.

By a miracle he survived, but at the price of having lost all ability to speak, read, write, or fly! Whereas he had previously mastered the saxophone, harmonica, and numerous stringed instruments, he found himself incapable of playing a note. Flying was out of the question, and his depression was absolute.

One night he made his way to the airport, managed to start one of the Spartans, and took off. Once in the air, he realized he had no conscious memory of how the controls worked or what coordination was necessary to land. Only raw willpower generated solutions to the various problems and permitted his safe return to earth. Once the ice was broken, however, he was able to regain his abilities or camouflage his deficiencies. A continuing speech impediment so intimidated him, however, that he surrendered any idea of flying for an airline or taking any position requiring spontaneous talk on the radio. Years later, after achieving fame for long-distance aircraft deliveries, he overcame this last hurdle and developed a reputation as a lecturer and after-dinner speaker.

During my own recuperation, whatever pain I suffered was minor compared to the despair I felt for depriving the squadron of an aviator who was just beginning to understand the intricacies of the fighter pilot's profession. Sixty-four Squadron was bearing the brunt of Germany's aerial attack, and I was not with them.

Those who have had military experience, or have been team members in one sport or another, may understand my feelings somewhat. I actually thought that I could make a difference: that I could protect others from having their lives irreparably shattered if I eliminated even one or two of the machines that were devoted to England's destruction. I believed that stopping the Huns at the channel would keep America from having to suffer the horrors of war. For me the Battle of Britain is more than a medal clasp on the 1939-45 Star decoration. It stands as a turning point in British history every bit as impressive as King Harry's victory at Agincourt a month shy of four hundred and twenty-five years previously. And I was one of those "happy few," one of the "band of brothers" who took part in it.

But I realize that for some the Battle, indeed World War Two itself, is—like Agincourt—ancient history imperfectly understood. Let me set the stage. The harsh terms of the Versailles Treaty ended World War One, dissolved Germany's armed forces, and led to the depression and political chaos that spawned Adolf Hitler's Nazi party. Speaking to its leaders in 1928, Hitler maligned politicians who espoused a "pitiable belief in possibilities—such as the belief in reconciliation, understanding, world peace." He went on to say, "we destroy these ideas. There is only one right in the world and that right is one's own strength."

Stung by inflation and unemployment, Germans in January 1932 elected 232 Nazis to the *Reichstag* and

Hitler's cohort, Hermann Goering, as its chief. Yielding to Nazi pressure a year later, President Paul von Hindenburg named Hitler prime minister or *Chancellor*. Hitler, in turn, directed Goering to build a secret air force.

Certain individuals in England perceived Germany's clandestine rearming. Chief among those seers was Hugh Dowding, an Air Vice-Marshal who'd directed the RAF's technical development since 1930. He knew three things: that England would be most threatened from the air, that defense of the homeland deserved top priority, and that a technology capable of directing England's aerial defenses must be installed. He, more than any other single person involved in the Battle of Britain, deserves to be memorialized.

We pilots may have been "the few," but for lonely and frustrating years, Dowding was seemingly "the only." Even Churchill, Chancellor of the Exchequer in 1925, had advocated reducing the home defense program. Other politicians supported the wishes of the Admiralty and the War Office to eliminate the RAF as a separate service. Nevertheless the organization survived even though, in 1929, it ranked only fifth among the world's leading air forces. A decade later—two years before Pearl Harbor—General Frank M. Andrews classified his own United States Army Air Corps as a "fifth-rate air force," and few Americans seemed to care.

In 1934 when Germany began to expose elements of the "black *Luftwaffe*" it had created surreptitiously, the British House of Commons took notice. Citing "private sources" that caused him to revise his past position, Churchill said that Germany's air force was nearly two-thirds the size of Britain's home defense units and would be stronger in two years than the entire RAF, even if a proposed expansion took place.

Following President Hindenburg's death, Goering enticed top *Luftwaffe* officers to swear allegiance, not to Germany, but *to the person* of Adolf Hitler. Subsequently, on the first of March 1935, *all* military officers and enlisted men took the same oath. Twelve days later Hitler announced that Germany was rearming. During the next four years, the *Luftwaffe* transformed itself into a first-rate air arm deficient only in heavy bombers.

When in 1936 Hitler moved troops into the Rhineland—German territory "permanently" de-militarized by the Treaty of Versailles—the world looked the other way. His annexation of Austria likewise went unopposed. Thoroughly intimidated by the *Luftwaffe's* reputation gained in the Spanish Civil War, English and French leaders acquiesced to Germany's subsequent takeover of Czechoslovakia. Then at dawn on the first of September 1939, Germany's air force destroyed nearly all Polish aircraft on the ground as invaders poured across the border. Two days later —too late to save the Poles—England and France declared war. Britain reinforced its ally with a ground expeditionary force and 474 planes including four squadrons of first-line Hurricane fighters.

After eight months of a do-nothing "Phony War," Germany took advantage of returning good weather in April of 1940 to invade Norway and Denmark, in May to conquer the Netherlands and Belgium, and then to drive 240 miles to the French coast in eleven days. German Messerschmitts decimated British bombers as well as French Morane 406 and American-made Curtiss fighters.

Only the Hurricanes had a chance, and they were overwhelmed.

Dowding, now in charge of Fighter Command, was beside himself as he saw his forces drawn far below the fifty-two squadrons agreed by the Air Ministry as being the minimum necessary for home defense. He couldn't understand how Churchill could acquiesce to French pleas for more and more aircraft. The reason was simple. In war there are always those "who don't get the word." In this case, the word was "fifty-two" and, as RAF fighter ace Peter Townsend later wrote, "Incredibly, Churchill got it into his head the figure was twenty-five." So as the prime minister dispatched Hurricanes to almost certain destruction in France, he thought he hadn't disturbed the agreed minimum force needed to protect Britain.

All of that was, of course, closely held within the government. Meanwhile, on the farm in Minnesota where I was helping Dad with the corn crop, I read of the debacle in France and became even more determined to throw in my lot with the British. Little did I know that my future squadron mates had seen their first action over Dunkirk, and that some had encountered disaster.

August twelfth, the day of my own disaster, saw the *Luftwaffe* hit the RAF's three airfields closest to the channel and its radar eyes as a precursor to *Adlerangriff* (Eagles' Attack), their all-out push to gain air superiority in preparation for invasion. Before my afternoon scramble, they had cratered the forward base at Lympne at 8:16 a.m., knocked five coastal radar sites off the air at mid-morning, shelled my staging base at Hawkinge with coastal guns firing from across the channel, and caught 65 Squadron just ready to take off from Manston. Despite the odds, however, eleven of 65 Squadron's twelve Spitfires managed to get airborne.

As I was sparring with Messerschmitts, a large formation of Ju 88 bombers again hit Lympne. They were the best the Germans possessed and the most difficult for a fighter pilot to destroy because of their high speed, well trained gunners, and air-cooled radial engines which could absorb a great deal of punishment before faltering. A separate raid of Ju 88s simultaneously plastered Hawkinge from five thousand feet, making two bombing runs and destroying a pair of hangars, several workshops, and other buildings. Subsequently both airdromes suffered additional damage at the hands of Dornier 17 bombers.

The Germans had selected the day after my shootdown as *Adler Tag* (Eagle Day), the actual kick-off of *Adlerangriff*. But solid clouds topping at twelve thousand feet caused Goering to cancel the planned morning raids. As usual someone didn't get the word, and sixty-plus Dornier bombers, called "flying pencils" because of their silhouettes, launched on schedule. Without fighter escort they pressed on to their targets of Eastchurch airfield and Sheerness naval base, breaking into the clear over the Thames Estuary where radar-vectored Spitfires and Hurricanes shot down five and damaged six.

In mid-afternoon a host of Messerschmitts swarmed across the channel in hopes of drawing a massive reaction by RAF interceptors. Radar controllers scrambled only one squadron, holding the rest to meet the expected bombers. Eagle Day exploded at half-past three when an armada of almost three hundred aircraft assembled over the Cherbourg Peninsula and headed for targets in western and southern England, an area protected by Fighter Command's

Number Ten Group, which launched all its fighters. Ju 88 bombers hit the seaport of Southhampton, heavily damaging the center of town and its docks but overlooking its prime target, the Woolston Spitfire factory.

Later the enemy returned to the realm of Keith Park's Number Eleven Group, the area most sorely tried throughout the battle. This time Ju 87 "*Stuka*" dive-bombers searched through scattered clouds for the airfields at Rochester and Detling, some twenty-five miles west of the hospital in which I was recuperating. Hurricanes repulsed the Rochester-bound formation, but the Detling raiders dived unopposed upon that Coastal Command base destroying twenty-two aircraft, killing sixty-eight persons including the station commander, and wounding scores. According to statistics compiled after the war, on this day the enemy lost forty-five aircraft in action, suffered three destroyed in accidents, and counted thirty-nine damaged. Our losses were thirteen aircraft destroyed and three pilots killed.

The fourteenth of August passed quietly except for a donnybrook involving some two hundred fighters over Dover some sixteen miles southeast of my hospital. Number 615 Squadron lost two pilots, and three pilots of 32 Squadron walked away from forced landings. We shot down two Messerschmitt 109s. Numerous raids by small formations kept Fighter Command on its toes, but the absence of mass penetrations convinced Air Marshal Dowding that most of the *Luftwaffe* was being prepared for a maximum effort on the following day.

Chapter Seven

Convalescence

All I could do from my hospital bed was doze fitfully or listen to the constant activity overhead. At first the sound would be like a distant storm approaching—just a heavy murmuring and rumbling that gradually grew louder. It still sounded like a great wind approaching until finally, as it was getting quite distinct, little individual sounds would separate themselves from the rest. The smooth high-pitched moan of a Messerschmitt in a power dive would rise above the rest of the sound momentarily, echoed by another doing likewise a few seconds later.

About that time we would begin to hear the barking of distant anti-aircraft guns and the sound of their shells exploding. As the great storm came closer, the guns near by would take up the chorus, barking fast and savagely. Then the raiders would be passing overhead with a tremendous convulsion of sound.

Sometimes they were being intercepted by our fighters, and then we would hear vicious, cascading staccato roars from the guns of Spitfires and Hurricanes, interspersed with the banging of the cannon on Messerschmitt fighters. Terrific outbursts of agonized whining from enemy Daimler-Benz engines in power dives mingled with the throaty *rhoom-rhoom-rhoom* of the Rolls Royces on our own fighters as they milled about. Sometimes the noise of one would rise to an earsplitting pitch as a stricken machine came diving to destruction.

For the next half-hour after a raid had passed going inland, there would usually be intermittent activity overhead: individual planes that had got separated from their units, scattered machines from broken formations, damaged Nazis making for home. Sometimes there was a quick burst of machine-gun fire as a fighter surprised an enemy.

Perhaps fifteen minutes or half an hour after passing inland, the main body of the raid would come back on its way home. Usually the enemy was pretty badly disorganized by this time and somewhat reduced in number. Most often there wouldn't be one big formation any more, just lots of scattered smaller ones, the pilots scared and shaken and flying with their engines wide open, and being harried by our fighters all the way.

I hadn't slept well the night before and dozed a good share of the afternoon. I wasn't bothered much by pain at that time. My arm and hand were just as swollen and tender, but I'd learned to keep from moving and had them propped up high. I was sleeping lightly, and I suppose the constant sound of airplanes passing overhead caused me to dream that I was flying on patrol. I seemed to be separated from my formation and cruising along looking for them.

Just then a Messerschmitt opened fire somewhere over the hospital with his cannon and machine guns. In my dream I saw a Messerschmitt behind me, and the firing was coming from him. Tracers were converging on my cockpit, cannon shells exploding in my fuselage, and I grabbed wildly for the controls trying to throw my Spitfire into an evasive turn.

The dream came to an abrupt end, and I found myself half out of bed, grabbing at empty air, and conscious of about the most intense agony in my outraged hand, arm, and fingers that I have ever experienced! It made me dizzy, and I cried out a little. The pain continued quite intense even after I got settled back and had my arm where it belonged. It was so ridiculous that I had to laugh even while it was still aching. Having heard me cry out, Nurse Green found me half laughing and half sobbing from pain and weakness. The discomfort quieted down finally, and I dropped off to sleep again only to have the same thing happen about half an hour later. After that I was afraid to let myself sleep during an air raid until my hand was better.

After about ten days I moved to "Rumwood Court," a beautiful mansion near Maidstone that had been turned into a convalescent station for officers who'd improved enough to be discharged from hospital. We had nothing to do but eat, sleep, read, play games, and otherwise amuse ourselves. My new location was about half way between Dover and London, so that we more or less had seats on the fifty-yard-line to watch the constant comings and goings. More wounded flyers kept coming in, one every day or two, so we got fresh news on how the fight actually was going. They all said the same thing: pilots were tired and the squadrons at times decimated, but the morale was good, and they were shooting down a terrific number of German machines.

The matter of aircraft accountability in wartime is a complex affair. At the time I believed the official Air Ministry communiqués because they seemed to jibe with my own observations and those of my friends. We lacked reliable gun cameras, and asking pilots to recreate exactly the swirling air battles was a bit much. I tried to be as conservative as possible in my claims, as did most of my mates, but in a battle with aircraft in sight sometimes only for an instant, who can say who rightfully deserved the individual "kill" or a portion of that victory? After the war, extensive research has pretty well defined the number of aircraft lost by either side on any particular day. Overall, Fighter Command reported that its pilots destroyed 2,692 of the enemy—a bit over one and a half times the 1,733 actual losses suffered by the Germans during the battle. On the other hand, the *Luftwaffe* claimed to have shot down 3,058 RAF aircraft—more than three times the 915 machines actually written off.

On the day I was shot down, for example, the official British communiqué said that sixty-one enemy aircraft were destroyed versus thirteen of our fighters. One of our pilots (presumably me) survived. Post-war records list thirty-one German aircraft destroyed versus twenty-two RAF fighters and eleven of their pilots. In this case Fighter Command claimed a bit less than double the actual German loss, while admitting a little more than half the loss it actually suffered.

When one peruses a book such as Kenneth G. Wynn's *Men of the Battle of Britain*, which features biographies and many pictures of the 2927 men who flew at least one operational sortie with Fighter Command during the battle, he or she is most powerfully struck by their youth and by the many who were lost quickly, including an amazingly large number killed during their first encounter with the enemy. During the course of the battle, which officially encompassed 113 days from the 10th of July until the 31st of October 1940, Fighter Command suffered 544 pilots killed. In contrast, during the next five years until the end of the war in August 1945, the command lost 791 pilots in all theaters. One can truthfully say that the Battle of Britain was "a bloody dear show."

In the fall of 1940, we fought against the best the Germans had: aces like Adolf Galland, Hannes Trautloft, and Werner Molders. Many had first tasted blood in the Spanish Civil War, and almost all were veterans of the campaigns in Poland, France, and the Low Countries. No matter that we called them "Huns" and detested everything they and their leaders had inflicted upon the innocent people of England and the continent, these men were valiant opponents.

When my leg finally got well enough, I hobbled outside and watched the action from the lawns of the mansion. Most of the actual fighting was too high to see, but we often observed stricken machines coming down. Sometimes one would dive straight in, and we could hear it before it was within sight, coming with an unearthly scream just like that of a big shell. A fighter could reach nearly seven hundred miles per hour in a vertical dive. It seemed that the Messerschmitts, when the pilot was hit, usually rolled over and dropped off in a vertical dive which they maintained all the way down.

One day some of us rode out to a farm where a Messerschmitt had dived into a stubble field the day before. There was a hole about six feet across and fifteen feet deep, but the only signs of the airplane were some fragments of the wings on the ground outside the hole. The fuselage of the machine was farther down, the guards told us, and dirt from the sides of the hole had filled in above it. They estimated that the engine was down about thirty feet! The pilot had baled out, so they probably wouldn't bother to dig the wreckage up.

Not all machines would come straight in. Sometimes they would tailspin down, spinning terribly fast, almost like a toy top. Sometimes they came down in flames, turning and twisting as they dropped, their bodies wrapped in bright flames and black smoke billowing out and leaving a long, ominous trail behind. Often, too, they just came in for a forced landing, with wrecked engines or punctured radiators or both, usually leaving a long white trail of steam and glycol behind them.

At this point I hadn't heard from anyone in my squadron since being shot down. I was visited by someone from *Life* magazine who made me a good offer for a story. Realizing that *Life* was primarily a photo-journal, I made no commitment preferring to hold off with the idea of hitting *Collier's* or *The Saturday Evening Post.* What I really wanted was word from the squadron. I knew the boys would come to see me if they could, but under the strain of the terrific fighting, they wouldn't have time. Finally I received a letter from my C.O. who had baled out unhurt four days after I "became a cropper." The first lines gratified me, for they related that, on the eighteenth of August, the squadron had been moved out of Number Eleven Group's realm where fighting was most intense and into the northern regions controlled by Number Thirteen Group where only occasional bombers or reconnaissance planes intruded. MacDonell wrote that "They came over by the hundred, and we fought them as long as hearts and nerves could stand it." I wondered which of the brave lads had fought their last battles. He didn't say in the letter, and I felt rotten because I had been forced to desert them in their toughest trial. I felt proud, though, because a man who had daily gone up to do deeds more heroic than any ocean flight had remembered to write and wish me well.

Our system of rotating fresh squadrons in to relieve wasted ones was an advantage we had at the beginning of the battle over our Nazi counterparts who couldn't support unit rotations. As the battle progressed through the first week of September, however, pilot losses in Eleven Group—especially among experienced leaders—caused Dowding particular concern. Roughly one in five squadron commanders and one in three flight commanders had been killed or wounded, and the unremitting pace of up to four— or more—sorties daily seemed unlikely to ease. Speaking of this period, Sergeant Pilot "Ginger" Lacey, whose eighteen "kills" made him the top scorer in the battle, admitted that his "nerves were in ribbons and I was scared stiff that one day I would pull out and avoid combat."

Sixty-four Squadron, therefore, was one of the last to be swapped as a complete unit not only because of the logistics nightmare involved but also because all possible Hurricane and Spitfire units had already cycled through Eleven Group or the sectors belonging to Ten and Twelve Groups most often involved in the heavy fighting. Dowding experimented with rotating only a squadron's aircraft, pilots, and a few key staff, and leaving the remaining support people to service the new replacements. Splitting up a squadron, however, proved a bitter blow to its morale. By the eighth of September, the shortage of pilots made even this scheme insupportable, and Dowding was forced to begin "cross-posting"—swapping pilots between squadrons—as individuals showed extreme signs of what we Americans later called "combat fatigue."

When finally discharged from Rumwood Court in mid-September, I took the train to Leconfield, an airdrome in east-central England too far north for enemy fighters to prowl, and reported to my squadron's medical officer. After examining my wounds, he told me to take two weeks of convalescent leave before getting back into a cockpit. Being on "sick leave" allowed me to use free railway tickets to any place in England or Scotland, so I decided to spend a few days in London and then travel to Cornwall to visit friends I'd made during my Atlantic crossing.

With this in mind, I got a ticket to Plymouth via London where I took a room in a lodging house. I didn't stay long. The "Blitz," short for "*blitzkrieg*" or "lightning war," had started on the seventh of September, and this was a time when London was "getting it" at the worst. The Germans had committed their costly blunder of suspending attacks on RAF bases and radars in order to try to break the British spirit and force Churchill to seek peace.

In the daytime the mass raids seldom got over the city in any numbers, so they were at most an inconvenience to me. The trains ran on time; buses, taxis, and subways operated normally. Even though some streets were blocked off and a number of buildings were damaged or destroyed, it seemed that about eighty percent of the businesses were carrying on as usual. Here and there one could see chalked on a derelict building the city's popular boast "London Can Take It."

But at night things were different! I got along fine for the first few hours of darkness. Venturing outside to watch the show, I could hear German planes droning overhead and continuous barking from anti-aircraft guns. Most of their activity was ineffective, but Churchill's orders were to "keep on shooting away, regardless." Far up among the stars, the exploding shells appeared as silent red flashes winking about first one point then another. No searchlights swung to and fro, as the guns relied rather on sound detectors to locate targets. Once in a while, I'd hear a little humming noise followed by the sound of something small and metallic dropping near by. Those were pieces of shrapnel falling from shells that had exploded overhead. I soon went back to my room and, since no one else in the building had chosen to go to the shelters, I retired for the night. Few noises bother me, and I got to sleep all right in spite of the gunfire.

About midnight I was awakened by a distant sound like steam escaping from a radiator. It was a ghostly sort of noise, as if something were slipping through the air in the distance at great speed. In perhaps four or five seconds, it intensified to sound as if a locomotive were letting off steam close by, and then rose to a fiendish shriek, ending in a heavy explosion that shook the building.

More bombs followed every two or three minutes on the average. They made various sounds. Sometimes they fell with a long wailing sound, like an American fire siren. Sometimes it was a whistle building to a crescendo; but when they were close, it usually sounded like a locomotive passing overhead and letting off steam. Sometimes a "stick" of four or five in a row, the entire load from one machine, arrived all at once. None landed really close, but each sounded, before it hit, as if it were aimed for a point midway between the washbowl in one corner of the room and the suitcase under my bed.

I'd have been exhausted if the bombing hadn't ceased after about an hour. Then I went back to sleep only to be awakened again at about four a.m. and kept on nerves' edge for another half-hour or so by more of the performance. That morning I went downtown to Oxford Street and found that several big stores had been hit. I stayed one more night then took a train for Plymouth and later to Southampton. My friends from the boat were overjoyed to see me. As far as that goes, wherever I traveled, my uniform was the key to the best hospitality imaginable. The people almost worshiped RAF pilots. Conductors on buses, policemen in the streets, everyone I approached just fell over themselves helping me find my way about. A number of times ordinary people said, "Words can't express how we feel toward you boys! Someone even said, "You're the greatest heroes we've ever had."

After seeing quite a bit of southern England, I returned to London to retrieve my belongings. Walking from the railway station, I found the street roped off about two blocks from my destination. Just before daylight that morning, a stick of four bombs had landed on the buildings right across the street from my room! That was enough for me. I decided to spend the rest of my leave with my squadron. I had learned not to mind being shot at very much, but I couldn't get used to being bombed.

As 64 Squadron had by this time lost most of its pre-war complement, it needed time for frayed nerves to soothe and replacements to be trained. I was warmly received, but there were many new faces in the mess. Our lads had earned three Distinguished Flying Crosses (DFCs) and one Distinguished Flying Medal (DFM). One of the DFCs had gone to our C.O. who had ten confirmed victories and several "probables." The DFM (presented to "other ranks" in situations where the DFC would be awarded to officers) went to Adrian Francis "Andy" Laws, a flight sergeant at the time of his exploit. He had worked up from the ranks to become an exceptional fighter pilot with four "confirmed" victories and a commission in the offing.

I loafed around for a few days until the squadron's doctor cleared me for flying. Then I hopped into a Spitfire for the first flight in six weeks! That night Andy appeared in the mess for the first time, wearing his new uniform as an officer, with the pretty, striped purple and white silk ribbon of his Distinguished Flying Medal looking very neat under his wings on the left side of his chest. If anyone deserved a commission and the right to wear the King's uniform, he did. He had been a mainstay of the squadron from the time of Dunkirk.

We were all happy afterward that he got to spend that evening in the mess, and I'm glad that I spent a pleasant hour with him in his room before we went to bed, chatting with him about America, in which he was very interested, and lending him some magazines my folks had sent.

Next morning Andy had to give a group of new pilots some practice flying. In doing so he became the victim of a mid-air collision which sheared off his tail assembly. His machine had gone all the way down, tumbling over and over, and for some reason he hadn't baled out. Nels, flying the other involved aircraft, managed to land safely as his machine wasn't badly damaged.

Collisions were not uncommon in the confused melees that were part and parcel of the fighter pilot's environment. John Gillespie Magee, Jr., the poet who wrote the universally acknowledged pilot's sonnet, *High Flight*, was killed in a similar collision while flying a Spitfire.

I didn't know Magee, but I've learned since that we shared a similar point of view about flying and the war even though our backgrounds and personalities were quite dissimilar. The off-spring of an American mother and Scotch-Irish father who lived on the channel near Dover, his rich and powerful family financed his education at Rugby in England and at the Avon School in Connecticut after his arrival in the United States in 1939. According to his biographer, he "drifted from his inherited spiritual moorings," dissipated his allowance, and felt the allure of worldliness.

When he found aviation, he seemed to have found himself. *Dawn Patrol*, a movie about gallantry and self-sacrifice in a British fighter squadron in the First World War starring Errol Flynn and David Niven, made a big impression on him, and events in Europe made a bigger one. "I've never felt so deeply about anything before," he had said, "I've got to get into this." He joined the RCAF, trained in Canada, and proved to be an exceptional student who soloed in six hours as opposed to the normal ten or eleven. He missed the Battle of Britain but saw action before the accident claimed him in December 1941.

The loss of Andy Laws three days after his commissioning was just another sacrifice among the many thousands to curb one man's savage desire for power, but I think for most of us in the squadron his death was one of the most painful we'd had to bear.

Chapter Eight

Eagle Squadron

I haven't been quite truthful about how much I loafed after rejoining 64 Squadron at Lenconfield. Ever since my first sortie, I'd been seething because reporters were embroidering my story. As far as I was concerned, my score was still minus one: one Spitfire, serial number X4018, a total "write-off," with no confirmed victories to balance it.

So I spent every spare moment writing about life and death in a fighter squadron. I wanted to put American magazine readers inside a Spitfire's cockpit, paint the many scenes I'd observed with words that triggered all their senses, and let them know how a country felt with its back against the wall. If that accomplishment happened to avenge past rejection slips, so much the better. When I explained my intentions to MacDonell and to our "Number One," Pilot Officer A. W. Fagan, the intelligence officer and one of the squadron's three non-flying "stooges" (the others being the chief mechanic, "Number Two," and the adjutant, "Number Three"), both pronounced the idea "smashing" as long as I cleared the manuscript through the censor. I believe all of us thought that a dash of realism written by an American participant in the struggle against Nazism would promote better understanding in the United States.

One of my reasons for stopping by London on my way to Plymouth was to show Quentin Reynolds what I'd written. He'd mentioned me by name in one of his own stories, "Boy in a Spitfire," which was printed in a British newspaper before its appearance back home in *Collier's.* The *Winona Herald* subsequently reprinted the article, much to my embarrassment because of the silly comment about combat being "fun while it lasted" which he'd attributed to me. He looked at my work, seemed impressed, and graciously offered to market it for me without commission, adding that he thought *The Saturday Evening Post,* having no correspondent of its own in Britain, might be my best hope.

I had spent a lot of time re-living the past during my hospital confinement, so once I moved to the convalescent station and could hold a pencil, I began scribbling my story and thinking of ways to achieve its publication. I even thought about applying for leave in the States in order to negotiate with publishers and, of course, see my family. On the twenty-first of September, I'd written a "Dear Folks" letter describing my stay in London, visit to Plymouth, and—to alleviate the distress I knew they were feeling regarding my going back into action—the possibility of arranging a flying instructor's job in Canada after completing a combat tour. Although I reminded them of this option from time to time, the more I assessed my situation, the more I realized the RAF had not only given me a home but also had provided high adventure, companionship, and the opportunity to make contacts I could never have made in Canada or the States. If my honest inclination at this time had been to remove myself from the danger zone for an extended period of time, a perfect opportunity was about to present itself.

As I awaited our imminent move south, the Air Ministry posted me to Number 71 "Eagle Squadron" forming at Church Fenton airdrome located ten miles south of York. Needless to say I wasn't happy to be pulled out of my squadron just as it was about to rejoin the "first-team" back in Eleven Group, but part of the deal I'd made in Canada was to rally to the Eagle Squadron whenever it was formed. Arriving with me on the twenty-ninth of September was an Englishman, Squadron Leader Walter M. Churchill, DSO, DFC, who'd been picked by the RAF to command the unit. Later described by some as the ideal man to oversee the squadron initially, Churchill probably had mixed emotions when he realized his resources included only five pilots, no airplanes, and a "figurehead" American squadron commander.

Colonel Sweeny's intention had always been to pattern the Eagles after the *Lafayette Escadrille*, the all-American unit that fought for the French in The Great War. Possibly he'd believed that pilots would volunteer more quickly if they thought an American would lead them. For whatever reason he'd named William Erwin Gibson Taylor, a former United States naval aviator, to be squadron commander. The British, on the other hand, wanted one of their own in charge so that the squadron would adhere to RAF standards. In Churchill, who'd flown with distinction in France and in the Battle of Britain, they had their man.

Whereas Churchill's emotions may have been mixed, mine weren't. When I looked at the pathetic quarters and officers' mess, saw only four other names on the pilots' roster, and realized that neither airplanes nor support equipment existed, I knew that the Eagle Squadron was no more a reality than the phantom "Heinkel 113" the Nazi propaganda machine had touted. Cornering Squadron Leader Churchill, I explained that I'd just come off six weeks of enforced inactivity and didn't wish to begin another endeavor that threatened to last six to eight months. I told him further that my own squadron was about to go into action with mostly unseasoned replacements and that I had a score to settle. I didn't tell him of my writing project, but it crossed my mind that the Eagles were going to be waltzing around the flag pole for a long time before moving into the line, and that made for dull reading!

Churchill listened politely as I ended my short speech by requesting immediate reassignment back to 64. I could tell that he was sympathetic, but I also surmised he'd been counting on me to take on a good share of the flight instruction we both knew was going to be required. To his credit, however, he didn't pull rank or try to prey on my compassion for the task he had before him. He simply told me he'd forward my request and accept whatever Fighter Command decided. Afterwards I called MacDonell and told him I'd appreciate anything he could do to pull the right strings. Then all I could do was wait: a job I didn't do well.

Looking at the backgrounds of the first six pilots (including Churchill) would have led one to believe that the squadron was going to be a pretty experienced bunch. All of us had tasted combat in the Battle of Britain, but none except Churchill could claim the title "fighter pilot." We Americans hadn't progressed through a disciplined military training program, some of us undoubtedly had lied about our experience, and all of us were still deficient in theory and practice.

Nevertheless I readily befriended the four Americans. I'd heard already of the first three—Andy Mamedoff, Vernon Keough, and Eugene Tobin. They were adventurers recruited originally to fly American-made Brewster fighters being sent to Finland for use against invading Russians during the "Winter War" of 1939. Before they could arrange travel, however, the Finns capitulated, so the trio diverted to France only to arrive as the Germans were racing for the channel. Joining the mass of evacuating civilians, they evaded capture and escaped on one of the last ships to get away.

A callous American Embassy in London threatened to send them home to face charges of violating the Neutrality Act until a Member of Parliament called in the RAF which signed them on as pilot officers. After three weeks at OTU, they all went to Number 609 Squadron whose commander chose not to put them in combat until they'd gotten more familiar with the airplane and learned what was expected of them. Each had about fifty hours of operational flying in Spits by the time he got to the Eagles. I was particularly glad to meet Vernon Keough, whose four-foot eight-inch height, when compared to my five-foot two, retained for him the nickname "Shorty."

Phil Leckrone, whom an Englishman later characterized as having joined the RAF "not for the glamour, if any, or the thrills, but to defend our way of life," had also flown in the Battle of Britain. He'd been a flight instructor in the States and had made his own way to England to join the cause. Sadly, he would be the first

Eagle to die, the victim of a mid-air collision, and the other three would follow him in death before the year was out.

The remainder of our pilots dribbled in, most with the same deficiencies as our little group, but many also infected with a bad attitude, stemming most probably from having received no training in military customs and courtesies. Someone was later quoted as having said, "Old soldiers around the station were amazed at the behavior of these young Americans who, in some cases, were plain saboteurs of military tradition." Fred Almos, an Eagle himself, said many years later that "eighty percent of the Eagle Squadrons were a bunch of renegades anyway." This indictment is too harsh, especially when considering that the two follow-on Eagle squadrons—Numbers 121 and 133—were composed of persons much better disciplined and trained. For the original complement of Number 71, however, it applied in a number of cases even if the percentage was much too high.

As week followed week in the company of persons who partied incessantly because there was little else to do, I came to wish I'd paid for my own ocean crossing so that I wouldn't have been tied to the Eagles. Perhaps at twenty-seven, and with a certain amount of maturity, I was just out of step with my more boisterous mates. Yet Carroll "Red" McColpin, an American volunteer who was my age and knew many of the unit's pilots, adamantly declined a proposed assignment to the first Eagle Squadron after having finished operational training. Like me he wanted action, not publicity; and he also wanted an all-business environment.

Finally after three and a half weeks, the Air Ministry countermanded my orders, so that I could return to

64 Squadron which had moved to Coltishall Airdrome in Twelve Group. In a letter home, I told the folks that I wasn't yet on the "front line" because "it's still too far from France for them to send fighters over, but we get all kinds of chases after bombers." I tried to play down the danger by letting them know that once a pilot "learned the ropes," which I thought I had, it became "wonderfully exciting and absorbing work, at which one must be very careful at the same time that we are audacious."

I had to walk a thin line especially when writing to my mother as she understood my personality completely and could tell when I was trying to spare her feelings. When I'd mentioned possibly getting an instructor's job, she wrote my sister-in-law that she hoped I could be satisfied at that instead of "combat pilot," but she didn't suppose I would. She'd also confided to having "sorta braced" herself for anything that might happen to me. But I too understood personalities and knew that my untimely death would shatter her and the others no matter how braced they thought themselves to be.

As for the Eagle Squadron, they received their first airplanes, three obsolete Brewster "Buffalo" fighters, the day after I left. Some comedian suggested that the RAF had probably reasoned that the "Yanks" would be happy to fly the American-built naval fighters first deployed to the fleet at the end of 1938. All of the Americans thought the Brewster an insult, or at the very least an example of subtle British humor at a time when Hurricanes or Spitfires were hard to come by. Regardless, the Eagles proceeded to demolish all three in ground loops caused by their pilots' not locking the tail wheel before attempting take-off.

My estimate of a long training delay turned out to be optimistic, as getting the squadron ready to mix it with Messerschmitts took ten months of arduous and painful effort. While flying Hurricanes on North Sea convoy patrol out of Kirton-in-Lindsey in the dead of winter, three pilots of 71 Squadron met death in a demoralizing series of training misadventures: nineteen-year-old Phil Leckrone died on the fifth of January, 1941, after a mid-air collision with Ed Orbison; a month later Orbison spun out of an overcast sky into the sea; and Vernon Keough, most likely suffering from oxygen starvation, plunged to oblivion from thirty-thousand feet.

Losing three aircraft and their pilots to non-operational causes over a forty-day period elicited the harshest cut of all—a complaint from Air Chief Marshal Sholto Douglas, who'd replaced Dowding at Fighter Command, to "Hap" Arnold, commander of the U.S. Army Air Corps, that the Eagles were "prima donnas" whose performance was unsatisfactory. This came on top of an earlier embarrassment when Douglas had banished to the States thirty-one-year-old Byron F. Kennerly because of his outrageously unbecoming conduct. The Eagles had accepted, even agreed with the Kennerly decision, but the Air Chief Marshal's blanket accusation was considered a "cheap shot." Later, however, they decided that perhaps he was right; so they determined to be the best prima donnas in Fighter Command.

But losses continued. Vern Haugland's *The Eagle Squadrons* and Philip D. Caine's *American Pilots in the RAF* catalogue the sad toll. In the month of August 1941, by then flying out of Martlesham Heath in Number Eleven Group, 71 Squadron lost four pilots: Bill Driver, Ken Taylor, Virgil Olsen, and Jack Weir. The first week in

September, three went "missing" during combat: Bill Nichols turned up as a prisoner of war—POW—, but Hillard Fenlaw and Eugene Tobin, one of the first three to sign into the squadron, were afterwards declared dead. The Huns bagged two more ten days later: Bill Geiger, who parachuted into the channel off St. Omer just twelve days before his twenty-second birthday, was picked up by a German patrol boat, and spent the rest of the war at *Stalag Luft III* as a POW. Killed outright was Tommy McGerty, an eighteen-year-old native of Los Angeles who'd led his parents to believe he was working as a ground-based operator of instrument trainers.

Times were hard and the Eagles were taking it, but they also dished it out. In July they had flown 586 sorties, a highly respectable total; in October and again in November, the "prima donnas" destroyed more enemy aircraft than any other squadron in Fighter Command. But the price of notoriety was additional casualties. In October three fell victim to Messerschmitt cannons. Gillmore Daniel, a Native American from Oklahoma, had been only fifteen when he worked his way into the RAF via the Sweeny organization. After baling out over the channel, he'd drifted in his dinghy for seventy-eight hours before coming ashore, getting his wounds tended in hospital, and then shuffling off to *Stalag Luft III* to join Bill Nichols, Bill Geiger, and the thirteen other Eagles who would later fall into enemy hands. Jack Fessler crash-landed his damaged Spitfire in France, set it afire to prevent the Germans from salvaging it, and later gave himself up rather than risk the lives of the farmers who'd taken him in and would have paid the price should he have been discovered under their roof. Oscar Coen baled out over France, made contact with the Underground, and returned to Martlesham Heath two months later.

Fate, which some had indicted in past incidents, seemed to continue dogging the Eagles. Only four days after joining the squadron, Roger Atkinson died in the mysterious crash of his machine during a training flight. A week later Larry Chatterton suffered the same lot. Technicians examining the wreckage discovered that both Mark II Spitfires had suffered cracked wing spars at some previous time; Atkinson and Chatterton just happened to occupy the cockpits when the spars failed. Fighter Command grounded all machines of that series and repaired or scrapped those in similar condition, but Atkinson and Chatterton were still dead, and the strain of losing comrades affected everyone in some way. Jim Goodson, who survived the war as a POW, told of eating dinner in his squadron's mess one evening after having lost a close friend: "I looked down at my plate and saw water on it. I looked up at the ceiling to see where the leak was but didn't see one. Then suddenly I realized I was crying."

No doubt many Eagles felt like crying in mid-November when the fifth in a series of squadron commanders, the much-respected, recently married Stan Meares died in another mid-air collision along with eighteen-year-old Ross Scarborough, an accomplished pilot already credited with four kills. In choosing a replacement, Sholto Douglas decided on an American who'd been one of the pilots originally publicized as being a member of the Eagle Squadron. Twenty-one-year-old Chesley "Pete" Peterson's first initiative was to control the unremitting flow of publicity. In closing the unit to the press, he signaled that Number 71 Squadron was fully integrated into the RAF culture. Commenting on his assumption of command, *Time* magazine wished to remind its readers of the toll the war had taken on the original group of thirty-four volunteers. Using information somewhat askew, it

100

reported that twelve were dead (true), twenty were prisoners (inflated), and only Peterson and Gus Daymond were left (not so). In any case *Time* forgot about me.

Chapter Nine

Back to Work

When Fighter Command ordered MacDonell to move 64 Squadron to Hornchurch Airdrome, I was one of the fifteen pilots chosen to fly our Spitfires back into the fray. The remaining two hundred or so squadron members —spare pilots, administrative people, maintenance personnel—would follow using ground transportation.

Immediately upon landing I made a bee-line for the officers' mess to stake out a place to live. Relics of German Zeppelins shot down by the station's fighters in 1915 and 1916 decorated the entrance reminding all who passed through of Hornchurch's distinguished reputation. I secured a nice double room for myself and Pilot Officer "Jonah" Jones, who was shortly to be married and living elsewhere most of the time. I was particularly delighted because we had a fireplace, for fireplaces are the English institution that I love most of all.

Our first shift at readiness was to be from dawn till one o'clock on the morrow: the Great War's Armistice Day. I went to bed with mingled feelings of tension and fear, of course, and a kind of fierce joy. I knew I'd soon be in action again, but from what MacDonell had told me, I was in for a new experience. Back in September when the *Luftwaffe* shifted its targeting from our airfields and dispatched its bombers to our cities at night, we Spitfire and Hurricane pilots realized we were almost useless as night fighters because the flaming exhaust stacks of our machines robbed us of our night vision. Airborne intercept radar, at the time just flickering to life, offered no solution to the most pressing requirement of finding the enemy in darkness. Until industry could conjure up a proper aircraft and scientists could equip it with a working radar, the cities had to depend upon anti-aircraft guns that generated more sound than fury.

Throughout October, and beyond, day fighters in Eleven Group mostly dashed hither and yon trying to intercept hit-and-run Me 109s and 110s hastily modified to carry a bomb or two. To improve reaction time, controllers often ordered us to loiter at altitudes above thirty-thousand feet in hopes of cutting off high-flying intruders. Those streaking in just above the tree-tops operated almost unopposed except by sparsely distributed anti-aircraft guns and by barrage balloons tethered at five thousand feet over major cities.

So that's the kind of war I expected as I began my "second tour" in the hot spot. The Battle of Britain had been officially terminated in RAF histories on the last day of October, 1940 knowing that we had "won" because German invasion arrangements opposite Dover were being dismantled. While suffering the loss of a bit over nine hundred aircraft and 544 pilots killed, Fighter Command had destroyed almost two thousand enemy machines and killed an estimated twenty-six hundred air crew. Bomber Command and Coastal Command contributed to the victory by attacking targets directly connected with invasion preparations—ports, landing craft, airfields—and by doing so lost roughly 250 aircraft and almost fifteen hundred crewmen.

Combining the combat losses of RAF fighters and bombers during the sixteen weeks designating the Battle of Britain, one realizes that we lost something over half the number of German aircraft destroyed and some five hundred fewer aircrew members killed. For us, the historical significance of the battle's outcome mitigated to some extent its heart-rending cost. We had demolished Hitler's invasion plans and, in so doing, had also destroyed irreplaceable numbers of Goering's men and a significant quantity of his machines. This loss of experienced aircrews hampered the *Luftwaffe*'s effectiveness for the remainder of the war.

Early on the eleventh of November, flying for the first time in the "finger four" pattern, we scrambled against what turned out to be a false alarm. Shortly after landing and being refueled, we and our companion squadron launched together against enemy formations attacking one of our convoys in the North Sea.

By the time we got there, other squadrons had jumped the bombers, shot down several, and scattered the rest. We finished the fight by sailing into a host of escorting 109s. They proved to be a very peace-loving bunch that scattered in every direction. Visibility was so poor that most managed to evade us, but I went head-to-head against one who unaccountably turned away thereby presenting me with the easiest shot at his unprotected side I'd ever had. About four hundred yards apart, I opened up on him, allowing for his speed and aiming just ahead of his machine. Once again I experienced the terrific thrill and sense of power that came from the sound and feel and smell of one's guns fired in combat.

He kept turning and exposing himself even more to me as we closed together, and at the last I was just firing point-blank at him and had to jerk back on the stick to avoid ramming his machine. Swinging back to see what had become of my victim, I couldn't find him. As we were so low over the water, I thought I knew where he'd gone.

Caught up in the thrill of the chase, I turned toward the convoy searching for other more worthy opponents among the swirling shapes filling my windscreen. There was something amusing about the way fighter pilots investigated each other in those days before radar, computers, and missiles mechanized the dogfight. It reminded me of the way two strange dogs approached: very much alert against any hostile moves, circling sideways until they decided whether they were going to be friends. This time all the dogs were friendly. Although none of our work counted as confirmed victories, we had suffered no casualties, and we had got the new boys safely through their baptism of fire.

About a month later, in a letter from Blanche containing a batch of clippings, I learned of other sorties flown back home because of events occurring on November eleventh. Those missions had exactly the opposite purpose as ours, a lifesaving goal more in keeping with the Armistice Day spirit that celebrated the end of World War One.

The sleet, snow, and gale-force winds of Monday, the eleventh of November, 1940, had supplied Minnesota with its most devastating blizzard. That day Minneapolis recorded over sixteen inches of snow along with winds of sixty-three miles per hour. Further north, persons faced drifted snow that was arm-pit deep. All forms of transportation stopped, people jammed hotels, schools, farm houses—anywhere they could find shelter. Blanche couldn't get home from her job in the city until Wednesday night and only then by catching an up-state bus going through Robinsdale. In Minnesota fifty-nine people died in the storm, a total of 144 died throughout the nation, and damage nationwide reached six-million dollars.

After a period of spring-like temperatures, the storm had come on so suddenly that many, especially deer and duck hunters, found themselves ill-clothed, lost, and freezing. As conditions on Armistice Day worsened, Max Conrad hangared his airplanes, closed the airport, and struck out for home. A little past dawn the next morning, an excited voice on the phone told him that many duck hunters were unaccounted for and asked if he could help search for them. Despite steady winds at fifty miles per hour that made walking difficult, he made it to the field, fired up a new Piper Cub trainer inside the hangar, and with five men holding down each wing, managed to taxi out. He headed into the wind, revved the engine, signaled his helpers away, and leapt backwards into the air. Flying never more than a hundred feet off the ground, he maintained eighty miles per hour on his airspeed indicator which gave him a ground speed of twenty to thirty upwind but a hundred and thirty downwind!

He had no difficulty locating overturned skiffs, bodies, and even survivors. In some cases he shouted instructions from a hover for men to stay put or to follow his airplane toward approaching rescue parties. Returning for landing he matched his airspeed with the wind's velocity, touched down into the grasp of his ground crew, and taxied into the hangar for fuel and a cargo of five-gallon cans filled with food, whiskey, and matches.

Using the same takeoff and landing techniques, he made uncounted sorties alone or with a spotter, circled over survivors to draw in the search parties, dropped his cans of supplies, or led those better conditioned to safety. He flew until dark then flew again the next day until all the missing were accounted for. Dozens of men vowed that he'd saved their lives. Later he told his biographer that he hoped he'd be remembered, if he were remembered for anything, for the mercy flights "into the wind."

Back at Hornchurch life settled down as did the weather pattern of low clouds, rain, and dense fog. An occasional raider or reconnaissance machine would try to penetrate our area using the clouds as cover, but generally they accomplished little and fled when they suspected we were running intercepts against them. The attacks on London and other cities continued each evening.

The night of Sunday, the twenty-ninth of December, was especially blitzy. No bombs were dropped near us, but Huns droned back and forth overhead for several hours starting around seven. The anti-aircraft kept up an unceasing racket and even "Alfy" (the heavy flak gun nearby) joined the chorus more frequently than ever before, making the boys drop their ale tankards and spill their sherry in the lounge during the evening, and afterward breaking our sleep frequently. Next morning we knew what it was all about. The great fire raid had been made on the City of London, causing England's worst fire in several centuries. We seethed at the news.

Our own bombers had been conducting night operations against targets in France and Germany for some time, but the number of aircraft involved was limited and success unspectacular. Often we longed for the time we could go on the offensive and give the Hun some of his own medicine. So when the big news came shortly after the first of the year, it was like the answer to a prayer. We were to initiate things with a daylight bombing raid on a target in northwest France! A formation of bombers was to be escorted by several squadrons of Spitfires and Hurricanes, and we were included. To add to the sting of the raid, two squadrons of Hurricanes were going to shoot up the St. Inglevert airdromes.

Over a hundred of us joined up and roared across Dover headed for coast-in between Calais and Dunkirk. Furious but ineffective anti-aircraft fire greeted us as we swept on, did our job, and returned home without loss. It was a nice little trip that boosted our morale. The papers played it up, and everyone in London was talking about it.

The weather turned foggy the next day, and at noon our squadron was released. Having heard that everything from Fleet Street to the tower of London had been obliterated in Sunday's raid, James (Jim) A. Thomson (my new flight commander of whom you'll hear more later) and I took the train downtown to see the damage for ourselves. The City of London was a borough containing, among its architectural treasures, the City's financial headquarters, the Bank of England, and St. Paul's Cathedral—Wren's masterpiece most beloved by Londoners. We found the burned section—the entire area between Liverpool Street and Ludgate Circus—roped off, but managed entrance on the strength of our uniforms. Our reward was a ghastly sight: silent streets lined with empty stone skeletons of once magnificent buildings, their fire-blackened walls still standing with blank windows and nothing inside but heaps of brick and rubble.

All about was the haunting smell of burned wood as we picked our way through the ruins of the Guildhall, the City's headquarters of local government which dated from 1411. The building had suffered major damage during the Great Fire of September 1666, to be restored by Sir Christopher Wren and remodeled by others throughout the years. Sunday's raid destroyed its roof, melted the stained glass windows, damaged the Nelson and Wellington monuments, and burned the fourteen-foot-tall figures of Gog and Magog carved in 1708 to replace those lost forty-two years earlier. The crypt and the library survived, but flames consumed roughly 25,000 priceless books. The art gallery appeared to be restorable, and indeed it was. I remember thinking that the Lord Mayor's annual banquet, the Guildhall's most majestic occasion, would have to be postponed for the duration. Before leaving, Jim and I told our escort that we'd remember this devastation the next time we got a Hun in our sights. Churchill as usual offered a more eloquent summation. Emphasizing that no possible military objective existed anywhere in the vicinity, he categorized this indiscriminate fire bombing as "an act of vandalism by the greatest vandal of all time."

But the prime minister knew that the vandal had benefitted from the raid's timing between Christmas and New Year which found some of the auxiliary services on holiday, the usual complement of "roof watchers" away from their posts, and water in the Thames drastically reduced because of an extremely low tide. Guardians, who in four months of Blitz had learned how to douse and smother incendiaries, had not been on duty thereby allowing the unimpeded roof blazes to jump across the narrow streets and rage unchecked after firemen had pumped the Thames dry.

St. Paul's survived because its fire watchers had been at their posts, and a bomb originally lodged out of reach high up on the dome had miraculously fallen to the ground without igniting. At his cabinet meeting the following day, Churchill had the Town Council order that all buildings would henceforth be guarded day and night by citizens directed to incorporate that task into their weekly duties.

Once back at Hornchurch, I settled into a routine of readiness, scrambles, and fighter sweeps into France when, on the nineteenth of February 1941, an order came transferring me to a different squadron, Number 91, located at Hawkinge, our forward staging base during the Battle of Britain. I hated to leave the old bunch whom I knew so well, but the order had come with little warning, and I had to leave right away. So I avoided long farewells and left that evening.

I arrived at Hawkinge the same day as Flying Officer "Chris" Le Roux, a South African who would become a close friend. The airdrome had suffered much bombing damage immediately after I was shot down in August, but most was repaired and our new squadron mates were fine fellows who took us on a party the first night we were with them. In twenty-four hours I was feeling right at home, but then my mother had always said I'd been to so many places, she thought I'd feel "right at home" anywhere.

Ninety-one Squadron had evolved from a smaller unit, Number 421 Flight, which was formed in early October 1940 just as the Battle of Britain was winding down. A complement of only ten pilots, flying lone Spitfires usually at extremely high altitudes, visually gathered information to supplement our command and control system—items such as types of enemy aircraft being plotted by radar, precise number, and probable targets. These sorties were code named "Jim Crows," as they, like that valiant bird, raised a ruckus whenever intruders ventured near.

Fighter Command's idea was to have one designated, highly experienced unit provide reconnaissance rather than having to task uninitiated squadrons to provide the service on a rotating basis. Headquarters soon tacked on the additional jobs of keeping track of ship movements in the channel and providing weather information. This necessitated flying sorties, often in the most intimidating weather, just above the wave tops in order to lessen detection by enemy radar. The unit's motto, "We Seek Alone," took on a more ominous tone as these tasks proliferated.

On the second of December, two months before my arrival, Fighter Command had "discouraged" single-aircraft patrols in all but the most unusual circumstances because of unexplained disappearances and unacceptable combat losses. This was a great tactical improvement because it decreased the chances of a patrol's being ambushed. In essence it allowed the lead pilot to discharge his reconnaissance duties knowing that his wingman was alert to an approaching enemy. In the case of a fight, it also allowed the leader to operate knowing his rear was being protected. Two-ship patrols also increased the chances of one returning with the information and the story in the event the other's luck ran out.

I had no illusions about the difficulty of our task of identifying traffic in the channel, poking into German-occupied harbors at daybreak in all kinds of weather, and flying a repetitious flight path that the enemy knew just as well as we. In a little over four months after 421 Flight had been formed, the unit had lost six machines in combat and three others in accidents. The enemy had damaged seven. Two pilots had lost their lives and five had been wounded. We had claimed twelve kills, four probably destroyed, and six damaged. So a fighter pilot couldn't complain of a lack of action!

Complicating the operational equation was the "Hawkinge Horror," a thick sea mist that rolled in periodically and stayed for several days reducing visibility to near zero and complicating reconnaissance, landing, and—in the event one went down in the channel—rescue. I must say, however, that the job called for a certain type of person who not only knew the flying trade, but also had the eyes and mind that could see, analyze, and remember everything that was moving or docked in harbor despite whatever countermeasures the Hun cared to take. To be placed in this category was a supreme compliment as well as a thrilling experience that would make for good reading.

A week or so after settling in, however, a message alerted me to report to an embarkation port in three days for transportation to Canada! I sat for a moment completely overwhelmed. The leave back home that Squadron Leader

MacDonell had worked so hard to arrange had finally materialized.

Art returns from a sortie (photo taken after posting to 91 Squadron). Battle of Britain service was with 64 Squadron.

Spitfire crash landed at Hawkinge Airdrome. Such aircraft were carted away, refurbished, and returned to duty in a matter of days! Battle of Britain

Refueling and re-arming Spitfire. Battle of Britain

Two landing Spitfires.

Macmillan published ten editions of Art Donahue's *Tally Ho!* and one British Edition in 1942. To conserve paper, no illustrations appeared in the British Edition.

115

Art at convalescent facility recovering from burns. This photo appeared along with a strong review of *Tally Ho!* by Publisher's Weekly October 4, 1941. Battle of Britain

Art and unidentified U.S. Army Air Corps Officers pose beside an RAF "Moth" Trainer.

Chapter Ten

Interlude

The voyage in convoy was rough and seemed endless. I'm a poor sailor, and although I managed to eat my meals pretty regularly, I found that there were a bunch of rules that my stomach dictated for me: principally that I couldn't concentrate my gaze on one thing while the ship was rolling, and that prevented my reading.

I was to have about a week at home where I planned to get some exercise on the farm to make up for the loafing I'd done through the winter. Little did I know what lay in wait. My sister, Blanche, later called it a "siege." Once the press learned I had arrived in Canada on the twentieth of March, they embarked on a full-scale invasion—an invasion of privacy. I had sorely miscalculated the level of celebrity the papers had bestowed upon me, but once I realized their interest, I determined to do what I could to explain the British position.

Immediately upon disembarking in Halifax, Nova Scotia, I arranged rail transportation to Windsor, Ontario, intending to shop there for civilian clothes before crossing to Detroit and continuing my journey. Somewhere along the way, I wired that I expected to arrive Friday night, so my father conveyed that information to reporters and friends who had kept the telephone line humming. Blanche left work early that afternoon so as to be in St. Charles for my arrival. At the farm she found my parents visibly upset. They'd received a second wire saying I'd been delayed until Saturday morning, and they knew a number of folks were preparing to meet the evening train.

I'd been detained by an immigration official who mistakenly thought I'd lost my citizenship and, therefore, could not enter the country. While I dealt with him in Detroit, Blanche sorted out the false alarm at home, arranging for representatives of the American Legion, the Commercial Club, and the home guard to drop by the house to discuss preparations for the forthcoming week. A United Press photographer from St. Paul joined them. Compounding their scheduling problems was the almost impassable condition of unpaved roads, particularly the axle-deep mud that constituted the final half mile leading to our farm.

At 7:40 the next morning, about a hundred people braved a heavy snow to greet me as I stepped down from the North Western local. Mother, Dad, Blanche, and Ora were there along with friends, schoolmates, and American Legionnaires. I couldn't believe anyone other than family would meet a train on a frosty morning in late March. Their greetings made me feel like a movie star for a second or two standing there in my new civilian suit, top coat, and fedora; then I was just the "kid brother" again. Mother hugged and kissed me, the people cheered, and the United Press man snapped a picture that hit all the papers.

The next thing I knew, I was at City Hall where everyone seemed to be talking at once and flash bulbs punctuated my statements. Once the reporters from Rochester, Winona, and our local paper, *The St. Charles Press*, got their stories, we drove out home where Mother insisted I have a second breakfast. She was thwarted by a series of telephone calls: two from out-of-town reporters, several from close friends, and one from Mrs. Charles Mayo who arranged a radio interview to support Bundles for Britain, the charity that sent food and clothing to the English people.

That afternoon a reporter from *The Minneapolis Star-Journal* paid a call, other friends dropped by, and the phone didn't stop ringing. I can't remember a great deal about Saturday night except for a heap of mail and telegrams. Buried in the pile, and discovered three days later, was a wire from J. B. Lippincott, the New York publisher, who wanted to negotiate a book deal.

We awoke Sunday morning to a raging blizzard with a temperature of zero and a 45-mile-per-hour wind which made getting to church impossible. About mid-morning a half-frozen admirer, someone I'd never previously met, pounded on our front door. He'd abandoned his stalled vehicle and trudged on, nearly losing his way in the drifting snow. I thought that incident was the day's high-point, but I was wrong.

I'd once foolishly said I'd rather see two Minnesota winters than one Texas summer, but I was wrong about that too. Despite roaring fires in each of our heating stoves, we couldn't seem to take the chill off the house. Mother's answer was to pile on more coal until, as the women-folk were taking up lunch, we heard an ominous crackling. Terror stricken, we instantly realized we had a chimney fire, a situation that could ignite the roof and consume the house.

Ora and a man named Holzer, who'd just arrived in a truck, went to work on the dining room stove while I scrambled onto the roof and dumped salt down the chimney. I suffered frost-bitten ears, but that was the least of my concerns until we extinguished the blaze. Only the foresight of my father, in having the chimney swept the previous week, had confined the fire to the stove's pipe rather than the flue itself.

Parachuting out of a fiery cockpit seemed a better alternative than the scene I contemplated after the excitement died down. The meal had been ruined, soot and water covered everything in the kitchen and dining room, and we'd all lost our appetites. At least I hadn't had to clean up my Spitfire's wreckage!

As Blanche needed to get back to work on Monday, and I had shopping to do as well as a Tuesday luncheon with the Minneapolis Kiwanis Club, we all decided to head for Blanche and Ora's home in Robbinsdale rather than sit in a cold house. With Holzer's truck breaking trail, we started off in Dad's car, stopping only long enough to dig the stranger's automobile out of the drifts. The closer we got to our destination, the less snow we encountered, so that we arrived without further incident.

Monday Blanche and I went to her department store where I talked to the employees at noon, got my picture

120

taken for their newsletter, and purchased items British friends and their wives had requested, such as bobby pins and nylon stockings. For myself I bought enough material to fashion frost shields for my Spitfire's windscreen and cockpit hood and tried, without success, to find a pair of boots that would protect me in case of another cockpit fire. After dinner we visited a family named Zurn, my sisters' neighbors, who served ice cream and a special St. Patrick's Day cake.

Tuesday was a day I'll always remember. After the Kiwanis luncheon, we returned home for the dinner in my honor. Over three hundred people filled the gymnasium at St. Charles High School. The Toastmaster, Father Thomas Duane, led us in singing "God Bless America." Following the invocation, we enjoyed a spectacular meal prepared by the Guild of Trinity Episcopal Church. Afterwards the mayor spoke briefly then handed off to Judge Leo Murphy who struck a patriotic note and predicted that the Lend-Lease Act, signed by President Roosevelt a week previously with an initial promise of seven billion dollars' worth of war material earmarked for Britain, would revitalize our economy and maybe even prevent our further involvement. Max Conrad, by way of introduction, recounted several flattering incidents from my days as a barnstormer and airport manager. Then it was my turn.

International law prevented my wearing the uniform of a belligerent nation, but it said nothing about showing it to people in a high school gymnasium. I held it high so everyone could see and said how honored I was to have been among "the few" to whom Winston Churchill expressed his nation's gratitude when it became evident we had won the Battle of Britain. I said that the audience, too, in spirit had flown along with me in the Spitfire I'd named "Message from Minnesota."

Holding up a gas mask, I refrained from donning it so as "not to frighten" them with its otherworldly appearance. Responding to their urging, however, I modeled the "Mae West" life jacket I'd brought along and then showed pieces of metal wing covering from a Messerschmitt our lads had dispatched near Hawkinge. I summarized my life in a fighter squadron and profiled several of my mates including, of course, Squadron Leader MacDonell. Thanking them for backing my choice to serve England during her greatest challenge, I then entertained questions.

Walter Feehan, president of the Commercial Club, presented me with a gold Hamilton wrist watch inscribed as being from the citizens of St. Charles. He concluded by reading a poem written for the event by Raymond "King" Kelly, Champion Speed Roller Skater of the Northwest. The two verses were quite sentimental, as you might imagine, but to me the last line was a huge, if overblown, compliment: "Even kids will yell from the house tops /`Cause you've shown the American way." Realizing I still had a bit of skating yet to do, I hoped some of Kelly's speed would rub off on me.

I spent Wednesday, my twenty-eighth birthday, chasing around some of my old haunts in Wisconsin, arriving back just in time for dinner. Thursday morning I spoke to students at St. Charles High School before picking up Mother for the drive to Rochester. By the time I gave my presentation at the Rotary Club luncheon, I was beginning to enjoy my speaking engagements. Being completely committed to the British cause gave me a sense of moral authority that pushed aside my natural shyness.

Mother and I had our first privacy on the way to Rochester and then on to Minneapolis where we were to meet my sister, Dorothe, who was to arrive by train from Montana with her two children. We talked of superficialities while, I'm sure, forbidden questions concerning risk, death, and fear circulated unspoken within our minds. Mother, being extremely hard of hearing because of a childhood accident, was frequently left out of everyday conversation, so she was used to withholding her thoughts. In my case, the answers she sought were not the words I wished to enunciate, much less shout.

The next morning we all drove down to St. Charles where I telephoned the British Air Attaché in Washington and learned that I had to be in Montreal on Wednesday. This caused a fury of re-scheduling that took up most of the day. One aspect of my visit that disturbed me was that I'd had little time alone with my dad. After all, he was the person most responsible for my getting off the farm. His own dreams to do so had been thwarted, and he made sure that we children did not suffer the same fate. He had been the first boy to graduate from St. Charles High School at a time when most farmers yanked their sons out to work full time. Afterwards he went to Wisconsin, learned telegraphy, and got a job with the railroad in Iowa. There he married Ada Gertrude Brandt, a tiny, gentle girl, one of three refined daughters of a Methodist minister and "music master" who'd once been a drummer boy with Sherman's army.

When my grandparents could no longer handle the heavy work, they agreed to sell the farm and move into town. At the lawyer's office, where the final papers awaited signatures, Grandmother reneged and announced that Dad would take over. Sure enough, at the age of twenty-three, my father returned. So a man with neither a liking nor a talent for farm work and a thin, musically inclined city girl with no preparation for hardship were committed to a life not of their choosing. Brother Bob best summed it up: "A man such as our father," he said, "was completely misplaced as a farmer."

Probably because his station in life was far below what he had envisioned, Dad became an irascible man who alienated or dismissed hired hands and, as a result, was often behind schedule. Despite his quick temper, he was gregarious—loving to "jaw," as he called it, with anyone who'd listen to him. In fact, into his ninetieth year he was writing letters to the editor which the Rochester newspaper published. That evening I tried to slip away with Dad and help with the chores, but a bunch of curiosity seekers followed giving us no peace.

I loved being with my friends, but the others tried my patience. Time didn't allow me to see my Texas friends, but one day during that hectic week a bunch of them called, so that I could talk to each for a few moments. They offered to pay my air fare if I came down to Laredo even for a few hours. Can you beat that?

Saturday morning a friend from Joplin, Missouri, arrived unexpectedly. Carl Lawrence, his wife, and their baby had driven all night to see me. They planned to return immediately, but we invited them to accompany us to Rochester where I was to consult with physicians involved in high-altitude flying research at the Mayo Clinic and then do my Bundles for Britain radio show. I also invited my friend, Elmer Zadtke, to go along because he'd been such a help since my arrival. On leaving the doctors after a mutually beneficial exchange, I learned that Mrs. Mayo had invited the St. Charles contingent to tea at Mayowood, the family estate.

We had a lovely hour at this story-book mansion, but all too soon had to rush to the broadcast studio. Afterwards we had invitations to Mayowood for dinner, but all except Elmer and me declined in order to return home at a reasonable hour.

Sunday's schedule of church, dinner, and departure was upon us before we knew it. Father Madden had asked me to do my Easter duties before leaving, so I had to be at church early for confession. Mother, Dad, Dorothe, and Blanche drove with me to Winona, where I was to board the train to Philadelphia at 2:35 p.m. Blanche, bless her heart, volunteered to answer all my mail then send the lot— even the crank letters—to me. My leave had passed in a twinkling, and I soon found myself once again on a railway platform embracing my mother and knowing that only great courage allowed her to release me back to the world and the fate that awaited.

Art (on right) returning to USA for short leave.

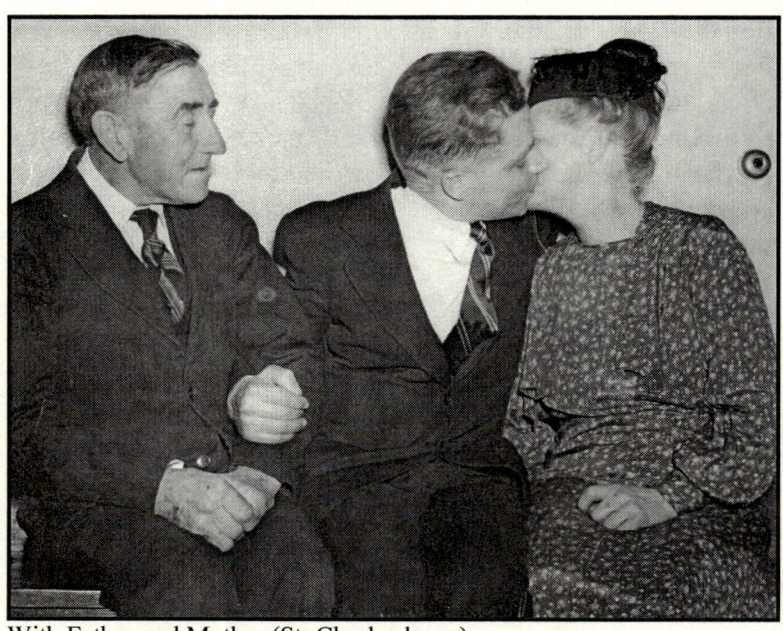

With Father and Mother (St. Charles leave).

126

Art showing his sister Blanche his "Mae West" flotation gear.

Receiving gold watch at banquet, St. Charles.

Art "pitching" the article he would submit to *The Saturday Evening Post* regarding his Battle of Britain experiences.

Chapter Eleven

Ferry Pilot

Once under way I reflected upon what I'd experienced. I found it hard to realize how much popular opinion had changed since my enlistment. People seemed solidly behind the British, although newspaper headlines trumpeted the wave of strikes sweeping Ford, General Motors, and comparable industrial giants. The year that was to bring war to the United States was also to witness over four thousand strikes involving more than two million workers.

At the time a pilot officer in the Royal Air Force earned the equivalent of eighty-eight dollars per month, out of which he had to buy his meals, keep up his uniform, and pay some six dollars income tax. It was hard to believe that, among a people ninety per cent convinced that their safety depended on England's victory, factory workers engaged in industries vital to that result were striking, delaying production, and jeopardizing England's chances.

If Germany won the war, I believed that America would be forced to impoverish herself in the greatest armament race in history trying to forestall the inevitable Nazi encroachment in the Western Hemisphere. With all of her other potential allies already defeated, I thought that America would be unable to maintain her accustomed living standards against the Nazis' advantage of slave labor. To me it seemed foolish for our workers to be using methods to raise their standard of living which threatened their very existence as free Americans.

Perhaps it all came down to self-interest. Striking workers were concerned with the welfare of their own families after a long depression whereas I, an unattached bachelor, could afford more of a world-view. Perhaps it sounds grandiose, but I had all along believed that my helping the British repel and then dislodge the Huns from their conquered lands would help prevent American boys from being drawn into combat and American mothers from being put through the tribulations that haunted my own.

During my visit I had tried to pass a message to Minnesota and to the nation that Britannia could prevail, but she needed lots of help. In some small measure, I believe I transmitted that message; and with that thought in mind, I was content to be going back into action.

I stopped in Philadelphia only long enough to wrap up details regarding the sale for a thousand dollars—fifty percent over their going rate—of my article to *The Saturday Evening Post*. Leaving their offices I believed I'd made myself clear regarding editing of the text, so I felt confident that nothing silly would appear. As I explained in a letter to my parents, I thought an article in a nationally circulated magazine would give them "cause to be a little proud of me—enough to partly atone for the worry I'm causing you."

I met my brother in New York where he had arranged a network radio broadcast which had to be canceled because of the time factor. We conferred instead with editors at Lippincott's and Macmillan's regarding my proposed book, an expansion of *The Saturday Evening Post* article then scheduled to appear in their May third issue. Both publishers expressed deep interest, and if more time had been available, I believe Bob would have invented the manuscript auction then and there. Late in the afternoon, we rushed out to LaGuardia and hopped an American Airlines DC 3 for Boston.

Bob wasn't comfortable flying; not that he was afraid, just that the cabin noise was bothersome. We joked about my flying him and his son, Bobby, out of Dad's field back in '34, and I confessed that I had been as sick as a dog on my first several flights with Max Conrad. Then I recommended that he focus on the front cabin bulkhead, as that was what I did when I was a passenger.

Bob's lovely wife, Dorothea, along with their boys (Bob Jr., Dickie, and Jim) met us at the airport, and we drove to their home in Lowell, had dinner, visited a bit, and then it was time to board the midnight train for Canada.

Montreal was the nerve center for the entire west-to-east ferry operation designed to supplant the inefficient shipboard delivery of aircraft from North America to the British Isles. I'd become familiar with Canadian Pacific Air Service recruiters during my prior visit to Montreal seeking employment as a fighter pilot. Desperately needing pilots qualified to fly the massive infusion of aircraft destined for

England, they'd practically salivated upon seeing my log book and advanced ratings. Previously they'd been sending all British purchased American aircraft as deck cargo to Liverpool. Upon arrival, American civilian mechanics would uncrate, assemble, and test fly the machines before turning them over to the RAF. Working with this group at Speke Airport became one of my options. Instead, however, it became the cover story I told my folks to ease their worries over my safety.

More than happy to ferry an aircraft back to the war zone, I assumed I'd fly a Hudson on the North Atlantic route, but after hanging around the British Consulate for two days, I was ordered to take the train back to New York. Once there, I was to embark on a ship bound for Bermuda where I'd rendezvous with a bomber of some kind and ferry it to England. In New York City, I had just enough time for a bit of sight-seeing and the purchase of a typewriter before learning that my ship was delayed and that I must return to Montreal.

Throughout this frustrating time, Bob and I exchanged telegrams concerning the book negotiations. Playing one house against the other, Bob got an exceptionally good offer from Macmillan; so we agreed they had won the prize.

Actually the prize for me was getting to know my brother as I never had before. Bob had left the farm when I was still a youngster of fourteen; consequently we'd had little time together as adults. Our correspondence after my enlistment had defined our characters, and the negotiations had cemented our closeness. He became my agent, business manager, and marketing consultant. It was he, for example, who suggested we insert in the book the Air Ministry communiqué summarizing RAF losses on the day I was shot down. He also recommended that "Yankee in a Spitfire" be added to the title in order to define the subject matter. Upon publication he and Dorothea mailed hundreds of descriptive post cards to prospective buyers.

Bob's life, with adventures as a singing actor (including playing the lead in the national tour of *Rose Marie,* which also included his future wife) and his subsequent move into radio during its early development, would make a fascinating biography. He was certainly my anchor—someone who could be trusted to oversee my affairs and respond at a moment's notice when I cabled a request from some exotic part of the world. He carried a load even heavier than the other family members; he knew how long the odds were.

Back in Montreal the Attaché gave me a railroad ticket and pointed toward Halifax. I made good use of my time by typing more of my manuscript on my new Underwood portable. Like most who'd struggled through the Great Depression, I wasn't a spendthrift, so I'd debated my purchase carefully. After considering that I was going to a place where its value would increase and where it would be worth a lot to me to be able to work around other people without disturbing them, I went all the way and made it a "noiseless" model. I wouldn't have dared work on the train with an ordinary typewriter because of the racket.

That peculiarity was another characteristic of my generation; we were raised to be aware of others and to respect their desires not to be distracted by thoughtless conduct. Quaint way of thinking, one must admit.

My ship arrived in Bermuda on the afternoon of the third of April. Steaming into the harbor was everything the most extravagant tourist advertisements ever described. The RAF put me up at the Belmont Hotel, an enormous complex with four or five hundred rooms. That night I sat outside typing by moonlight and the flickering fire of little garden lanterns.

First I wrote to my folks describing my circumstances in case they should be worried about my comfort. I still couldn't quite believe my surroundings, but I settled once again into my project knowing that I could finish the manuscript if I were to stay in Bermuda any length of time. I also knew that every day I could save in completing the story would be worth a lot of money to a person who had yet to see much financial gain from his aviation career.

By the fourteenth of April, I was virtually finished with a manuscript of roughly fifty thousand words, needing only to retype it for official review. After having idyllic writing circumstances for a week and a half, duty called once again. I was to work my way to England as co-pilot on a brand-new PBY-5 flying boat (dubbed "Catalina Mk IB" by the Brits) financed by the recently signed Lend-Lease bill. Ours was one of fifty-nine selected by the British Purchasing Commission. Forty similar aircraft, ordered by the French but diverted to England after France's capitulation, also were to cycle through Bermuda. All in all the British were to receive more than five hundred of the aircraft, which proved second only to the four-engine Short S.25 "Sunderland" flying boat in usefulness as a long-range patrol bomber.

Aware that the PBY prototype, the XPY-1, had first flown in January 1929 and that the U. S. Navy had taken its last delivery of the design two years previously, I wondered if the ungainly looking beast that had flown in from Elizabeth City, North Carolina, was up to droning some 3100 miles non-stop to Greenock in Scotland's Firth of Clyde. I was suitably impressed, however, to learn that the navy had thought enough of the product to equip nineteen squadrons with the aircraft, and that the Museum of Natural History had used a civilian version to complete in 1939 the first circling of the globe's greatest diameter and the first global flight by a seaplane. During the museum's year-long expedition, their aircraft had performed flawlessly and had flown the South Atlantic from Africa to New York non-stop. Later in the war the PBY went on to achieve a sterling combat reputation and ultimately became the most produced flying boat design ever conceived.

As I inspected the aircraft more closely the day before departure, I came to appreciate the spacious crew accommodations, rugged construction, and graceful lines of the stressed-skin fuselage sweeping upward to join the massive empennage assembly with its huge rudder and high-riding horizontal stabilizer. Most impressive were the twin, twelve-hundred horsepower Pratt and Whitney R-1830-82 radial engines, each sporting twelve-foot diameter, three-bladed Hamilton-Standard adjustable-pitch props. The engines were positioned close inboard of the fuselage and shrouded by nacelles molded into the 104-foot wing, itself parasol-mounted aft and above the flight crews' station. Amazingly the stabilizing floats that extended for water operations folded upwards in flight to form the wing's tips. The only compromises to an overall streamlined effect were the two sets of external struts connecting the hull and the wing on either side of the fuselage and the bulbous Plexiglas blisters protecting the left and right waist gunners' positions.

Of one thing I was certain: although our progress would be plodding, it would be infinitely faster and much safer than zigzagging in convoy through stalking submarines. Had we been given the luxury of a choice of route, we'd have taken the one flown by commercial flying boats with refueling stops in the Azores and Lisbon, but neutral Portugal had closed both those way-points to military traffic. Flying a great circle would take us northward nearly as far as Newfoundland and would require at least a fifteen-knot tail wind to assure our safe passage. Awaiting this fortuitous condition accounted for my extended stay in Bermuda.

At the crack of dawn on the fourteenth, as we cruised through a light swell around Darrel's Island and out to where we'd begin our take-off run, the thought struck me that the rugged old girl seemed well suited to handle an open-sea emergency landing, an option the land-based Hudsons, Flying Fortresses, and Liberators didn't possess. Heavily loaded with twenty-nine hour's worth of fuel and stripped of all non-essentials including extraneous radios and machine-guns, we accelerated ever so slowly before lifting off. Settling onto an east-north-easterly heading, we clutched in the autopilot and climbed to find the tail wind we expected to ride all the way to Scotland.

Just before sunset our navigator took a celestial sun shot in order to plot our longitude and compute how far we'd progressed. Had we not made our "point of no return," we would have had to return to Bermuda to await a more favorable wind. Fortunately we proceeded on toward the approaching darkness.

136

The long, monotonous flight gave me plenty of time to review the bidding. In the nine months since I'd rejected a thousand-dollar-a-month ferry pilot's job back in Montreal, the aircraft delivery system had matured significantly, but a shortage of experienced people was still its major deficiency. The Atlantic Ferry Organization now managed the "Atlantic Bridge" which the Canadian Pacific Air Service had set up, but it too was about to gain a new name and an influx of military people.

Even though the massive air bases being constructed at Dorval outside Montreal, Goose Bay in Labrador, and Prestwick in Scotland wouldn't come on line until the end of 1941, by that time 748 aircraft would have already passed through a ten-day-long pipeline that beat previous factory-to-destination delivery time as deck cargo by some three months. Maintaining its headquarters in Montreal, the newly hatched RAF Ferry Command would oversee the development of an additional series of airfields in Greenland and Iceland which, by spring of 1942, would allow short-range fighters to hop from one base to another without at any time exceeding eight hundred miles flown on any overwater leg.

Just two months after my crossing, the Air Ministry earmarked six of their first contingent of four-engine Liberator bombers—they called them LB-30s—to initiate a shuttle operation carrying returning ferry crews and other important persons and freight between Scotland and Montreal. This aerial taxi service replaced the prolonged and dangerous shipboard crossings that had tied up crews and caused a huge backlog of aircraft awaiting delivery.

I don't mind admitting that I did some second guessing as to whether I'd made the right choice of career paths. Sure, the pay of a ferry pilot was good, but danger—much of it beyond his control—lurked at every step of the way. Although the overall delivery process was amazingly routine, the unexpected still happened. Occasionally an aircraft just disappeared; once a Hudson rammed a hillside approaching Prestwick; and three separate crashes of LB-30s flying the west-bound shuttle wiped out forty-seven ferry crew members returning from the war zone.

In my mind the ferry pilot was a gypsy engaged in a necessary but uninspiring milk run. The fellowship, the thrills, the sense of being on a crusade—all were missing. Even though my family might rest better at night if they believed I was out of combat, I knew as a ferry pilot I'd become hostage to ill winds, mechanical breakdowns, and even—after a while—complacency. As I twisted uncomfortably in my seat, lulled by the mind-numbing beat of the propellers, and fighting the effects of spirit-sapping boredom, all I could think about was rejoining the squadron and putting my name on the morning's dawn patrol.

I remember the crossing primarily for its duration and the fact that we were most often out of radio contact. We did manage to get a bearing passing abeam Iceland and were able finally to home in on our destination. Precise navigation was supremely important because of our limited fuel reserve and the knowledge that a forced landing in neutral Ireland would condemn us and our airplane to internment for the duration. One reason I was aboard was that I knew the RAF's radio identification procedures, so that we'd not be harassed upon arrival.

My pilot settled the majestic bird gently onto the protected waters opposite Greenock and taxied directly to the facilities of Scottish Aviation, the company responsible for fitting out arriving flying boats for RAF service. We'd been airborne some twenty-eight hours and awake at least five before that. But I'd gotten my second wind, so it was some time before I could settle down to an afternoon nap before catching a ride to Glasgow and boarding the night train.

I arrived in London early on the seventeenth of April, the morning after the greatest bombardment it had yet absorbed. The sun was a red ball glowing feebly through the haze of brown smoke that covered the city. You can imagine my feelings upon seeing this most recent sacrilege. I had just returned from the light, the glamour, and the laughter of the United States only to see the results of villainy rained indiscriminately upon innocent people.

Waiting for the train that would take me to Folkestone, I entered the crowded restaurant at the station for tea. A lady sat down at the same table, looking tired and a little stunned. She told me she lived just outside London but had a little restaurant in town. She'd spent the day winding up her business as best she could, because her place had been blasted to bits the night before. And she was only one of many. Those Americans who preferred to have war come to them, rather than letting their sons fight abroad, could have taken a lesson from that woman's suffering. I left the restaurant itching to strap into a Spitfire.

Chapter Twelve

Channel Watch

It was swell to get back to 91 Squadron, although I felt like a shirker after being away so long. We'd had successes, but also losses. Sergeants Arthur W. P. Spears and Jackie Mann fell to Major Adolf Galland, commander of the third *Gruppe* of *Jagdgeschwader* 26, and his wingman, *Oberfeldwebel* (Warrant Officer) Robert Menge. The Germans were flying new Messerschmitt 109Fs which were faster than their predecessors, and better armed with a more rapid-firing cannon.

Spears, the nephew of Major James T. B. McCudden, the fourth-ranking British ace in World War One and winner of the Victoria Cross, was a veteran of the Battle of Britain and a founding member of the original 421 Flight. As his machine disintegrated around him, an exploding cannon shell mangled his right arm and machine gun bullets ripped into his cockpit. He baled out and was taken to Royal Victoria Hospital at Deal where doctors removed splinters from his arm and bullets from his leg.

That incident ended his operational flying, but he survived the war to retire in 1970 as a squadron leader.

Mann, who had fought in the Battle of Britain with me in 64 Squadron, found himself over the channel with a wrecked engine. He managed to glide back over land, where he committed himself to a forced landing. Descending through two hundred feet—too low for bale out—his machine burst into flames leaving him with no alternative but to ride it in. After sliding to a fiery stop, he crawled out of the cockpit and, despite terrible burns, took his camera from his pocket, carefully adjusted it for light and distance, and snapped two pictures of the blazing wreck before staggering across two fields to a farmhouse!

The odds had finally caught up with Jackie Mann who had been credited with five Me 109 fighters destroyed and who himself had been shot down six previous times. He underwent plastic surgery becoming (like Richard Hillary, Geoffrey Page, and many others) a member of Archie McIndoe's "Guinea Pigs Club." Awarded the Distinguished Flying Medal while in hospital, he subsequently gained a commission and left the service after the war as a Flight Lieutenant.

I wish I could say that Jackie lived happily ever after, for if anyone deserved that outcome it was indeed he. Forty-eight years after the ambush by Galland, while retired from an airline career and living in Beruit, he was kidnapped by Lebanese members of a splinter group of the terrorist organization *Hezbollah* and held hostage for twenty-eight months in solitary confinement punctuated by regular sessions of torture.

Like his encounter with Galland, he'd been in the wrong place at the wrong time and had been undone by superior forces. I suppose in his loneliness he sometimes compared his incarceration to time spent as a Guinea Pig under McIndoe's merciless routine of recurring surgery and physical therapy. In neither case had he brought such terrible consequences upon himself, yet one must believe that the toughness of spirit that allowed him to shoot photos of his downed Spitfire had ridden herd on his sanity and carried him through physical and mental torture.

His release on September 24, 1991, was part of a complicated prisoner exchange of western hostages for Lebanese and Palestinian prisoners held by Israel, and it occurred just six days shy of the last mass daylight bombing raids of the Battle of Britain, fifty-one years previously. A Spitfire fly over saluted his return to his homeland.

The legendary Galland, whose fifty-eighth victim had been Spears, achieved a final score of 104 kills and went on to become a general commanding all German fighters. Subsequently he served in the post-war *Luftwaffe*, wrote a superb memoir entitled *The First and the Last*, and died in 1996 at the age of 83.

When I rang up the mess at 64 Squadron to thank MacDonell for helping to arrange my leave and to tell him about the book, only sadness greeted me. The C.O. was a prisoner of war held at *Stalag Luft III* after having been forced to parachute into the channel while nursing a crippled fighter home from a sweep in France. "Pip" Pippet went missing, later to be declared killed in action, and Norman, a new replacement unknown to me, had been killed outright. I wasn't prepared for the number of

143

casualties suffered during what was considered to be light action.

Immediately I cabled Bob asking him to dip into the money my article had provided and purchase a blanket, food, and other items for the Red Cross to deliver to MacDonell. We received a signed receipt for the first package and repeated this practice several times for him and others who subsequently joined him in captivity.

I fell back into the routine that was not a routine for 91 Squadron. We always launched a low-flying dawn patrol to see what the Hun was up to, but seldom did the pilots know what to anticipate. One day it might be a minesweeper or a motor torpedo boat or even, in one case, a tender towing a floatplane. These and the aircraft on occupied airfields were always inviting targets for strafing. As you might imagine, machine gunning surface targets isn't the easiest pastime. In fact it's the most hazardous. To hit anything one must fly a straight, predictable path taking care not to get target fixation which causes one to fly into the ground. The approach, no matter how low or fast, often has to run the gauntlet of anti-aircraft and small arms fire. Anything really valuable, of course, will be protected by active ground defenses, obstructions, and patrolling fighters. Pulling off the target calls for abrupt and frequent changes of heading.

But for all its hazards, or more likely because of them, strafing is just plain thrilling. And so is air-to-air combat where you're matching your experience, skill, and courage against your opponent's; "letting it all hang out" is the phrase coined by fighter pilots in another war at a later time. My first "go" after returning from America was on the homeward leg of a dawn patrol with Tony Lee-Knight, my flight commander. We were at five hundred feet abreast of each other in a loose formation so that we could watch each other's tail. I was flying a brand-new Spitfire Vb armed with two 20mm cannon and four Browning machine guns mounted in the wings. On the left side of the fuselage, forward of the cockpit, she sported a name identical to her predecessors: "MESSAGE FROM MINNESOTA and she was a little darling. Alerted by our radar controller's warning of Huns in the area, I spied two 109s streaking along just above the water a few hundred yards behind us. They were camouflaged dark, with their noses painted yellow. Behind them were six more in close formation.

We maneuvered to engage. I took a snap shot at long range, and it was swell to hear the bedlam again and smell the powder smoke and feel a Spitfire shudder and slow from the recoil as the guns roared. Twice I saw small pieces fly back off his machine as I was firing. Our beautiful little dogfight continued among broken clouds by Calais with me hammering another adversary, so that he pitched down in a forty-five degree dive, with black smoke rippling back from under his fuselage. He had no chance to recover before hitting the water, but I didn't observe him crash, so I was awarded only a "probable." The first engagement, which resulted in my seeing pieces flying off the aircraft, gained me credit for one "damaged."

With a description of this action, I ended my book and sent the manuscript to my squadron commander, Jean Demozay, formerly of the *Armee de l' Air* who later died a hero's death destroying a V-1 robot bomb and is remembered as the war's second-leading French ace. Afterwards the station commander had a crack at it, and then the formal censor gave it the official reading. While all of this was going on, I began searching for a quick way to get the manuscript to the publisher. Someone mentioned knowing a woman who planned a trip by Pan American Clipper to New York toward the end of May. The timing seemed fortuitous, so I contacted this person, whom I will call "Miss Evans," and thus began a bizarre, but thankfully short, relationship.

She turned out to be a wealthy grass widow who was approaching middle age, homely, and I believe, a little unbalanced. When I asked if she would carry my manuscript, she assured me she would be happy to do so. Since I had typed five copies, I planned to send one with her and one through regular air mail as soon as the censor gave the go-ahead.

Because Macmillan wanted the manuscript quickly, I spent an entire week's leave in London revising to satisfy the oftentimes nonsensical objections of the censor, arranging for photographs from the Ministry of Information, and trying to get a straight answer from Miss Evans who told me her trip had been postponed but would be rescheduled.

Soon I realized she was infatuated with me, and I must say she became more than a little brazen. When I went back to Hawkinge, she called every day using her transportation arrangements as a ploy to speak with me. One afternoon she arrived unexpectedly at the airdrome in her automobile and invited me to dinner at a Folkestone hotel. Her mentioning that she had already engaged a room confirmed for me that she was quite immoral, and I determined to have nothing more to do with her. I told her in as harsh a manner as I was capable that I was unable to accept her invitation and that I had made other arrangements to have the manuscript delivered.

Subsequently I refused to accept her calls or answer her letters, and in time I heard no more from her.

Finally the censor gave his approval, and I mailed my personal Bundle from Britain on Saturday, the thirty-first of May, thereby beating by one day my self-imposed goal. Somewhere along the way, the package was delayed until the twenty-first of June. My editor at Macmillan, H. S. Latham, was beside himself. Perhaps anticipating the book's having a positive affect upon public opinion, the Ministry of Information sent a back-up copy via diplomatic mail. At about the same time, I got a letter from Blanche and Ora with a clipping of my article from *The Saturday Evening Post*. A thousand dollars is a thousand dollars (actually a lot more in those days), so I suppose I shouldn't have cared about the layout of the story. But I did. Strongly!

Reading the text I came to believe that I was being treated to another lesson on how material could be manipulated to enhance or decrease its impact. Although I assumed the editors would cut some of my words, I never dreamed they'd write the stuff they did, especially the first couple of paragraphs which put the focus on me rather than on my story. Particularly embarrassing was the choice of a two-year-old photograph of obsolescent Hurricane Mark I fighters (sporting fixed-pitch, wooden, two-bladed propellers) to illustrate a story of Spitfire operations. More subtle, but nevertheless calculated to my way of thinking, was the placing of Charles Hanson Towne's four-stanza poem, "Fog: In time of War" exactly in the middle of the last page of my article, so that my words framed the poem in a way that would cause a reader to assume the poetry related to the text or even summed it up.

Nothing could have been further from the truth. Whereas *Tally Ho!* was precise, well defined, and optimistic, Mr. Towne's poem envisioned a fog of war that "confounds and frightens . . . / Clouding our vision, confusing our blind hopes / [So that] I shudder at the dimness all about me." It spoke in a pessimistic tone completely foreign to me and to those of the RAF who met the enemy knowing exactly what was at stake and where our duty lay.

This is not to attack Mr. Towne's poem which, in proper context, is a quite acceptable rendering of the atmosphere which has enveloped wars since the beginning of time. I should imagine he shared my feelings of the inappropriate placing of his work juxtaposed to mine.

Was the placement haphazard? Certainly little in a major magazine is arranged without forethought. Was it the calculated work of someone ill-disposed toward the British and to any American support of their cause? Plenty of that ilk existed; one, Joseph P. Kennedy, happened to be United States Ambassador to England when I arrived in July 1940. Many others belonged to the America First Committee that championed isolationist neutrality. Whatever the cause, I couldn't help but feel that someone had consciously undercut me just as a saboteur would snip the control cables of an unattended Spitfire.

Over time I've seen the growth of an insidious movement which seeks to mix propaganda (some call it advertising) with news or history. The Nazis honed the practice as they rose to power. Could it be that Adolf Hitler's most atrocious contribution will have been the perfection of techniques of manipulation that strip from any particular subject all that is good, ethical, and true?

What I didn't know at the time was the extent of the competition between Germany and England to sway American public opinion. Dr. Joseph Goebbels' Ministry of Propaganda and the New York-based German Library of Information vied against the British Ministry of Information and their United States-based compatriots, the British Embassy in Washington and the British Library of Information in New York. All of that is material for another book, one that Nicholas John Cull wrote under the title *Selling War: The British Propaganda Campaign Against American Neutrality in World War II,* which Oxford University Press published in 1995.

According to author Cull, the British won that competition, rallying from a point in 1939 where 74 percent of Americans surveyed disagreed with Churchill's belief that the war was a struggle "to defend Christianity." By the spring of 1940, however, many out-spoken Americans had associated themselves with The Committee to Defend America by Aiding Allies or with The Century Group, which shared the same views. In the United States, numerous comic books and newspaper strips were politicized, and pulp fiction was overwhelmingly pro-British as, "presses ran hot with tales of RAF Gallantry." Leading hardcover best sellers of 1941 were written either by "Anglophile Americans" or British writers, and "an Eagle Squadron pilot named Arthur Donahue wrote *Tally Ho! Yankee in a Spitfire,* a rousing memoir that mixed Nazi brutality with a polemic against American neutrality."

I don't know about the "polemic," but I must say I like the sound of "rousing." It's also nice to know that, after almost seventy years, someone still remembers my first book!

Despite reservations over the *Post* article, I felt mighty proud to see my by-line beneath the title, and I had high hopes for the book that would follow. Writing the manuscript had taken a tremendous amount of my time, so I felt like an anxious father as I awaited its birth. I knew that Bob would be the mid-wife, and he wouldn't allow the "doctors" in green eyeshades to make more than minor corrections of grammar and syntax. Actually Bob told me the manuscript needed little editing: another tribute to the St. Charles public school system!

Writing the book also took its share of time that a young bachelor might otherwise have invested. But it kept my mind focused, made me see things more intensely, and allowed me to be able to purge my emotions when fate dealt some hard knocks. Parts of me were scattered throughout the pages along with parts of people who meant a great deal to me: squadron mates such as Peter Kennard-Davis, Jackie Mann, and Donald MacDonell (to whom I dedicated the book even though the censor wouldn't allow me to identify him by name).

Later, upon reading the published version, I realized that it was in the tradition of much American literature: a young man's movement from innocence to experience. As I wrote on the penultimate page, I had considered "touching on the emotional side," but I rejected that in the event "it might look melodramatic." I had come a long way from St. Charles, Minnesota, and I had a long way to go before I returned again, but my choice of style was, I believe, the correct one. *Tally Ho!* is a young man's book: an optimistic book composed of experiences, heartache, and growth within a moral framework. Maybe it was meant to be read especially by young men who might be called upon to make the same journey.

150

Perhaps in its own way, it was the book that was meant to be for that particular time. Others would follow—Hillary's *The Last Enemy* for one—that would be more mature, more philosophic. Maybe even I would write one, or two, or three. Who could know? But for a brief respite in June of 1941, I knew I was happy and at peace with myself.

Chapter Thirteen

Toward the Unknown

Once I learned my publisher had the manuscript, I was able to catch my breath and take stock. Life was good. June 1941 brought sparkling, invigorating weather. I remember trying to describe my environment to the folks in a letter dated the sixth of June, three years before the date none of my generation would forget. "This is lovely country this time of year," I wrote. "The temperature is nice and warm most of the time, but not hot or sultry, and it's very green, like the Whitewater Park if not more so. The soil is dark and rich, and grass grows thick and luxuriant everywhere. The trees are also thick and leafy, and as a good proportion of the land is wooded and most of the rest sheep pasture, you can probably understand how green it all looks. There are also a lot of wild flowers, including millions of bluebells and buttercups, and some white flowers that look like buttercups except for color. I usually walk from the house where we sleep to the airdrome these days, just for the pleasure of walking through the country. Most roads are narrow and winding—with turnout places where cars can meet, and where the road passes through woods, you often can't see the sky for the heavy branches of trees overhead. Half a mile from the airdrome you'd never dream there was a war; it's so peaceful and nice, with sheep grazing in the meadows, little children playing about, and farmers doing their normal work."

I went on to describe my feelings when flying over occupied territory: "The strangest thing is flying over France, cruising over the countryside and seeing farmers driving along the road in little carts or working in the fields, and trying to realize what a tremendous barrier separates me from them, wondering how hungry they are, what their thoughts are. I'd like to drop down and wave to the people sometime, although there's seldom a chance to do that safely."

It was easy to be optimistic in such surroundings and with the war news generally favorable. I remember in the same letter trying to tally up the score: "The fortunes of war seem to swing back and forth; at least they aren't going against us all the time. We lost out in the Balkans while we finished winning in Abyssinia. Lost the *Hood* and won the *Bismarck*. Lost Crete, but are winning the fight against night bombers and actually stopping them. The 'Battle of the Atlantic' seems to be anybody's right now, but time is working in our favor. Now we've just started moving into Syria forestalling Germany there and winning a big diplomatic victory in that the French aren't fighting us. If that's successful the Huns will probably have to fight either Turkey or Russia to continue their advance in that section. The whole setup looks encouraging to me."

Sixteen days later, on the twenty-second of June, three German army groups smashed into the Soviet Union

154

and drove to within sixty miles of Moscow in three and a half months. Worse was yet to come before 1941 had run its course, and I would find myself involved in a far more desperate enterprise at year's end. But for a time in early June, life was indeed good.

I had left unsaid in my letter that I was tiring both of the lull that had followed the Battle of Britain and of the reconnaissance mission of 91 Squadron and felt drawn toward a more active theater, a place where a fighter pilot could mix it up. At that time Malta or the Middle East seemed to be the hot spots. Little did I know what fate had in store for me, for surely fate had a hand in the events that were to follow.

Several days after writing that letter, I went up to London for a bit of leave and to negotiate regarding my book. This time I went first class staying at the Regent Palace Hotel on Piccadilly Circus, a place favored by Americans of the Eagle Squadron. The almost nightly raids initiated on the seventh of September, 1940, had ended in May, so the Huns cooperated with my plans and refrained from bombing.

Returning to Hawkinge, I wrote a letter home describing my stay and mentioning that I had been offered a night fighter slot but had turned it down. I did so for three reasons, only the last of which I offered the folks: first, the machines we used (mainly twin-engine Blenheims and Beaufighters) were verging on obsolescence and were awkward at best; second, I'd have to waste time learning the aircraft and the tactics; and third, I thought I could accomplish more by staying at Hawkinge for the time being. Even though I had only two confirmed victories, I thought that some of the information I had brought back

155

from patrol had benefitted the overall effort. Because my letters had to pass the censor's review, I thought it best not to mention my belief that the night fighter mission would atrophy as German raids on Britain petered out.

As I was writing, Paddy Barthropp, who the previous day had got his first confirmed Hun since joining the squadron, popped in and asked if there was anything to do. I told him he could help me finish my letter, so he immediately penned the following to my mother and dad: "Art asked me to write you a note. I have never been to America but hope to get over after this thing is all over. As you know Art is in the Squadron. We try to keep the little chap under control (it's a bit of a job at times). The Germans seem very frightened of him. Being an Irishman I am taking him over to Ireland on our next leave (July 4th —11th). I don't think they have any food over there but we will exist somehow."

We did more than merely "exist." As I was detained for a few days, Paddy went on ahead. Anticipating seeing my first bright lights since Bermuda (Eire being neutral and having no blackout), I made the three-hour crossing from Holyhead, an English port south of Liverpool, to Laoghaire, near Dublin. Paddy met me at the dock with our dates, two sisters, one of whom was returning the next day to her nursing duties in England. Paddy and I spent the night in Dublin then journeyed some thirty miles southwest to Portarlington and the country estate owned by his Godmother.

"Rath House" was elaborately furnished, full of brass-framed paintings, statuettes, hand carved furniture, ornamental vases and pottery. The meals were absolutely luxurious. I had hoped to visit Cahirciveen, Grandpa

Patrick's home village, but it was on the western side of the island and impractical to reach in terms of time and distance.

Paddy and I returned to Hawkinge by way of London where we were treated to a show at the Victoria Palace Theatre courtesy of Lady Manton. She was a fairly wealthy woman past middle age, but a live wire with a passionate love for fighter pilots in general and 91 Squadron in particular. When I arrived back on station, I found that the RAF had rewarded my year of service with a promotion to Flying Officer, the rank equivalent to First Lieutenant in the U. S. Army Air Forces.

Then it was back to dawn patrols and snoops into France flying in shirt sleeves with canopy open at low level, walking through the country lane to our quarters at "Whitegates," taking a dip in the pool, or writing beside it. The reviews of my book were beginning to come in, and I had reason to feel even better. One critic wrote that *Tally Ho!* was "a thrilling and inspiring story that Donahue tells and he tells it simply without affectation." He concluded by saying "Donahue packs into his tale the most vivid accounts of combat that have yet appeared. The Air Ministry ought to blush in shame for not getting out anything like it a year ago." Maybe that's why they sent my second manuscript copy in the diplomatic pouch!

Publishers' Weekly gave me a two-column write-up complete with a picture taken when I was convalescing. They reported that reaction to the first edition published on the thirtieth of September was good enough to merit an immediate second printing. In addition to mailing post cards to everyone they could think of, Bob and Dorothea began promoting the book at all sorts of civic and social gatherings. The resulting publicity provided more clippings for the scrapbooks that Dorothea had started when my adventures began to interest the newspapers.

Determined to do her part in Minneapolis, Blanch inspired a window display at the downtown Dayton Company department store where she worked. It featured copies of *Tally Ho!*, reviews from major newspapers and national magazines, pages of my typed manuscript showing words and sentences deleted by the censor, and the fabric I'd cut from the bullet-riddled fuselage of a crashed Nazi raider. She also made sure that surrounding editors and journalists didn't ignore my book's publication and reader acceptance. *Tally Ho!* ultimately went through ten editions and, at two dollars and fifty cents per copy, made the company money. A separate edition, published in England without pictures because of the paper shortage, also sold well.

When my sister, Ora, complimented in a letter my choice of words in the book's descriptions, I wrote her that "I had the advantage of being able to describe things that I had seen and experienced, and remembered vividly. I had only to search for words and phrases that painted the mental pictures I already had impressed in my memory." I volunteered that I didn't "think I could do anywhere nearly as well writing anything fictional, where imagination would be required." I went on to write, "It was the changing of words and phrases in those descriptions that angered me regarding the treatment of my story by *The Post*. I expected them to cut out lots of parts, but many descriptions were changed without being shortened, so they didn't give the impression I meant."

About the first of July, the Ministry of Information had me give a three-minute account on the BBC Home Service of my trip to the States. Several weeks later I received a packet from Fighter Command forwarding a letter written to the BBC by Father Horan's niece who had once lived in St. Charles and who had heard my broadcast. She was living in Ireland, and I wrote to tell her I'd stop to see her on my next leave, as Paddy and I were planning another trip in August.

The pieces forecasting the next phase of my life began to fall into place later in the year. Winter was fast approaching with its weeks of foggy weather and inactivity in England, while big things appeared to be in the offing abroad. Japan wasn't in the war yet, of course, but Hitler's armies in Russia had reached the northeastern shores of the Black Sea and a drive down through the Caucasus Mountains looked imminent; besides we'd heard rumors and opinions (which soon proved correct) that one side or the other would be starting something big in Libya before long.

The scenario started with an invitation to a party being given as a farewell for the officers of 258 Squadron, who were preparing to leave for overseas service. Jim Thomson, my flight leader during the Battle of Britain, now commanded 258, and it was undoubtedly he who invited me. I was in extra high spirits that noon because my wingman, Pilot Officer Andrews, and I had chewed up a German motor launch that morning in clear weather without cloud protection along the part of France where the *Luftwaffe* had its greatest concentration of fighters.

My own strafing had been textbook-smooth, and I turned in my cockpit to watch Alan initiating his attack, his distant Spitfire looking wicked and panther-like from in front as only a Spitfire can, seeing the row of little lights break out, flashing along the front of his wings, and the twin streams of grey cannon-smoke puffs ripping back like taut strings of soft grey beads. After that the two of us scooted for home side by side and low down over the waves as hard as we could go, engines bellowing raucously at full throttle and controls stiff with the speed, squirming in our cockpits to look furtively backwards for signs of 109s in pursuit, feeling for all the world like a couple of kids who'd just stolen a watermelon!

I re-emphasize the word "fate" in connection with my future activities because any number of events in the sequence could have prevented my seeing Squadron Leader Thomson before he departed. Having a spot of lunch before taking off in the squadron's de Havilland Tiger Moth trainer for the party, I learned from one of the pilots who had just landed that a line of thunderstorms and low fog lay between Hawkinge and Debden airdrome. The duty pilot confirmed the bad weather with reported fog right down to the ground in places. I thought of canceling the trip but decided to wait until later to make my decision. Toward mid-afternoon Operations said I could give it a go if I wished.

Even then I nearly didn't make it, for, after I'd flown about fifty or sixty miles, the weather got thick and dark all around. A thunderstorm loomed ahead with white curtains of rain hanging to the ground. I was miserably cold already in the open cockpit of my little biplane and sick of shivering, my face blue and my nose running, and of bouncing around in the rough air which tossed the little machine about like a chip; I was sick above all of the slow speed—exasperated since I was used to streaking about the countryside at two and three hundred miles an hour in Spitfires.

Again I almost called it off; but then I saw a lighter patch ahead on my left and decided to make a try at it. By swinging off my course and edging close to the London balloon barrage, I managed finally to get by the bad area, and then it was clear sailing the rest of the way to Debden, where I landed triumphantly.

The duty pilot gave me bad news: the boys going overseas had received an extension to their embarkation leave, the party was canceled, and I should have got a telegram to that effect. Disappointed to say the least, I determined to return to Hawkinge but was told that one of my engine's magnetos needed repair and would not be ready until morning.

The next day fate intervened again in the person of Squadron Leader Thomson who had returned early and subsequently invited me to deploy with 258. The squadron had a short and rather undistinguished five-month existence at the end of World War One flying D.H.6 single-engine bi-winged bombers on maritime patrol, was reactivated as a fighter squadron flying Hurricanes a month after the Battle of Britain, and had seen limited action other than fighter sweeps until it was stood down for its move overseas. It certainly lacked the historical credentials of 64 Squadron or the elite status of my present posting, but its motto of *In medias res*— "In the thick of things"—appealed to my inner drive not to be left out of the action. Although no one knew where that action would take place, we speculated that it would be either Russia or Libya. Either way, it seemed likely that the squadron would have a chance to write some history.

Moving in with my new mates, I found three other Americans in the crowd, two Californians and one from Florida, all swell fellows. The California boys were Don Geffene and "Red" Campbell; the latter was to become the squadron's first Ace. Cardell Kleckner had quit a government job in Washington to join the Royal Canadian Air Force. There were five New Zealanders also, besides boys from Australia, Rhodesia, Canada, and, as we put it, "even a few Englishmen," who were generally known as "the foreigners."

Actually I was the "foreigner" as only I had been recruited by Squadron Leader Thomson, who told me later that he had been concerned that I would be thought of as "the C.O.'s boy." Fortunately nothing of the kind materialized, but remembering the undercurrent of distrust and intrigue I sometimes encountered in The Conrad Flying Service, I realized that such things happened among lesser men. More potential for discord existed within the organization because of the British system of having two groups of pilots, commissioned officers and sergeants, each doing the same job but the lower caste doing it for less money and in less comfortable surroundings. My innate sense of fairness caused me to attempt to resign my commission sometime later, but the particular incident blew over, and I realized that my job was not to revamp the English social system, just help save it.

In the few days remaining before we were to embark, I had my hands and arms full: hands full of a Hurricane fighter which I'd not flown before, and arms full of shots such as yellow fever, tetanus, typhoid, and others to ward off various tropical diseases. After all of that, I had a couple of days to wind up my affairs. In London I met Tex Marchbanks, a friend of mine from Waxahachie,

Texas, who was also now wearing RAF blue. He told me he had just been posted to Singapore. I informed him I was going overseas, too, but didn't know where, and we wished each other luck.

At Hawkinge, where I needed to pick up some personal belongings, I found my flight off duty and only a couple of boys around. All the Spitfires were standing in their dispersal bays, like tired cavalry horses asleep, each as familiar to me as an old comrade, each bringing me memories.

Paddy's old machine, marked on each side of its fuselage with its white identification letter, "N," was there. It had always been lucky. Paddy had shot down at least two 109s with it; Chris was using it the day he was out on a recco and surprised a formation of three 109s over Le Touquet, dropping on them out of the sun and shooting down two before they knew what had happened, and then coming home so excited he couldn't talk, having completely forgotten to finish his reconnaissance! Gilli was flying it the day he blundered into a whole bunch of 109s in a thick haze low over the sea north of Nieuport, shot down one, damaged a second, and got away unscathed, leaving the rest dog-fighting with each other in their confusion.

Chris's assigned "P" was in line with Gilli's "U," Roy's "V," Alan's "T," and all the rest, including "S"—the one everybody hated because it didn't perform as well as the others. And of course there was my own "O," my MESSAGE FROM MINNESOTA, which I knew and loved the best. Personalities, all of them known to me; for one of us would fly another's airplane when his own was laid up for repairs, checks, and so on, and I knew all the peculiarities of each.

There wasn't one in whose cockpit I hadn't experienced unforgettable thrills and scares, flown through unbelievable scenes of grandeur and beauty among and above the clouds. And how often I'd seen each of them taxiing back to its place after a flight across the Channel, displaying evidence of a battle fought or a target attacked— the tattered remnants of what had been fabric covers fluttering about the holes for the machine guns in the wings, and the ugly bared cannon muzzles, dirtied with powder smoke, their covers likewise shot away. Sometimes it was I who taxied in with my machine bearing these signs, my heart still pounding, while I grinned behind my oxygen mask with an amount of pride proportional to whatever it was that I had accomplished. And now it was all over. I was saying good-bye to it all and to them all, and it was very hard.

The wind was still blowing and the sky overcast that night as I rode along the dark highway and through the blacked-out city with the friend who drove me to the station, and my heart was heavier than ever. I'd planned to stay overnight and take a morning train, but a telephone call at supper time informed me that our date of embarkation had been advanced and that I had to take the train right away.

It meant I hardly had time to say good-bye to any of my pals, which was probably just as well because I know I'd have broken down. When I got on the train, I could hardly keep my eyes dry as I fumbled my way into one of the darkened compartments and slumped down, utterly miserable, beside a couple of soldiers going on leave, who moved their rifles to make room for me.

Hoping to see something familiar, I pulled the curtains aside for a last look after we got out of town, and as if the elements sympathized with me, I found that the clouds had blown away and that the countryside now was bathed in brilliant moonlight. The airdrome was out of sight from the railway, but "old Baldy," a high, rounded hill that was a landmark beside it, was plainly visible; and I took a long last look at it, trying to photograph it in my memory. Then I replaced the curtain, resolving to keep my mind on the future.

Receipt for Red Cross package sent to Squadron Leader MacDonell, who was shot down and imprisoned.

Art returning to Hawkinge from a dawn reconnaissance in his beloved
"Message from Minnesota."

91 Squadron Pilots in front of Officers' Mess, Hawkinge Airdrome. Art
stands at left.

At the tip of the spear, 91 Squadron pilot.

Chapter Fourteen

Fortunes of War

I arrived back at Debden in time to draw "tropical dress" including sun helmet and, burdened with ninety pounds of kit, joined twenty-one other pilots for the rail trip to Abbotsinch, near Glascow, Scotland. In convoy with the aircraft carrier *HMS Hermes,* we sailed on the third of November, 1941, aboard *HMS Athene*, a seaplane tender loaded with seventy-two Hurricane IIC, cannon-equipped fighters and pilots from two other squadrons: numbers 242 and 605.

I suppose that if you rounded up a score of two-year-old colts from a Montana range and penned them in a half-acre corral for a few weeks during the fresh new days of spring, you could get an idea from watching them of how we fighter pilots felt and acted during our long imprisonment aboard ship.

Accustomed as we were to flying an hour or two in going from one place to another, this business of spending days and even weeks between stops was appalling. We read until our eyes ached, played cards, and argued endlessly about everything from air tactics to women's suffrage. Our tempers grew shorter until we were constantly snapping at one another over insignificant things, so that our C. O. was at his wit's end trying to keep the peace, and still our voyage had scarcely started!

We arrived at our first port of call, the British crown colony at Gibraltar, late on the seventh of November still not knowing our final destination or departure time. In school I had always been fascinated with the rock fortress that dominated the western entrance to the Mediterranean Sea, so I lit out early the next day trying to see all the sights before we departed. I needn't have bothered because we were in for a long stay dictated by the fortunes of war. That night I wrote the folks that the small town of Gibraltar reminded me of a Mexican village with its buildings all of stone. I wanted them to know that my education was continuing and that seeing the coast of Africa right across the bay made the third continent and tenth country I had seen.

We were happy to find plentiful food, particularly fresh oranges, bananas and grapes—and no blackout. Shortly after arrival, half of our total pilot complement (all of those belonging to 242 Squadron and half of 605) left to board the aircraft carriers *HMS Ark Royal* and *HMS Argus* which were to take them and thirty-six of *Athene's* Hurricanes through the Mediterranean to a point where they would take off, fly to Malta for refueling, then continue on to Alexandria. The carriers were to return for the rest of us and repeat the same operation. So at last we knew where we were going; we just couldn't tell anyone!

The first part of the plan worked perfectly, but on the thirteenth of November, within sight of Gibraltar, the German submarine U-81 slammed a torpedo into *Ark Royal,* and she went down almost immediately. Her sinking delivered a tremendous blow to the Royal Navy's prestige, as one of her ancient Fairey "Swordfish" biplanes had laid down a torpedo that jammed the rudder of the *Bismarck* just six months previously thereby assuring the German battleship's subsequent destruction. This tragic incident, within twenty-five miles of safety, committed us to an additional six weeks marooned on "The Rock," and you can imagine what that did to us colts milling around the corral! We continued living at dockside aboard *Athene* which allowed those of us holding commissions to make friends with many British naval officers. They always expected us to join them in their wardrooms and share a meal, most often a sumptuous event.

Our enforced vacation was less than idyllic, especially for our sergeant pilots who, classified as "other ranks," couldn't socialize in the officers' wardroom of *Athene* and certainly weren't welcomed aboard other ships of His Majesty's Navy. In fact they complained that in the town of Gibraltar "all the few places of quality were out of bounds to other ranks."

Rather than let a resource as expensive as ours go completely to waste, the Air Ministry decided some of our machines should be assembled, given external fuel tanks, and flown in search of Fw 200V-10 "Condors," which were Focke-Wulf 200-series airliners modified as long-range maritime raiders.

What Churchill called "the Scourge of the Atlantic" because of the deadliness of its mast-height bombing altitude was an absolutely splendid machine developed in 1936 for trans-Atlantic service being planned by Lufthansa, Germany's national airline. The streamlined giant carried four BMW radial engines beautifully cowled and molded into a wing spanning almost 108 feet. Its tapered fuselage, six inches shy of 77 feet in length, hosted a tail assembly featuring a single vertical fin similar in shape to that of the Douglas DC 3. To *Luftwaffe* engineers looking for an airframe to modify for the maritime role, it was the only candidate that not only had established unrefueled distance records (Berlin to New York in four minutes less than twenty-five hours being one) but also was currently being produced on an operating assembly line.

Designed to carry only modest transport loads, the Fw 200 wasn't easy to modify for a military mission. Mechanical bugs plagued the up-graded engines that sported an innovative water-injection system supplying increased power for take-off, and cracks soon appeared in fuselages incapable of carrying the weight of guns, bombs, extra fuel tanks, and a beefed-up undercarriage necessary to exploit the aircraft's potential. Combat missions begun in late April 1940 with twenty-six aircraft flying from Denmark were canceled in mid-May after several had their backs broken during hard landings and only two remained in commission.

Hastily re-equipped with fifteen new machines—the 200-1 series featuring reliable engines and reinforced fuselages—Condor crews flying from Bordeaux-Merignac, France, began deep Atlantic reconnaissance and anti-shipping flights in mid-July, just before the Battle of Britain heated up. A typical out-and-back mission armed with two 1,012-pound bombs and two 550 pounders would see a raider cross the Bay of Biscay at 7,000 feet, arc around the western reaches of the British Isles, then land in occupied Norway for servicing and a return the next day.

They found hunting particularly good where the homeward convoy routes from Gibraltar converged in the Bay of Biscay with those from Sierra Leone. During August and September, Condors and U-boats had sunk thirty-one ships and three escorts. Another favored area was northwest of Ireland where the troopship *Empress of Britain* suffered damage from two hits by a Condor on the twenty-sixth of October and was finished off two days later by a U-boat responding to the aircrew's radioed strike report.

Putting the colts into airplanes and getting them out of the corral was just what the doctor ordered. Our mission was to find Condors rumored to be flying out of Cadiz on the Spanish seacoast, and all of us took to it enthusiastically if dubiously because of the lack of radar surveillance which would have taken our interception problem out of the "pure luck" category. But nothing would have given us better satisfaction than to have saved countless lives and priceless cargo by pumping cannon shells into so potent a menace.

Aside from the possibility of combat, our patrol duties gave Squadron Leader Thomson a chance to hone the flying proficiency of our "Sprongs"—low-time graduates of the OTUs who formed the majority of our complement. As for myself, I was elated to have a chance to learn the idiosyncrasies of the Hurricane, which seemed much more docile than the debonair Spitfire which still dominated my dreams.

We found no Condors even though we saw our share of convoys—some with as many as forty or fifty ships. I imagine, however, that seeing Hurricanes in the role of guardian angels was a reassuring sight to those brave men afloat. Our escort flights proceeded routinely until bad luck cost us the services of our fellow American, Don Geffene, who'd flown previously with two of the three Eagle Squadrons and was someone we'd counted on to watch over our neophytes.

Returning from a patrol with Red Campbell, Don had experienced engine problems that forced him to deadstick onto the nearest strip of beach, which turned out to belong to Spanish Tangier across the Strait from the Rock. Knowing that Don would be interned and his plane impounded, Red realized that Fascist Spain would quickly allow *Luftwaffe* technicians to swarm all over our fighter and its tank-killing cannon unless something dramatic occurred quickly. Deciding that risking an international incident was a small price to pay for a nice little strafing demonstration, Red reduced Don's evacuated Hurricane to a heap of molten metal.

We all knew that Don would be interned, yet we wondered how long he'd consent to being held. The rules suggested it could be for the duration of the war, but we made bets it wouldn't be long. The story's a bit obscure, and may someday be clarified by Hollywood, but supposedly the governor-general's daughter arranged for a *New York Herald Tribune* correspondent to slip Don a gun and maps, thereby allowing him to escape to allied control. He just missed our departure and was unable to rejoin the squadron until it had reconstituted itself in Ceylon after our Singapore fling. Sadly he was fated to meet the enemy in a match where even the governor-general's daughter couldn't help.

Red and I got a pleasant surprise about this time when Oscar Coen, who'd been shot down on an Eagle Squadron strafing mission in France some two months previously, suddenly appeared in Gibraltar. After parachuting from his riddled machine, the twenty-three-year-old, college educated, former teacher from Illinois met up with the French Underground who dressed him as a teenager and escorted him through German lines without difficulty. Thereafter he made his way to Portugal only to find Lisbon crowded with escapees waiting placidly for repatriation. He and a British squadron leader teamed up and walked through Spain to the Rock. Leaving us he shipped back to England, rejoined 71 (Eagle) Squadron three days after Christmas, and was the guest of honor at a number of "Happy New Year Oscar!" parties scattered inside a seventy-five mile radius of London.

While all of this was going on, I made the most of my spare time by polishing two articles based on my adventures since the Battle of Britain, catching up on correspondence (a one-way channel since I was to receive nothing from home for some five months until Bob's cable on the twenty-first of April), and exercising my Spanish around town and on jaunts into Spain itself. I found the dialect so much different and the speech so much faster than I was used to, that I was hardly able to understand anything. But Red Campbell thought I was fluent and credited me with keeping us out of serious trouble with the constabulary.

We heard the dreaded news on a Sunday evening when most of us had been away from our ship attending a movie. Returning after the show, we were met on the ladder by Red, his face flushed with excitement. "America's at war!" he shouted. "The Japs have raided Hawaii! Here, read this!" He waved a piece of paper in our faces. It was a general message to all British ships: "COMMENCE HOSTILITIES WITH JAPAN REPEAT JAPAN AT ONCE."

My personal reaction to Pearl Harbor was one of muted outrage. I found myself more truly mad at the Japanese than I had ever been able to be towards the Germans, with all their crimes. Somehow the fact that it was my own people who'd been attacked seemed to make a tremendous difference. I could accept any catastrophe inflicted on other countries and not be surprised because I'd never seen Europe except at war.

It seemed impossible Americans should be having blackouts and building shelters and taking other air raid precautions, and that the sirens could actually have sounded in some parts of the country. I guess what hit me so hard personally was that I had failed in my goal of keeping the United States out of war by helping the British hold the line against Hitler. I hadn't counted on Japan, nor had I understood the political and economic currents that swirled in the Pacific.

I wrote the folks after things settled down that night telling them that the Japanese air force should be easy meat, as that was what we'd been led to believe. Little did I suspect the depth of our ignorance concerning everything Japanese.

To a man we all wanted a crack at our enemies on the other side of the world: the Americans among us because of the "sneak attack" on Pearl Harbor and the others because Nipponese troops had also made landings on the west coast of Malaya and were driving toward

Singapore. We Americans realized that our movements would be directed by the RAF for some time to come, and we knew we were already committed to the Middle East. Unbeknown to us was the turmoil the Japanese attack had created in London. The British government, after ignoring the vulnerability of Singapore and Australia for years, was desperate to reinforce a potentially catastrophic situation now that the American Pacific Fleet—which they had assumed would deter the Japanese—had been mauled at Pearl Harbor.

Chapter Fifteen

Long Road to Singapore

On Christmas Eve 1941, *Athene* finally sailed for Freetown, Sierra Leone, with a cargo of thirty-six Hurricanes and associated aviators. We pilots were assigned four-hour shifts manning two pom-pom guns which were part of our defense against the very aircraft we'd so recently stalked—the Folke-Wulf Condor. As an aviator, I have always felt that anti-aircraft guns should be abolished, and Cardell Kleckner ("Kleck" for short) grumbled that asking a pilot to crew such weapons was like asking Charlie McCarthy (the wooden dummy of a well-known American ventriloquist) to care for a pair of woodpeckers.

At night the sea was "phosphorescent," one of the wonders of nature which most of us had never seen. Every disturbance in the water caused little flaky green lights to flash beneath the surface, so that the water churned from the ship's sides seemed full of fireflies. Every whitecap was a shower of fiery little green jewels; every fish left a trail like a small green skyrocket in the darkness, and the wake of the ship was like a great mass of colored fire.

Sailing into warm tropical seas, we changed from our blue uniforms into tropical dress of open-necked khaki shirts, khaki shorts, and tan-colored pith helmets instead of caps. At night we slept in hammocks on deck because of the heat in our cabins. We made port in Freetown on the last day of 1941, a year that marked a dramatic expansion of the war yet one that had been memorable and educational for me. That evening we sailed on an overnight voyage to Takoradi where we said goodbye to *Athene,* which continued down the west coast of Africa, around the Cape of Good Hope, and across the Indian Ocean to Java where its cargo of Hurricanes would be assembled and sacrificed piecemeal.

As the major port of entry for lend-lease material sent to build up British forces in Egypt, Takoradi was thriving. An industrial complex capable of processing two hundred fighters a month had been constructed just outside of town. There men uncrated aircraft and prepared them to hop-scotch over impenetrable jungle and blistering desert east to Khartoum and then north to Cairo. Scattered along the way were emergency airstrips featuring few navigational aids, short runways, and minimum facilities. British aviators had pioneered the air route between Takoradi and Khartoum some five years earlier, and it had remained extremely primitive until October of 1941 when Pan American Africa, a subsidiary of the famous air line, received a contract to set up scheduled service with seven Douglas DC 3s and thirty aviators to fly them.

We pilots from *Athene* boarded two of these DC 3 transports, called "Dakotas" by the British, and flew east

180

northeast to Khartoum, Sudan. After relaxing for several days, my fellow officers and I departed on a 489-mile journey by rail to the country's only deep-water harbor, Port Sudan. The high point of the journey for me was getting my picture taken beside a camel at one of the stops along the way. Our sergeant pilots, however, were flown to the airfield nearest our destination where they were given the frustrating and nerve-wracking task of taxiing forty-eight brand-new Hurricanes over narrow and dusty roads from the airstrip to the docks where they were hoisted aboard the aircraft carrier *HMS Indomitable*.

The palatial hotel in which we stayed as we awaited our sailing date made up somewhat for the cramped quarters we'd shared since leaving England. Terence Kelly, one of our sergeant pilots and later a playwright and writer whose books include three devoted entirely to the squadron's activities, summed up the way many of us felt: "It seemed the most exciting, remarkable trip imaginable. All was new to all and we had no idea where we were going." Still without mail from home, I consoled myself by thinking my Sudanese air mail letters, advertised to reach the States in a week, should give the family a welcome position report. Three months later my letters reached Bob in Lowell.

Awaiting embarkation we all enjoyed frolicking in the marvelous swimming pool and partaking of the lavish meals. Even seeing more camels and all sorts and colors of tropical fish could not, however, erase the secret desire I had to see another Minnesota blizzard!

On the ninth of January, 1942, *Indomitable* sailed down the Red Sea, passed through the Gulf of Aden, and set course toward the Indian Ocean with our Hurricanes lashed to her deck and the pilot complement of two full-strength squadrons. Twenty-four men belonged to my unit (two had been added to the original twenty-two who left Scotland), twelve were our 605 Squadron friends who'd accompanied us on *Athene* and were now integrated into Number 232 Squadron, whose twelve members had joined us in Port Sudan.

Once at sea we assembled on deck one evening for a lecture. It began with a talk by the First Lieutenant on the Far Eastern situation. Using a large map for reference, he showed us where the Japanese had attacked in the Philippines as well as in Borneo and other islands. Next, he pointed to where they had invaded Burma and were working toward Rangoon, and last of all to Northern Malaya, where they were pushing down the long Malay Peninsula toward Singapore at its southern tip. Everything hung on Singapore. If it fell, the enemy would be able to conquer the Dutch East Indies, which would give them rubber, tin, and oil that they needed to continue the war.

Then the captain addressed us saying that his ship would proceed through the Indian Ocean to a point near Christmas Island—not to be confused with the American possession of the same name in the Pacific—some three hundred miles south-southwest of Batavia, Java. There we would take off from the carrier's deck with a final destination of Singapore! A cheer went up from our crowd. We all wanted action, and now we had drawn the jackpot! The forty-eight of us were then divided into three groups of sixteen for the trip.

I was in the second bunch scheduled for launch on the twenty-seventh of January. Squadron Leader Thomson would command the first group that would rendezvous after takeoff with two Blenheim bombers sent to provide navigational assistance to the first refueling point at Kemajoran airport outside Batavia, Java. Each of the two follow-on formations would be provided Blenheim pathfinders also.

The prototype of the Bristol Blenheim had first appeared in 1935 as a privately funded twin-engine medium bomber candidate for the RAF. The first production model arrived two years later carrying a three-man crew and featuring a low wing, all-metal, stressed-skin construction, and an hydraulically operated top turret equipped with two .303 Browning machine guns. Its range loaded with a maximum of a thousand pounds of bombs was 1,090 miles. At the time it was faster than the first-line, bi-winged fighters found in RAF squadrons. When the "Phony War" turned hot in France, German flak and the *Luftwaffe's* Messerschmitts quickly relegated the Blenheim to theaters where the opposition wasn't as formidable—the Middle East and Southeast Asia.

Naturally we all shared a certain hesitancy to be among the first to take off from the flight deck, preferring instead to be in the rear of the pack where a longer take-off run would be possible. As Christopher Shores, Brian Cull, and Izawa Yasuho report in *Bloody Shambles*, the deck officer quickly tired of our bickering over who would be among the first to take-off and stamped out a spot "about mid-way down the deck" where he announced "'First or last, you'll all bloody well take off from here!'" This alarmed everyone, but it gave each of us the same amount of take-off distance and settled the issue. It was one of the most brilliant examples of decisive leadership I'd seen. If that deck officer had been the supreme commander in

Singapore, things might have turned out a good deal differently.

Unfortunately for our plans, leadership of another kind was lacking. On the day of our departure, the Blenheim sent from Java to provide escort for our first group of sixteen could not locate our ship. This slipped the scheduled nine o'clock take-off time. Two more bombers suffered the same consequence; however, a third pair had no difficulty, as they first navigated to Christmas Island only fifty or sixty miles from our carrier then took up a heading for our announced position. Squadron Leader Thomson and his charges lifted off without incident at four in the afternoon, causing my group and the next to be rescheduled for the following day.

Since I'd talked at length with some of the carrier's pilots who regularly flew Sea Hurricanes (the navy's version of our fighter) off and back onto the ship, I was confident of my ability to launch handily. When my time came, I simply dropped flaps, locked the brakes, revved up to full power, and let her go. Nothing to it for an old barnstormer; although looking back as I pulled into formation, I was glad this barnstormer didn't have to return and land on that little postage stamp. We clustered around our Blenheims in sections of four and followed them into Kemajoran airport which in peacetime hosted KLM, the big Dutch airline.

We had lunch and then took off on the next leg of our trip, a flight of three hundred miles or so northwest to a jungle airdrome in Sumatra. It was a beautiful jaunt, for the sun was out and the fertile, well-cultivated farmlands of Java appeared rich and green as we cruised over them. Scattered fluffy clouds under us glistened softly in the sunlight and set off the beauty of the landscape underneath. Then the seacoast, the water a beautiful blue-green and the white-capped waves gleaming in long lines of snowy crest as they collapsed majestically along the beaches far below us.

On out across the sea for half an hour or so and then Sumatra appeared—a far different kind of country from Java. This was where everyone said, "If you ever have a forced landing, you've just HAD it!" No cultivated farm lands here. No sign of any kind of civilization. Just endless dark flat jungle stretching off into the steamy horizon in all directions, broken only at great intervals by some silvery stream winding its way across our course and off into the distance. Many, many miles of this, until at last a broken patch appeared ahead of us. As we drew nearer, it took shape as an airdrome cleared out of the jungle—our stopping point.

The RAF was just getting established at this secret airfield located south of the city of Palembang and called "P.2" to differentiate it from "P.1," Palembang's civil airdrome. The Officers' Mess was a large wooden shed with concrete floor and wooden benches and tables. We lined up at mealtime and drew tea in tin cups from a big boiler, and dipped stew from another boiler into tin plates. Bread, margarine, canned strawberry jam, fresh bananas and pineapples completed our fare.

We slept on camp cots and learned the intricacies of enclosing ourselves in those overhung mosquito-netting affairs. The air had been very hot and muggy when we landed, but during the night little showers accompanied by some thunder and lightning occurred every hour or so, and

185

it became comfortably cool. By the time we got up next morning, however, it was hot and steamy just as before.

The next day, the twenty-ninth, featured weather too unsettled to allow us to push on. Instead we spent the day working on our planes, especially disassembling the twelve .303 Browning machine guns that provided our armament and stripping the heavy grease that muzzled them. We washed the parts in gasoline then oiled and reassembled the mechanisms before re-installing the guns into their bays in the wings.

We worked beside the airplanes, sitting on empty gasoline cans, and retreating under the wings to work during the frequent showers. By chatting with the armorers who had been in the fighting zone in Malaya until recently, I came to realize some of the challenges that lay ahead. It was from them that I first heard of the Navy Zero fighter ("Navy-naughts" we called them). These fighters were reputed to be sleek little jobs with great maneuverability and an exceptional cruising range. Whereas we believed our Hurricanes would be a match for them individually, we had to expect to be badly outnumbered. What we didn't know but would soon find out was that our opponents, especially the naval aviators, had been superbly—albeit brutally—trained, that many had combat experience against the Chinese, and that their A6M2 "Zero-Sen" machine was a premium specimen of a single-engine fighter.

The armorers told me Japanese bombers seemed to be good machines, too, and could fly at more than twenty thousand feet with full bomb loads. They flew in beautiful close formations; and when attacking airdromes did "pattern bombing" all letting their bombs go at once, so that they plastered the whole area evenly. After our

186

conversation I was beginning to understand that the fight for Singapore, like the Battle of Britain, would be no game.

The next afternoon we followed our Blenheim leaders another three hundred and fifty miles to our destination. We flew nearly straight north for the first fifty miles until we could see the coastline in the distance on our right, at first paralleling our heading and then gradually angling closer. After perhaps an hour, we crossed the coastline and droned out on our one-hundred-and-fifty-mile crossing of the Strait of Malacca.

About now I was getting tired and stiff from being cramped in one position, and I squirmed in my seat, loosened my straps, and tried to do some primitive sitting-up exercises for relief. I'd gone for so long without flying that the posture was hard to get used to again. My engine, throttled down almost to idling speed to keep pace with the slower bombers, purred endlessly on the same note, which was broken only when I held my head to one side of the cockpit and got the staccato crackling of the exhausts from that bank of cylinders. Like most of the rest, I flew with my sliding cockpit hood open to keep cool, for the sun was out and the air hot; we were actually crossing the equator on this very hop, Singapore being only eighty miles north of it.

After a long time the sky grew darker ahead. The Blenheims started losing altitude, and we did too, keeping in formation with them. Then the unmistakable outline of land began to emerge along the darkened horizon, and we knew that after months of anticipation our destination was finally in sight. We began passing under heavy, blue-black storm clouds that forced us to fly lower and lower, and looking ahead I could now make out a great harbor on the coast, with the dim shapes of several ships anchored in it. Singapore harbor!

I noticed one ship that contrasted strangely with the rest, because it was all white except for a narrow green stripe around it and large red crosses on the deck, sides, and funnel. It was the first hospital ship I'd seen, and it looked grimly suggestive there. Little did I suspect that I was to see it as a passenger within a month!

Art's first meeting with camels on his 489-mile journey from Khartoum to Port Sudan.

Hurricane Pilots bound for Singapore.

188

Chapter Sixteen

At the Front

Singapore Island lies at the southeastern end of the Malay Peninsula across the three-quarter-mile-wide Johore Strait. It's roughly diamond-shaped, about twenty-five miles long east and west, by fifteen miles north and south, and our destination was Tengah Airdrome on the northwest side. We made it just ahead of a heavy storm that was bearing down from the north, and we had to fly through a curtain of rain as we approached for landing. This was the season of the wet monsoon, so we could expect some dicey weather along with whatever the enemy put up. Even circling the airdrome, we could see we were in a war zone, for it was spotted with filled-in bomb craters just like the ones in England and quite a few unfilled, too.

What we couldn't see beneath the jungle foliage on this thirtieth day of January was the disposition of Japanese troops under orders to be ready to assault Singapore Island by noon on the seventh of February. The invaders had begun their conquest of Malaya by making three near-simultaneous night landings early on the eighth of December, 1941, along the east coast of Thailand and Malaya.

The first began two hours after midnight following a naval bombardment of the Eighth Brigade, Ninth Indian Division, defending the fortified beach at Kota Bharu, Malaya. Its goal was to capture three airfields in the vicinity. The first objective, Kota Bharu airdrome, was occupied twenty-two hours later following some of the most violent action of the entire campaign. Tanah Merah and Kuala Kulai fell on the thirteenth and the nineteenth respectively.

At four in the morning, two separate forces assaulted Thailand's eastern shore some thirty miles north of the Malayan border. Even though the Thai government had agreed in secret to allow Japanese troops "peaceful transit" in their plan to conquer Malaya, not all local military and police units had been informed. At Singora Beach the Japanese braved seas running nine feet high to dispatch light resistance, seize two airstrips, and overrun British defenders in an hour of sharp fighting at the border. In short order the Japanese off-loaded over thirteen thousand troops, five tanks, and some four hundred vehicles. The companion landing at Patani went as planned meeting sharp but relatively short-lived Thai resistance.

Because these landings in Thailand weren't confirmed by Headquarters until a mid-morning aerial reconnaissance, they weren't subjected to any air or ground challenge of significance. This allowed the Japanese easily to secure the two beachheads and adjacent areas. Shortly after seven that morning, Ki 27 fighters had swarmed from their Indo-China bases to occupy the rain-soaked airfield at

Singora. Soon afterwards four-engine H6K flying boats settled onto Singora Lake to establish a base for future long-range patrols.

At Kota Bharu the appearance of enemy troops on the beach explained previous scattered sightings of Japanese naval activity in the South China Sea as well as overflights by high flying reconnaissance aircraft. Until that moment the British had been unsure of Japanese intentions and hesitant to violate Thailand's sovereignty. This prevented their crossing the border to occupy the beaches at Singora and Patani which seemed to beckon an invader hungry for Malaya's tin, rubber, and unmatched harbor at Singapore. Air Headquarters had, however, ordered all flying units to "full readiness" and placed on "armed alert" at Kota Bharu a mixed bag of twenty aircraft: eleven Hudson bombers, two Brewster Buffalo fighters, and seven ancient, fabric-covered "Vildebeest" torpedo-carrying biplanes.

Defending Indian troops occupying prepared concrete pillboxes pinned down the assault wave for a time: time enough for seven Hudsons of Number One Squadron, Royal Australian Air Force (RAAF), to launch and immediately roll onto their bomb-run headings at wave-top altitude. At approximately the same time as Japanese bombers dived on Pearl Harbor, Flight Lieutenant J.M.H. Lockwood put two bombs square amidships of *Awagisan Maru*, one of three transports off-loading her portion of 5300 men belonging to the 56th Regiment. In quick succession six more Hudsons bored through withering anti-aircraft fire thrown up by the cruiser *Sendai* and other escorting vessels. Badly crippled during its run-in, Flight Lieutenant Leighton-Jones' machine faltered then slammed into a loaded barge accounting for sixty soldiers. Japanese

191

witnesses reported the incident as the last willful act of a true warrior. A following crew overflew its target unable to jettison bombs hung in their racks, others missed completely or weren't able to observe results.

The six surviving Hudsons dropped into the landing circuit for rearming even as a three-ship flight roared off. They met intense flak that severely damaged the first aircraft and wounded the gunner on the second. None observed the results of his bombing.

A second wave rammed home its attack but suffered the loss of another Hudson whose observer survived crashing into the water only to be picked up by a Japanese patrol boat. Even though the machines were being riddled and crewmen pierced by bullets and shrapnel, the stalwart Australians had the pleasure of seeing all three transports blazing and beginning a slow withdrawal to the northeast. *Awagisan Maru* had absorbed ten direct hits, *Ayatosan Maru* six, and *Sakura Maru* several. By five a.m. the Hudsons had flown seventeen sorties.

Eager for the kill, Air Headquarters launched seven Vildebeests into lowering clouds to head off the transports. Battling constant rainstorms and restricted visibility, the flimsy museum pieces stumbled upon and engaged a light cruiser. Not able to coordinate their attack, only four pilots released their torpedoes and nothing was accomplished.

As the battle raged on Malaya's northern border, Singapore's harbor, naval base and airfields at Seletar and Tengah became targets. Having threaded their way through massive thunderstorms that caused forty-eight others to return to base, seventeen Japanese Naval Air Force (JNAF) Mitsubishi G3M bombers found clear weather, a full moon,

192

and a brilliantly illuminated and unsuspecting Singapore fast asleep at quarter past four. Later the military commander, Lieutenant-General Arthur Percival, admitted his surprise as "we hardly expected the Japanese to have any very long-range aircraft."

At dawn Hudsons, Blenheims, and Buffaloes cycled in and out of British airfields all morning to bomb and strafe ships, barges, and troops on the beach at Kota Bharu in desperate attempts to keep the airdrome from being overrun. In time, however, the Japanese secured the beach in hand-to-hand fighting, rolled up the second line of fortifications, and pushed ever closer to their prize. In hindsight one realizes that a good bit of the morning's air effort would have been better directed northward had the landings at Singora and Patani been known.

The first Blenheims airborne from Sungei Patani after daybreak encountered only blinding rainstorms. They returned to find that their base on Malaya's west coast had been devastated by five Ki 21 medium bombers. By this time small groups of Ki 27, Ki 43, and A6M fighters—operating from captured airfields in Thailand—prowled the countryside looking to destroy all vestiges of Allied air power.

Sergeant Pilot Charlie Warham, stationed at Singapore with the 4th Photo-Reconnaissance Unit, was tasked to photograph from his unarmed Brewster Buffalo "a place called Singora." Finding no charts of his objective available, as "it was considered not the thing to have maps of somebody else's country," he ripped a map from a World Atlas, flew up-country to Alor Star for refueling, got his pictures of the invasion activity, then hustled back to Singapore. The results of his reconnaissance caused other

193

groups of Blenheims to target the Singora and Pattani areas. Weather, anti-aircraft fire, and patrolling fighters made their lives miserable and their efforts generally ineffective. By mid-morning none of the RAF airstrips in northern Malaya was safe from marauding Japanese flyers, and Sungei Patani was evacuated leaving 1500 drums of fuel, ammunition, and supplies after two dozen Ki 21s again worked it over. Light fragmentation bombs, which destroyed aircraft and people but left runways intact, were the enemy's preferred ordnance.

With snipers infiltrating the south end of the Kota Bharu airfield and flights of enemy fighters strafing its facilities at fifteen-minute intervals, flyable aircraft were ordered out as conditions allowed. Five Hudsons and six Vildebeests escaped. Confusion, rumor, and pressure resulted in the enemy's gaining another useable runway later that night along with stocks of bombs, torpedoes, and fuel. Simultaneously with the decision to evacuate, commanders of the nearby auxiliary fields at Gong Kedah and Machang received orders to destroy their buildings and fuel storage before abandoning their strips.

Despite the great valor shown by individual crews operating in a fluid situation, Japanese plans suffered few holdups. Had it not been for atrocious weather, "friendly fire," and accidents, first-day Japanese losses would have been slight or non-existent. Because of weather the 62nd *Sentai* lost its commander's and four other Ki 21 bombers, 22nd Air Flotilla three of eight A6M Zeroes, 59th *Sentai* two Ki 43 fighters, and 75th *Sentai* one Ki 48 "Lily" light bomber. Friendly fire, mostly from ships, cost the 60th *Sentai* two Ki 21s that ditched and one that force-landed. Two more Ki 21s received damage and a 64th *Sentai* Ki 43 ditched. Accidents, mostly during landing attempts on soggy terrain, claimed eighteen additional machines.

Incredibly W. G. S. Dobbie, General Officer Commanding Malaya, had predicted this very scenario in 1939. Insisting that the peninsula's jungles were not impenetrable, he secured sixty thousand pounds to construct weapons positions in southern Malaya and on the northern coast of Singapore Island. Dobbie's successor was thwarted, however, when he petitioned to further barricade Singapore's back door. Concerned by the war in Europe, and not perceiving a threat from Japan, the region's governor concentrated on developing his rubber and tin production in order to generate export revenue for defense of the Empire.

In sixty-two days combining audacity, innovative tactics, and splendid discipline, the Japanese used their own bicycles and captured vehicles to propel themselves five hundred miles down the Malayan peninsula until they were poised to cross the Johore Strait separating them from Singapore Island. Protected by virtual air supremacy, they had plunged into the jungle to outflank, and then destroy opposition where they found it. To maintain momentum they exploited "Mr. Churchill's supplies"—food, fuel, vehicles, and weapons—abandoned by retreating Empire forces.

What we arriving reinforcements couldn't know as we spaced ourselves for landing was that their assault on Singapore Island, to begin with a bombardment by 450 guns on the night of the eighth of February, would be embarrassingly successful. Under no circumstances would we have believed that, within a week, defending forces would be routed, reservoirs captured, and 130,000 troops surrendered in Britain's greatest military disaster.

Blissfully unaware of events to come, we bedded down our aircraft and joyfully greeted the others of 258 Squadron who had arrived two days before. Actually they had landed first at Sembawang Airdrome north of the city but had been driven out by Japanese artillery fire from occupied Malaya. Eager to get word of my friend, Tex Marchbanks, whom I'd last seen in London, I sought out Red Campbell who also knew Tex. Red broke the news that a Navy Zero had shot him out of the sky. He was dead.

Details were few: just that he and his commanding officer, Squadron Leader Landells, had been killed, and Pilot Officer Norman Williams shot down on the twentieth of January during 232 (Provisional) Squadron's first action. Some fifty years later Christopher Shores, Brian Cull, and Yashuo Isawa, writing in *Bloody Shambles, Volume I*, presented a detailed description of what transpired. That Tuesday morning saw the heaviest yet bombing of Singapore city, its airfields, and harbor. Twelve Hurricanes led by Landells intercepted a force of some eighty bombers—Army Ki 21s and forty-four Navy G3Ms escorted by countless fighters.

Lieutenant Yoshio Hatta killed Squadron Leader Landells and was, in turn, destroyed by Landell's wingman, Pilot Officer Parker. Williams baled out with burns, was rescued by natives, and evacuated to India. Tex Marchbanks chased after the bombers only to be sent spiraling into the jungle some twenty miles north of Kuala Lumpur. His body was never recovered.

My friend and his cohorts had been overwhelmed by a vicious combination of Mitsubishi Zeros and Nakajima Ki 43 *Hayabusa* (Peregrine Falcon) fighters, extremely capable machines of which they knew little or nothing. Indeed the *Hayabusa* was not even in our vocabulary! Many of the subsequent claims we made of attacks by or upon "Navy Naughts" actually involved similar-appearing Ki 43s that were much more numerous in the Singapore Theater. Both appeared amazingly similar, being low-wing, radial-engine single seaters with retractable landing gear and great big red circles dominating their wing tips and aft fuselages. During my first several encounters with these opponents, it seemed that the red insignias were their chief characteristics!

Later I realized that the Zero was a bit more chunky in the engine cowling, featured a longer, more hump-backed canopy, a thicker aft fuselage, broader horizontal stabilizer, and fully retractable tail wheel whereas the Ki 43's was fixed. Because our squadrons lacked intelligence officers to debrief pilots as was the custom in the Battle of Britain, we had no system to collect, sift, and disseminate information about the tactics and performance of Japanese aircraft. Our ignorance of enemy types was almost complete. Rumors filled the void, and soon everyone seemed to accept the fiction that the Hurricane was outclassed. That wasn't true! The Zero may have been a bit faster at altitudes up to 15,000 feet, and both the Zero and the *Hayabusa* could out-turn us, but the Hurricane could best either in the vertical—a diving and climbing mode rather than a circling dogfight. Our plane could dive at speeds that would pull the wings off the Japanese machines; its armored seatback, bullet-proof windscreen, and self-sealing petrol tanks allowed it to absorb punishment that would destroy its adversaries; and—best of all—its eight guns could disintegrate its opponent. But no one put this together for the uninitiated pilots, and even if someone had, the usual odds of eight to one against us didn't bode well for our survival.

With the benefit of hindsight, the modern tactician might surmise that the British should never have committed the Hurricanes to Singapore. Indeed, one could argue they should have established the force in Sumatra (or even Java) along with the remaining Hudson and Blenheim bombers and used this significant amount of air power to hold out until reinforcements arrived.

In his books examining this period, *Hurricane over the Jungle, The Battle for Palembang*, and especially *Hurricane and Spitfire Pilots at War*, my squadron-mate, Terence Kelly, argues convincingly that the Hurricane could have held its own against Japanese fighters and supports the plan put forth at the time by Wing Commander Harold Maguire, who proposed that Hurricanes not be committed piecemeal. Maguire advocated holding back the ninety or so Hurricanes coming into the theater in January until all were mechanically prepared for battle, their pilots briefed, and "a cogent tactical scheme" formulated.

Militarily sound, this idea was politically unacceptable at a time when Britain's force of obsolescent Buffalo fighters had been decimated, Japanese bombers routinely—and with impunity—attacked Singapore, and its defenders and civilians alike looked to the RAF for deliverance. The job of the Hurricanes, therefore, was to contribute as quickly as possible whatever they could to the military equation while providing an illusion of reinforcements yet to come.

198

The situation resembled that existing when France was being overrun in 1940. The French had screamed for modern fighter planes, and Churchill accommodated them by sending Hurricanes that became fodder for Messerschmitt cannon. Finally convinced that he was reinforcing defeat while simultaneously stripping England's home defense, the Prime Minister turned off the tap. Similarly, in the case of Singapore, Hurricanes reached the island too late and in numbers too few to make a difference. They, along with the British and Australian soldiers who arrived in harbor on the twenty-ninth of January, had been thrown into the shambles that was Singapore even though its fate was already determined.

On land the Japanese were coming in the back door where no permanent fortifications barred entry. At sea their land-based bombers had sunk two of England's mightiest dreadnoughts—the brand-new battleship *HMS Prince of Wales* and the World War One-era battle cruiser *HMS Repulse*—which had sortied without air cover. This disaster left no existing Allied naval force, other than a thin screen of Dutch ships, in a position to challenge the Imperial Japanese Navy. In the air the enemy enjoyed superiority verging on supremacy. Knowing full well what he was doing, Churchill dribbled Hurricanes into the cauldron in order only "to prolong the defense of the Island to the last possible minute." It was a half-hearted and futile effort; as he had already in mid-January faced up to the inevitable, shifted his priority to defending India and Burma, and hoped for the best where Singapore was concerned.

In the Battle of Britain, "the few" had prevailed against the German onslaught and prevented an invasion. In the Battle of Singapore, however, the island lacked a twenty-two-mile-wide protective channel, a steady source of replacement aircraft, and a radar intercept network. At Singapore "the very few" were expendable, and they were sacrificed to a degree that stripped Sumatra and Java of any chance of surviving.

Fortunately none of the foregoing occupied my thoughts as I observed the scene at Tengah airdrome. Having managed an airport in civilian life, I could see that much was being left to chance. It seemed the Station Commander wasn't on top of the rapidly fluctuating situation. We in 258 Squadron were particularly at risk because our own ground staff (riggers, fitters, and armorers) had been diverted to Sumatra, and we had to depend upon volunteer or on-loan maintenance people.

Even though our chaps were spoiling for a fight, I was concerned because only a few of us had combat experience. Some, like me when I plunged into the Battle of Britain, had fired their guns only once during training! Additionally, it was more than three months since any of us had flown in action—and that flying had been the cautious, sparring sort of game we played with German fighters back and forth across the Channel through most of 1941. According to what I'd learned at Palembang, we were going to have our hands full when we tangled with the "Navy Noughts."

Since the twenty-fifth of January when our mobile radar unit evacuated Mersing, some seventy miles up the Malayan coast, Singapore's defenders had operated without the marginally adequate, thirty-minute warning of air attack they'd previously enjoyed. That meant we had little chance to scramble and gain an altitude advantage on approaching bombers. I'm sure the C.O. shared my apprehensions, but more mundane details occupied his mind: how to provide the squadron with food, housing, transportation, and aircraft maintenance. In any event, he could do nothing to rectify the warning problem.

We prepared for action on the morrow—the last day of January. The first group to arrive, "A" Flight, had the readiness. My bunch was on deck to fly the next day, but still I joined the pilots' meeting after supper. First we discussed what we could expect from the enemy. Once the Japanese realized the inadequacy of our defenses, they had abandoned night operations and switched on the twelfth of January almost exclusively to daylight attacks which markedly increased their bombing accuracy. Using heavy bombers based on captured airfields in northern Malaya, the Japanese launched an average of 120 sorties daily.

Next we speculated on how many fighters we could expect to have ready. Seven or eight appeared to be the most optimistic figure. Our brothers-in-arms in 232 (P) Squadron, launching from Seletar on the east coast near the naval base, would augment whatever number we came up with. Those pilots had been diverted to Singapore on the seventeenth of December as their ship cruised off South Africa bound for the Middle East. They arrived on the thirteenth of January with fifty-one crated Hurricane IIbs. A unit consisting of 232 Squadron's ground maintenance party and these twenty-four pilots, who formerly belonged to four different squadrons, had been quickly mustered to reinforce Singapore. The designation (P), indicating "Provisional," was added to their unit identification to differentiate them from the bulk of 232 Squadron which had accompanied me and my squadron mates on *Indomitable*.

Working around the clock, their ground crews had assembled twenty-one machines in four days. These particular aircraft, earmarked originally to operate under desert conditions as were ours, carried Vokes sand-intake filters which were installed as an integral part of the engine cowling. That meant the bulky contraptions, worthless in a jungle environment, couldn't be removed. This configuration created enough drag to reduce the Hurricane's top speed some thirty miles per hour, and there was nothing anyone could do about it! Despite that handicap, and the dearth of combat experience possessed by its pilots, Air Headquarters had thrown the Squadron into action on the twentieth. A week of constant effort against overwhelming odds resulted in a loss of seventeen Hurricanes; so considering their damaged or otherwise unserviceable machines, we didn't foresee a mass formation joining us in confronting the enemy.

Details were settled on the basis of what we'd picked up from other pilots about enemy tactics and aircraft capabilities. The standard raid consisted of twenty-seven bombers flying in close formation at twenty-two thousand feet escorted by twenty or thirty fighters. The enemy usually staged one or two of these intrusions every forenoon, in addition to little raids and reconnaissance flights at odd hours. We agreed to attack the bombers either head-on or from the side in deference to the volume of machine-gun and cannon fire the rear turrets pumped out. Denny Sharp would lead our boys.

When we awoke next morning, we learned the explosion we'd heard during the night had been our engineers blowing a portion of the Johore Causeway which connected the mainland of Malaya with Singapore. Enemy armies now massed three or four miles from our airdrome, so that we had arrived just in time to defend an island under siege.

Since I'd seen Britain through such a threat, I thought I could do the same for Singapore. Missing in the Crown Colony, however, was the spirit present in England. An aura of defeat pervaded the island: native workers had to be rounded up for runway repair at gun point, "evacuation" rather than "resistance" seemed the watchword, and a mantle of invincibility cloaked the enemy. Those precise formations wheeling unchallenged over the island had a disastrous impact on everyone's morale, but we were determined to change all of that.

Hurricanes scrambling to intercept Japanese bombers.

Chapter Seventeen

Shade-tree Mechanic

"A" flight scrambled after breakfast, bolting from the dispersal huts and racing toward their airplanes, ground crews running to help, clouds of dust billowing up as the Hurricanes left their parking spaces, coolies running in all directions to get out of the way. The field became alive with planes, all heading for the end of the runway, the pilots taxiing jerkily, as fast as they dared, dodging bomb craters, racing in clear stretches, slowing down again, stopping to avoid collisions or to let others by, speeding up again, all in a bedlam of noise from the dozen Rolls-Royce engines, each roaring fiercely in spurts, quieting momentarily, bellowing out again, and slowing once more, in response to the hurried manipulations of throttles as the pilots made their way by fits and starts across the drome.

The two leading machines turned onto the runway, pausing momentarily, their mighty engines trumpeting at idling speed. Then great stentorian roars swept across the field to us, drowning the other din, as these two machines gathered speed down the runway and were off, skimming over the boundary, wheels rising upward and inward to their recesses, like pigeons folding their legs. The others followed, swinging left to cut off the leader, and quiet returned but for a minute or two. Then air raid sirens began their familiar, spirit-draining wail. Later we heard then saw an enormous cluster of bombers far above, appearing as tiny, close-grouped, silver flecks against the bright blue tropical sky! Strangely they turned away without dropping their bombs. Our interceptors were nowhere to be seen.

Later, failing to make contact, our mates dropped into the landing circuit, looking not nearly so grand as previously. Within thirty minutes they were refueled and back on readiness. A half-hour later, led again by Denny Sharp, they scrambled—this time climbing toward disaster. After some time a lone Hurricane appeared from the northeast, losing height until it was near the airdrome, when its pilot opened his engine and roared low and fast across the field, rocking his wings in the victory signal. After landing Red Campbell was grinning from ear to ear: "I got a fighter, Art!" he yelled at me from the cockpit. Jumping down from the wing, he yanked off his helmet showing a shock of hair turned deep burgundy by sweat and began filling in the details like an over-speeding phonograph. "We sailed right through the formation from one side to the other, shooting at everything in sight. When I came out the other side, I saw two fighters coming at me, little chubby fellows with great big radial engines in front and painted bright green all over. I got real close before I let one have it. His machine just seemed to explode, with pieces flying off and smoke pouring out. The last I saw of him, he was just a ball of fire going down."

More Hurricanes were stringing back at intervals until all except four had landed safely. Finally we got a call from Sembawang Airdrome, a few miles to the east, informing us that three had force-landed there unhurt with their airplanes shot up. Denny Sharp had flamed a bomber, but took bullets in his engine and radiator from the rear gunner's return fire, so that his oil tank and radiator went dry causing his engine to overheat and "seize." Cardell Kleckner damaged two bombers, got hammered by a fighter, but stayed with his machine and landed wheels down among Sembawang's craters. Mickey Nash claimed one bomber damaged, noticed "funny little holes" appearing around him, was blinded by steam, glycol, and oil but managed to make the airfield wheels-up.

The real disaster hit when we learned that Bruce McAlister, a New Zealand boy who was both an experienced pilot and the best-liked person in the squadron, was listed as "missing, believed killed." His body wasn't recovered, and all we had to remind us of our friend was a small bag of personal effects I collected from his room and vowed to return to his folks.

Shortly after things had settled down, we got a call from our airdrome at Tengah reporting that they also had scrambled against the raid and that Sergeant Ron Dovell had claimed a Ki 43 fighter which he watched spiral into the ground. As his flight commander had verified the crash, the machine was being credited to Dovell. After the war when historians consulted surviving records of the 64th *Sentai* of the Japanese army air force, they found that the Japanese had listed only one of their fighters as having been destroyed. It's possible, of course, that during the swirling melee Red and Sergeant Dovell could have claimed the same aircraft, or that the records are inaccurate.

More likely from my perspective, Red's insistence that he bagged a navy Zero rather than its look-alike Ki 43 is correct, for Japanese naval aviation records have never surfaced and are presumed to be lost. There's no way to be certain, since gun cameras were another luxury we had to do without, but from personal experience, I can testify that observing an enemy's machine explode in one's face leaves an indelible record more vivid than any black and white film. Red's integrity of character and his exuberance upon landing convinced me that he had indeed drawn our squadron's first blood, and Dovell's claim leads me to believe that our sister squadron had also racked up a victory. As for our adversaries, returning enemy pilots reported having engaged fifteen intercepting Hurricanes and claimed to have shot down eight—double the actual losses we suffered.

Air Headquarters scuttled my turn at the Japanese when they ordered our squadron back to Palembang to "contest anticipated raids on that city and on shipping in the Bangka Strait." That was the official reason, but actually they were evacuating all but eight Hurricanes belonging to 232 (P) Squadron and a like number of Buffaloes in view of deteriorating conditions. We were all terribly disappointed. And so it was that I felt anything but sorry when the C.O. told me I was to remain in charge of a group of the boys who were being left behind to repair six unserviceable aircraft: the three force-landed at Sembawang the day before and three others with us at Tengah. The only order the C.O. gave me was to do what I could toward getting these machines into flying condition. I'm quite sure he knew I'd have my own ideas about what to do with them after that!

I'd inherited for my use a beautiful new '42 Ford sedan which had served Squadron Leader Thomson; but Kleck, who was one of the group staying with me, wasn't to be outdone. He appeared later in the afternoon triumphantly driving a '41 Chevy he'd promoted. It had been left behind by a bomber pilot whose unit was unexpectedly moved away!

Although the countryside was quiet and the afternoon sunny and pleasant, I realized we were besieged by a great army just across a narrow strip of water no wider than the Mississippi River and that my task was formidable. Not having our own mechanics and spare parts meant that we were little better than orphans, so we drove all over the island procuring needed parts and tools. This was a highly interesting way of passing the time until we could start flying again, for it gave us a chance to see what the island was like. We got a radiator here, a wingtip there, a couple of propellers from different sources, a propeller installation tool kit from another place, and so on. We made frequent trips to Sembawang, of course, taking spares for the three machines and checking on the repair work.

You may wonder that I relate such a seemingly intimidating task in such matter-of-fact terms. To me this was almost play. In the thirties, pilots were much closer to the mechanical aspects of their aircraft than those who followed in succeeding decades. We had to be if we expected to get anywhere—literally and figuratively—in aviation. The reliability of airplanes back then was nothing like their modern counterparts. We always expected forced-landings and knew that we couldn't be assured of finding technical help even if, highly unlikely, we could pay for it.

I'd become a pretty good "shade-tree mechanic" working on the farm where we were always tinkering, always fixing our machinery. When barnstorming or working at Conrad Aviation, I seemed to spend more time with a wrench in my hand than a joystick. One time, after a charter flight to Wisconsin, I'd left my Parks bi-plane overnight in a pasture only to find the next morning that a freak wind had thrown it into a fence and cracked a wing spar. I went into town, got some materials, repaired the damage, and flew on back to Winona. That's why getting my engine mechanic's license had been so important: better to learn to do it correctly than to bluff through a job where lives depended on my work.

In Singapore I was fortunate to be working on Hurricanes rather than Spitfires. The Hurricane's fuselage, with its conventional bulkheads, longerons, and fabric covering, was constructed like the older planes I'd serviced. Doing field repairs on Spits, with their more modern, but fragile, monocoque construction would have given me real headaches.

Salvaging the planes at Sembawang was the bigger challenge. In the first place, the airfield was within artillery range of the enemy, its runway had been cratered by bombing raids, and most of its people had evacuated. In the second place, its planes had been badly knocked about, and Mickey Nash's was resting on her belly after he'd folded the gear during landing rather than hit a string of craters.

Additionally I spent quite a bit of time working on airplanes at Tengah. On one occasion I was putting a wingtip on a machine, working alone, and was so engrossed that I failed to notice the drone of an approaching bomber formation until I had been listening to it for perhaps three or four minutes. Suddenly coming to, I looked up to see them almost overhead. I jumped into my car and started with wheels spinning. As I approached the trenches, I just yanked the emergency brake handle and landed running, without waiting for the car to stop. The bombers were directly overhead. I dived into a trench and crouched down, but the aircraft passed on and no bombs fell.

At the Officers' Mess, a beautiful building of dark grey stone at the top of a gentle, grassy incline overlooking the airdrome, the Malay waiters and batmen had all run off after the news that the enemy were so near, but the two elderly Chinese cooks and "Tichi," a little Malay boy of ten or eleven who worked in the bar, remained on the job. The meals were still lavish, the only difference being that we had to serve ourselves. There was always plenty of beer, as well as ice-cold Coca-Cola and other soft drinks, to be had.

On February second, two days after they had been withdrawn to Palembang, the squadron returned. They'd come to escort a raid on occupied Kluang Airdrome by Hudson and Blenheim bombers of 62 Squadron at dawn next morning, and I promised the C.O. I'd have three of my machines ready to go with them.

My crews and I had to work a good share of that night finishing repair jobs and doing final inspections on the three fighters. We worked and sweated and toiled in bright moonlight until about two o'clock in the morning. Then with the last engine checked, the last fuel tank filled, the last gun cleaned and loaded, and the last cowling clip fastened, I told the men they could go to bed and take the morning off. Then I drove wearily back to the Mess for two or three hours' sleep myself before the raid. I was to take part in it, so naturally I was looking forward once more to getting my first action against the Japanese.

After the mission briefing, I was again disappointed. Expecting to find the Hurricanes they had flown from Palembang ready for take-off, my squadron mates instead found them sitting virtually as they had left them, with ground crews no where to be found. Rather than launch only my three aircraft, Headquarters scrubbed the escort mission. An hour later Squadron Leader Thomson was ordered to take his aircraft and my three serviceable birds back to Palembang.

Consequently, when 62 Squadron's six American-made Hudson bombers arrived at the rendezvous point, they found neither the Blenheims nor the Hurricanes. Squadron Leader Lilly courageously decided to strike the target knowing that he would face certain fighter attack. Bombing from six thousand feet, he was jumped by three Ki 43s that immediately shot Sergeant Doug Hunter's aircraft down in flames. No one survived the crash of the young New Zealander's bomber. The Japanese erroneously claimed a second aircraft as being probably destroyed. Its rear gunner reported sending a fighter down trailing smoke, but the enemy's destruction was not confirmed. The Blenheims, failing to rendezvous with either the Hudsons or the promised escort, opted to bomb an alternate target.

Shortly after the Hurricanes had departed for Sumatra, leaving me to patch up my three remaining cripples and two of the Palembang machines that had refused to start for the squadron's departure, I was saddened to hear that the Station Commander, Group Captain F.G. Watts, had used his service pistol to commit suicide. A former C.O. of 62 Squadron, "Poppa Watts" had been in charge at Tengah for two years. Having seen his own and other squadrons decimated by the Japanese, having been stymied by the influx of evacuees and the collapse of morale and discipline among native workers, and having been directed by Command Headquarters to explain why the escort hadn't launched, he'd simply had enough.

One of the two pilots whose aircraft couldn't deploy with the squadron was Denny Sharp who now assumed command of our small detachment by virtue of his rank as Flight Lieutenant. Sergeant "Pip" Healy was the other stay-behind. Both were treasured friends, as was Cardell Kleckner, my American expatriate companion, who departed with the squadron in one of my repaired Hurricanes. Kleck was quite put out about leaving Singapore and groused about the prospect of seeing little action in Sumatra.

He shouldn't have worried on that score. He was destined to get more action there than I got in Singapore, and I was never to see him again. The day following our squadron's return to Palembang on the fifth of February, I got a preview of what fate had in mind for me. Eleven Hurricanes, flown by pilots of 232 Squadron who had accompanied me on *Indomitable*, came winging into Tengah. They had been ordered up from Sumatra to Sembawang Airdrome, but enemy shelling immediately forced them to join us.

Lunch at the Mess took on a party atmosphere until a muffled blast, a whistling noise, and a loud explosion announced that we had become an item of interest to the enemy's batteries. The barrage lasted over an hour, but nothing landed nearer the Mess than a hundred yards or so, and most of us ate our food unperturbed. The time had

213

come for what was to be my first of five evacuations under fire in the next two weeks, but we weren't going to let them spoil our meal.

Chapter Eighteen

Into the Fight

With all three of the RAF's bases under shellfire, the only possible haven was Kallang Airdrome, the former municipal airport of Singapore located on the south side of the island just east of the city. Two Thirty-two Squadron was now ordered to move down there, and our small party did likewise, taking our two Hurricanes and two automobiles. We'd remedied the engine troubles on their aircraft, but the weather was reported bad in the direction of Sumatra, so that Denny Sharp and Pip Healey couldn't rejoin 258 Squadron in Palembang. Instead, they flew the Hurricanes to Kallang while I drove my Ford, and "Brownie"—Arthur Brown (RCAF) who'd survived the sinking of *Ark Royal* back in December—and Ted Tremlett followed in the Chevy. I brought along the bag of personal effects belonging to Bruce McAlister, the New Zealand boy who went missing from the squadron's first engagement.

The road entering the airdrome passed under imposing dark stone archways, now pitifully scarred and chipped by blast, shrapnel, and bullets. The beautiful hangars and terminal buildings of what had once been a great airline base were barren and empty, with windows gone, walls gashed and torn. It reminded me of the buildings at Croydon Airdrome, London's once magnificent airline terminal, with ticket and information booths silent and empty, their counters covered with dust, windows blown in and walls shattered and scarred: results of the mass bombing in August 1940. The vast concrete aprons between and in front of the hangars at Kallang were torn and pitted with bomb craters, as was the entire field. The saddest sight of all was the remains of several Hurricanes and Buffaloes, along with three or four trucks and tank wagons scattered around the outside of the field, all victims of bombing and machine-gun attacks. It was heartbreaking.

The Hurricanes had already arrived from Tengah and stood dispersed around the field with mechanics working on them. I found the Officers' Mess a burned-out ruin. Denny and some of the others poked among the debris salvaging the bar stock. Squadron Leader Llewellin, 232's commander, was out scouting for something more elemental—a place for us to sleep! By nightfall he had us ensconced in the Sea View Hotel located on the shore several miles east of town and reputed to be one of the most luxurious places in Singapore. In my room the illusion of being in a movie star's boudoir was compromised only by six-inch-wide strips of tape crisscrossing the mirrors to inhibit flying glass.

One side of the hotel looked out on the sea, but the main entrance faced onto a manicured lawn, its beauty spoiled by shelter trenches and by automobiles parked beneath the palm trees for concealment. Dinner that evening was seven courses served by Chinese and Malay waiters in a spacious dining hall filled with wealthy civilians including the first white women we'd seen in some time, wearing the first evening dresses we'd seen in months. Altogether, it was a strange lair from which to go forth to battle. Before going into action, however, we had to resolve the matter of just whom we worked for. Denny was as eager as I to stay in Singapore where we believed our airplanes would be more useful. So after a good night's sleep, he volunteered our services on Friday, the sixth of February, to Squadron Leader Llewellin. After receiving approval from Air Headquarters by telephone, our new boss gave us the rest of the day off. Denny, Ted, Brownie and I piled into the Ford and drove to town.

The business section might have been an American city except for the welter of Chinese and Malays all about and the rickshaws mingling with automobiles on the streets. People seemed to have little interest in the hot breath of approaching history. Getting a haircut appeared to rank high on their priority lists along with reading the *Free Press* or the *Tribune* over morning coffee. Those queuing outside the cinemas caused me to think everyone preferred not to contemplate the future until I realized that one such line ended at the door of a veterinary surgeon, and its members were Europeans clutching their unsuspecting pets.

As it was a hot day, we soon lost interest in sight-seeing and stopped for refreshments at the Raffles Hotel. Standing at its world-famous long bar, I experienced another of those periodic disconnects when an incongruous setting caused me to probe the connection between time and space. How would it all turn out? Who would control Singapore in fifty or sixty years? What would the city look like? Had I but glimpsed the answers to those questions, I would not have believed the vision. At that time would

Denny have believed the Raffles itself would become the most expensive hotel in Asia with 104 suites priced from five hundred U.S. dollars to five thousand for a single night's stay? Could Ted have predicted that Singapore would be an independent nation where, in the words of its patriarch, "Oriental traditions, values, and tastes thrive within an efficient, Western-style national infrastructure?" By what magic could Brownie have conjured up a Camelot boasting a spotless subway system; skyscrapers including the planet's tallest hotel; trees, open spaces, parks, restored historic buildings; regulated automobile ownership, safe streets, no drugs, guns, chewing gum or pornography; the world's busiest port, and three million residents claiming Asia's highest standard of living?

In the hotel's lobby, we saw an advertisement for the film *Ziegfeld Girl* showing at the Alhambra Theatre nearby, so we voted for a matinee. It wasn't the show we would have chosen if we had been given a choice, for though the music and lavish pageants were wonderful, the sight of so many beautiful girls was almost more than we could take after being away from feminine companionship for so long. The shock was quite rude for us when it was over: completely lost in the atmosphere of American girls and song and gaiety, we stepped outside into the teeming oriental traffic and the sweltering tropical sun, to be reminded that we were half-way around the world from America with our enemies only a few miles off.

Towards mid-afternoon we returned to the hotel; there we learned to our keen sorrow that Squadron Leader Llewellin had been killed as he scrambled to intercept a raid. He was a fine C.O., loved by all of his boys, and we ourselves had known him well enough to like him very much. Two of the others had been shot down but escaped

218

injury, although their machines were wrecked. One pilot, Joe Hutton, learned a basic lesson the hard way. Intent on confirming the crash of a Ki 27b, Type 97 Fighter, he allowed two others an opportunity to riddle his Hurricane. Perhaps having expected to meet the sleek *Hayabusas,* he'd let down his guard against the stubby Nakajimas sporting a fixed gear and wheel pants belonging to days gone by. Joe quickly learned, however, that the Ki 27 defined the concept of maneuverability, so he dropped his nose, firewalled the throttle, and dived for mother earth. Racing low over the sea, his engine wide open with its radiator shot through and running dry, he managed to get clear of his assailants before his engine seized, thereby causing him to force-land near the shore of an island. Rocks just beneath the water's surface almost tore his Hurricane to pieces, but it stayed right side up, and he managed to get out safely.

Joe's luck was holding. While landing on the previous day, two artillery shells had bracketed his aircraft almost causing him to cartwheel. In this second incident the rocks actually prevented his fighter from nosing under water. We all knew the Hurricane's penchant for diving like a submarine following a ditching because of its heavy, twelve-cylinder engine. A pilot dazed by the impact would be hard pressed to unstrap and get out in time to save himself. The Spitfire had the same tendency.

Whereas luck sometimes rescued a pilot who had done something unwise or had neglected in his haste to properly position a switch or control lever, one never knew when Dame Fortune would refuse to smile. Squadron Leader Llewellin's death proved that axiom and pointed out how accidents could happen to the best of us when fatigue, strain, and haste joined forces. Examining the cockpit of his machine after it had been recovered from the water, we found that he had attempted to take off with the propeller lever in "course" rather than "fine" pitch. This prevented the engine from attaining maximum revolutions thereby drastically increasing his take-off roll and fatally restricting his climb, so that his wing clipped a junk's mast causing the aircraft to plunge into the sea. He had also neglected to lock his safety harness, so that his head was thrown violently into the gunsight on impact. Whatever the primary cause, Llewellin's luck had run out. You can imagine our feelings when, in his effects, we found a small black rag cat, the lucky charm he always carried when flying.

Fatigue extracted a heavy toll whether it claimed a life or merely debilitated it. A case in point was my meeting at Kallang with an old friend, John Noble MacKenzie, DFC, who'd served on Spitfires with 41 Squadron when I was with 64 at Hornchurch. We were almost the same age; he being a year younger. The grandson of a former Prime Minister of New Zealand, John traveled to England in 1937 to join the RAF. On the sixteenth of January, 1941, he was promoted to Flight Commander and decorated by the King in recognition of 245 sorties flown during the Battle of Britain. He'd arrived in Singapore early in September assigned to 488 (New Zealand) Squadron flying the obsolete Buffalo and had been in on all the fighting.

Imagine trading a Spitfire for a Buffalo! The American-made Brewster Buffalo was a stubby, radial-engine monoplane with an embarrassing rate of climb and a top speed almost 50 miles per hour slower than the Zero at 10,000 feet. Produced in 1938 as a carrier fighter, ordered by the British when they were desperate in 1940, and re-directed to Singapore when the RAF determined it to be grossly outclassed by German fighters, the Buffalo was dead meat for Zeros or Ki 43s in 1941.

John was so worn and haggard and had lost so much weight that I hardly recognized him. He said he had just been promoted to squadron leader and was going down to Java to re-form his unit, as most of their planes had been lost and most of their pilots killed. He himself was off flying for at least a week or two because of shock from a bomb that had landed too close a few days before. I advised him to try to get sent away for a rest, even if it meant losing his promotion temporarily. He looked much too tired and ill to carry on. But carry on he did, eventually retiring in 1957 after a distinguished career and subsequently returning to New Zealand.

Flight Lieutenant Eric "Rickey" Wright replaced Squadron Leader Llewellin and Denny moved into Rickey's former position as commander of "A" Flight, one of the two sub-units within an RAF fighter squadron. I was in Denny's flight. Contrary to our situation during the Battle of Britain, machines—not men to fly them—were the problem as we had twice as many pilots as Hurricanes.

After breakfast the next day, as we sat waiting to go to the drome for our shift at readiness, for the first time in more than three months I began to experience the familiar tension and nervousness, with the sickish pain in the pit of my stomach unusually strong. I suppose it was the realization coming home that I was "in it" once more, with all the uncertainties and dismaying possibilities to get used to and subdue again into their places as normal parts of life.

Denny and I spent a little time talking over the formation we'd use. We planned to fly in two sections of four, Denny leading one and I the other. I would endeavor to engage the fighters with my four to keep them diverted while Denny took his section into the bombers. Then the next time we'd change around, and he'd do the dirty work. As we talked and I visualized the situations we were discussing, I found my excitement increasing until my heart was pounding and my knees trembled a little—and after eighteen months of mainly front-line service, too!

It seemed so strange to be there relaxing, or trying to, in the cool quiet veranda of the hotel, nonchalantly discussing how we should go about the bizarre and unearthly business that might occur in that eerie world miles above us before the morning was out, while civilian men and women lounged around us, finishing their coffee, reading the morning papers, chatting as ordinary people anywhere might, not planning to kill anyone. Their greatest danger was a probable sea voyage to Java in a few days. I had my helmet, gloves, and Mae West in my lap, having just unpacked them from my things, and their significance helped to make it all seem too incongruous to be real!

About quarter past eight, we strolled out to the Ford and piled in. I was wondering how long it would take me to get over feeling like a little boy on his first day at school. At the single dispersal hut that served both flights, I changed from my shorts to a pair of slacks to give my legs some protection from fire, shouldered my parachute and went out to get my airplane ready. It took about ten minutes to set my 'chute on the seat, arrange the straps, hang my helmet over the gunsight and tuck my gloves behind it, then run a few checks—oxygen supply, air pressure system, electric gunsight—and finally position the switches for a quick start. As the field was soft and muddy, I pumped my wing flaps down a little to assist in getting off the ground quickly. I made sure the seat was raised as high as it would go, and then I realized that I was slipping quite rapidly into my old mental attitude: combining fighting fever and resignation to "come what may."

Around mid-morning we launched against "Thirty plus bandits, above twenty thousand feet, approaching from the northwest." There was the old feverish fumbling at parachute and seat straps, helmet and gloves, the glancing around to see if I was late and whether the others were taxiing out yet. All tucked in and ready to go at last, I found my tenseness relaxing its hold a little. A moment's wait with engine idling, for Denny's four machines to taxi out ahead, and then I was following after them onto the rain-soaked field, fast but carefully, dodging the newly filled bomb craters in which the earth would still be soft. Because of the field's condition, it wasn't safe to take off in formation. We followed each other off the ground like beads on a string. Once airborne we turned to cut off the leader and slip into our places in a loose arrangement of two sections, each flying in "finger four" style so that we could guard each other against surprise attacks, and either act independently as two units, or close in and work together as circumstances dictated.

We climbed furiously, whipping our engines hard, the noses of our airplanes pointed steeply upward where we could be "up-sun" of our enemies. Singapore Island was now a miniature in brilliant tropical green far below, landscaped with miniature jungles, orchards, fields, roads, villages, and towns, with the miniature city and harbor on its south coast, all partially screened by a layer of low broken clouds sprinkled over it like hundreds of tufts of white cotton fluff, pretty in the bright sunlight.

It was dwarfed by the green expanses of the great Malayan Peninsula which half swallows it in the hollow of its southern tip into which the island fits, and by the endless reaches of warm blue-green sea stretching in all directions. Over it ran the long dark mantle of smoke from the oil fire, stretching from its source on the north side, down across and southward out over the sea into the southern horizon. The bombers were nowhere to be seen. We'd be lucky if we could reach their altitude by the time they were over the island. Starting a fight with a disadvantage in altitude is one of the most reliable ways of committing suicide.

Despite our best efforts, the enemy dropped their cargo of bombs and a few leaflets, put their noses down, and poured on the coal heading for home. We didn't have a prayer of catching them. Had we been under radar control as we were in England eighteen months previously, we would have scrambled in time to have been above and up-sun in perfect position to attack. So much for the narrow appreciation given to the RAF's pre-war needs in Southeast Asia.

It was disappointing not to intercept, but one gets used to disappointments in air warfare. We didn't realize what the target of the raid had been until we were nearly back. Coming over our airdrome at three or four thousand feet, with the layer of broken clouds making a sort of carpet just under us, I noticed a light pall of thin blue smoke floating over the field. Beneath the clouds the truth sank home, as I saw that the drome was littered with dozens of fresh bomb craters! So it appeared that our enemies, not content with shelling us out of all the airfields on the north side of the island, were determined to drive us out completely by bombing this, our only base left.

I circled for several minutes "shooting" the field in fake approaches at low altitude from various directions, just as I had often done over pastures and stubble fields back in America in my barnstorming days. Finally I made my choice, a short narrow stretch between the paths of several sticks of bombs, with water standing in the low area at one end and a cracked-up Hurricane, which appeared to have just landed, lying on its belly near the other end. By this time I was leading a procession of all the rest of our Hurricanes around the field, all the pilots likewise trying to figure out how to get down. I made a try at my "runway," and landed all right, with room to spare, and then the rest followed one after another. Everybody made it safely.

One bit of gallows humor provided a rare laugh. While we were attempting our intercept, three of the boys not on readiness had decided to drive from the hotel to the drome to see what was happening. They were caught in the open by the bombing and had time only to throw themselves on the ground. Their car was holed by shrapnel, and they were badly shaken up. One of the three was Joe Hutton who'd been bracketed by artillery shells on landing two days previously, had been shot down the next day, and had now been bombed on the third. Even Joe shared in the laughter when he reminded us that his luck was still holding!

Unbeknownst to us at the time was another bit of humor that someone inserted in the official communiqué covering the day's action. Reporting the morning's bombing: "Fighters of the Far East Command intercepted the raiders, destroying one enemy aircraft, probably destroying another, and damaging two. All our fighters returned to their bases." In truth, we had one bomber credited to Second Lieutenant John "Stewie" Stewart of the

South African Air Force. Engine trouble had forced Stewie to drop out of our formation, but returning to Kallang he stumbled into the enemy and sent one down in flames before suffering a wound to the hip. The rear gunners had directed so much tracer ammunition at him that he "thought they were laying down a smoke screen!" Afterwards he dived for Kallang with oil and glycol covering his windscreen.

Turning onto his final approach, he judged the field's location by the buildings and high trees on each side, steered between them, and hoped. "I came in real fast," he told me later, "touched down at well over a hundred miles an hour, and slid to a nice stop in the middle of the field." It was Stewie's machine that I had seen as I circled for landing. He had done by luck what I agonized over before picking my landing site. So the communiqué was right: all fighters *had* returned. In their understated British manner, headquarters simply chose not to say that one landed on its belly! Neither did they report that the entire fighter defense of Singapore was reduced to using just one strip of sod between rows of bomb craters.

Our two flights were now sharing the daily load with one on duty from nine in the morning until one in the afternoon to cover the most active period of attacks and the other on readiness during daylight hours either side of that period. My turn pulling the "short shift" came on Sunday, the eighth of February, but again we failed to intercept, and my subsequent convoy patrol was uneventful. Our new C.O. managed to get himself shot down during a melee in which we claimed two of the enemy. Like Stewie the previous day, Rickey managed to land wheels up on the airdrome so that the communiqué could again report "All our fighters returned to their bases."

226

Chapter Nineteen

Last Flight from Singapore

Enemy air activity had been light for a few days; but things started popping early on Monday, the ninth of February. When our flight reached the drome, the others were still airborne on their second sortie of the morning. They looked pretty tired as they left their machines, but most of them were grinning triumphantly. There'd been numerous skirmishes and chases with low-flying bombers, and nearly every pilot had taken one or more shots.

Scrambled immediately, we raced to our aircraft where I found the ground crew still working on mine. I'd drawn "Z," the machine flown earlier by Sergeant J.A. Sandeman Allen, whose seven "kills" would subsequently classify him as the leading ace involved in the defense of Malaya, Sumatra, and the East Indies. "Sandy" warned me that his Hurricane had a runaway gun that wouldn't cease firing once it was activated, yet he'd claimed two bombers destroyed, and I thought perhaps my ill luck would change. The armorers were working feverishly snatching out empty ammunition tanks, fastening new ones in, and threading fresh belts through the chutes that led into the guns. Roar after roar of sound swept across the field as the four planes of Denny's section took off, one after another in quick order. Then my own section was taking off without me.

Finally, with the last panel in place, the men slid off the wings, and the sergeant waved the "go ahead" signal. Denny's formation was out of sight, so I knew I would have to "freelance" in hopes of finding prey. I spent an hour or so circling like a hawk ready to pounce, but nothing came my way and the radar-blind ground controllers could offer me no help.

The scenery at high altitude was magnificent that morning. Gigantic tumbled masses of cloud rose to twenty thousand feet, beautiful and awe-inspiring with their great misty mountains, valleys, and chasms with here and there a detached cloud like an island suspended by magic in the sky. It was so enchanting that once or twice I surrendered to temptation and swooped down among them to play about for a couple of minutes: diving at their tops, careening at four hundred miles an hour through great foggy valleys and in and out of weird mystic caverns half a mile deep, occasionally shearing away to practice a few rolls.

Somewhere under the south part of a level carpet of broken fluffy clouds would be our hotel—no bigger than a pinhead—and the old grouch who tried to chase our boys out of the swimming pool, still sitting on the veranda, no doubt, with his pink gins, his enlarged liver, and his dislike for the world. What a narrow life he led. Perhaps most of ours were fated to be short, but they were wide as we could make them while they lasted!

228

I returned to the drome with nothing accomplished except a burst into an enemy truck, a complete fire-out of the runaway gun in my right wing, and a feeling of acute frustration. Shortly after being refueled and rearmed, we scrambled against another high altitude raid. During the climb, Ground Control asked Denny to dispatch two aircraft to break up a strafing attack on our troops fighting in the northwest section of the island. He chose me and my wingman, Sergeant Bill Moodie.

Approaching the area we saw what appeared to be one of the fixed-geared Ki 27 fighters streaking for home just above the treetops. Disregarding possible ground fire, we swooped to attack. As I settled into firing position, one of those nightmare experiences that last only a moment but live forever in inescapable memory began to unfold. First a bright flash of color caught my eye: a green Navy Zero wheeling across below and ahead of me, turning steep left just above the treetops. Without conscious decision I twisted viciously into a diving turn after him. I closed in, still diving, pulling my nose around until my sights lined up with him and a little ahead, leading him, then let him have it. The quick, shattering roar from my guns startled me as my white tracers reached out to caress the graceful little green wings with their strange red discs painted near each tip. I zoomed up hard, just missing the trees, while my runaway gun chattered and spewed its tracers aimlessly over the jungle. At that moment I spied Sergeant Moodie's Hurricane diving steeply, obviously hit!

He plunged straight into a small clearing and exploded. I recall circling to confront any new enemies and, in the process, losing sight of both the one we'd been chasing and the Navy Zero. Anti-aircraft gunners of Japan's Twenty-fifth Army, which was in action in this sector, reported shooting down four aircraft this day, so hindsight suggests that Sergeant Moodie fell at their hands. Nevertheless, with a heavy heart, I turned back toward Singapore to face the sad task of reporting his loss. I hadn't known him well, but the mute faces and glistening eyes of some of the boys told me how much they thought of him. I wondered if any of them felt it was my fault.

Brownie had taken command of my flight and claimed one bomber damaged. Denny and Pilot Officer Tremlett each claimed one damaged. As we gathered to compare notes, I heard the incredible news that the enemy had forced the Strait of Johore during the night and were established on the northern part of Singapore Island itself! Shortly before midnight, following heavy artillery preparation, fifteen thousand men of the Fifth and Eighteenth Divisions had swarmed into armored landing craft and collapsible launches powered by outboard motors to assault the shore of Singapore Island itself. The first wave of four thousand veterans of the China war suffered heavy casualties at the hands of the Twenty-second Australian Infantry Brigade, but the weight of successive attacks overpowered the twenty-five hundred defenders. By morning the Japanese were attacking Tengah airfield some five miles inland.

The siege was over and the enemy inside our gates. Was the thing we couldn't let happen, really occurring? Was Singapore falling?

That evening we learned from the boys of "B" flight that the air space over the island had teemed with small groups of bombers and dive-bombers flying at low altitude, mostly unescorted. Everyone had got at least one crack at them, and they had destroyed five or six and claimed a bunch of probables. Late in the afternoon, responding to an army request for air cover, Squadron Leader Wright, with his flight of four protected by rain showers and the smoke from burning oil tanks, surprised a number of fixed-gear bombers. Flight Lieutenant Julian claimed one destroyed, Wright damaged another, and Sandy (again in "Z") claimed three damaged "because there were no witnesses," he said, "but, in fact, I saw two go into the ground." Pilot Officer McKechnie had to break off because of an overheating engine which caused him to land "dead-stick" back at Kallang.

During these afternoon melees, the flight lost two machines, but Sergeant Tom Young, RAAF, got away unhurt and Sergeant Fred Margarson escaped alive although badly wounded. Both pilots had stories to tell. Young had attacked a formation of twelve bombers, most likely Ki 21s of the 7th Flying Battalion. He claimed one as probably destroyed, but enemy gunners riddled his aircraft putting the hydraulic system out of commission and causing him to head back to Kallang. Finding the drome under attack, he elected to land wheels up in what was essentially "no-man's-land" between our lines and the advancing Japanese. Pistol in hand, he cautiously picked his way southward until he made contact with British forces.

Margarson's survival was little short of miraculous. Preparing to attack a bomber formation, he heard and felt bullets slamming into the armor plating behind his seat. Breaking downward he sailed through the bombers scoring hits on the port wing of one before again coming under attack by escorting Ki 43s which sent explosive bullets into his engine cowl and shattered his right wrist forcing him to fly left-handed for the rest of the engagement. Attempting

231

to accomplish a half loop from a half-roll, he came to grief. Describing it to us later, he said, "I must have misjudged the height and the aircraft did a high compression stall into the sea. My next recollection was regaining consciousness underwater."

His miscalculation probably saved his life as he was convinced he could not have returned to Kallang, and he knew—as we all did—that a pilot's chances of surviving a ditching were not good. He believed that the impact of hitting the water tore the engine from its mountings thereby allowing the fuselage to sink relatively slowly so that he could abandon the cockpit.

Once in his inflatable dinghy, rifle fire from shore punctured the raft on either side of his body. He spent the next two hours bobbing in his Mae West until two Australian soldiers rowed out to pick him up. The gunfire had come from members of an Indian artillery battery who had taken him for a Japanese!

As we talked with our friends about the day's events, we were all looking forward to the next morning in anticipation of good hunting. No doubt there'd be loads of bombers operating in close support of enemy troops, flying at low altitude where we could get at them easily. Despite our hopes, the action of the ninth of February was to be the last over Singapore for 232 Squadron as Air Vice Marshal Maltby ordered Rickey to evacuate to Palembang at dawn the next day.

Although we were crestfallen, our protests carried little weight. Air Headquarters considered our situation hopeless and determined to regroup its resources in Sumatra. Yet they, like we and our counterparts in the other services, had no inkling of what was taking place at the highest echelons of power.

In light of the catastrophes brewing in Singapore, Churchill had cabled General Sir Archibald Wavell, commander of allied forces in the Far East, "the defenders must greatly outnumber Japanese forces . . . and in a well-contested battle should destroy them. There must at this stage be no thought of saving the troops or sparing the civilian population . . . ." Churchill's instructions continued as dispassionately as if he were addressing the toy soldiers of his boyhood: "Commanders and senior officers should die with their troops. The honour of the British Empire and of the British Army is at stake . . . the whole reputation of our country and our race is involved."

For various reasons the on-scene commanders, cut off from reinforcement and at the mercy of Japanese artillery, bombers, and fighters, did not comply with the Prime Minister's dictates. From the perspective of London, and in theory, General Percival's eighty-five thousand troops should have been able to handle their enemy. A third of that number, however, had just arrived in the theater and had no experience or training in jungle warfare. Most of the others had been on constant retreat down the Malay Peninsula, had abandoned their equipment, and were exhausted. Even a charismatic leader—which he was not—would have been sorely challenged to rally such a force. Alas, Percival was not to glimpse the Grail but was fated to drink from the bitter cup.

Tuesday, the tenth, found only eight Hurricanes serviceable for evacuation. Rickey chose their pilots from the 232 Squadron roster, so we five from 258 Squadron were among those staying behind. We didn't mind, as rumors circulated that a fresh squadron might return in a day or so if the military situation stabilized. If there were any chance to do some fighting, we wanted to be in it. Singapore just couldn't be allowed to go under!

The "fortunes of war" continually asserted themselves, and the evacuation of 232 Squadron provided new anecdotes. Sergeant Gordon Dunn, RCAF, was assigned to fly the aircraft that McKechnie had deadsticked the previous day because of an overheating engine. He and his close friend, Sergeant Tom Young, discussed stripping the parachute from the cockpit so that Young could ride "piggy-back." They gave up the idea when Young was offered a seat on one of the Hudson bombers that was also leaving for Palembang. As fate would have it, Young discovered at the last moment that space was not available, and by this time it was too late to get back to Dunn's aircraft. Good thing! On the trip Dunn's engine again overheated forcing him to bale out. He landed minus one boot lost when the parachute blossomed at nine hundred feet, and after further adventures found a village headman who drove him to Palembang. Had Young been with him, they would have been committed to a forced-landing without benefit of shoulder harness and lap belt: a chilling thought!

At the Sea View, I realized that the hotel routine went on as usual even though the enemy might be approaching and the number of guests was rapidly decreasing. At four in the afternoon, the same friendly Chinese boy brought tea and cakes to my room. Supper in the evening consisted of seven courses as usual, delicious and expertly cooked, complete with French names on the menu that always made the dishes a surprise when they were served.

234

The guests who still remained were dismayed when they learned that our Hurricanes had left. They commented to us, as others had, that one of the biggest helps to the morale of the people during the last few days had been the sight of our little band taking off and climbing over the city time after time each day to engage the enemy. No matter how bad the news, they felt there was hope as long as they could see the RAF still flying.

That night the artillery fire was definitely much closer, so we knew the battle was going badly. A sullen red glow lit up a large part of the sky north of us. As always in Singapore, I slept with my revolver under my pillow, and this time I kept my doors locked, too. But my only intruder was the grinning Chinese boy who brought in my cup of tea early next morning.

Denny had detailed two of our remaining 258 Squadron pilots, Ted Tremlett and Ian Newlands, to drive to Seletar Airdrome on the northeast side of the island and bring back a couple of damaged Hurricanes which had been repaired. They turned up again before breakfast, having done their job, and told of a creepy trip going over there in the darkness, being stopped and examined frequently at bayonet point along the blacked-out road, scared each time that they'd run into an enemy trap. They said the Japanese had captured the airdrome the afternoon before, but our troops had retaken it in the evening and were preparing to blow up the field as soon as the boys had taken off.

Still it was cool, quiet, and peaceful where we sat on the veranda of the hotel that morning, only a few miles from the fighting—less for all we knew. The artillery fire had quieted down with the coming of daylight. Denny and I were enthralled for a while watching an exotic, dark-haired

English girl clad in shorts and a light sweater, exercising with two greyhounds on the lawn among the palm trees. She was swinging a scarf about for them to leap at. Her movements and theirs were so graceful that I thought she must be a dancer, but someone said she was a nurse. It seemed that either she or the approaching enemy and the terrible fighting must be unreal. It just didn't make sense— but neither did a lot of things in the last days of Singapore.

The Singapore Free Press—"NO.16,541. ESTD. 1835. WEDNESDAY, FEB. 11, 1942. 5 CENTS."— arrived at breakfast time just as usual, though we could now see a fire started by shelling in the northern part of town. We read the news just as usual over our lavish breakfast. The paper's front-page editorial called on everyone to be "determined and defiant." It informed the reader that our defenders weren't greatly outnumbered and that the enemy had no fifth columnist friends behind our lines. It reminded us that much was at stake and that we must fight with no thought of surrender. It prophesied that the names of men who defended Singapore would "for ever shine in the annals of all freedom-loving nations."

Near the bottom of the front page, I read with pleasure a story with a London dateline summarizing the Red Army's advance on the whole Eastern Front as it drove toward Smolensk. Adjacent articles chronicled successful attacks by submarines against enemy convoys in the Central Mediterranean; the number of Italian casualties in Libya and elsewhere according to a Reuter's dispatch; and the sad news that Lady Thomas was unwell, would be confined to bed for a week or ten days, and would not be leaving Singapore. Four lines without headline immediately beneath the report on Lady Thomas' condition mentioned that "Civilian casualties due to enemy action in Singapore areas on Monday were 51 killed and 262 injured." A four-inch-square advertisement in the lower right-hand corner advised of the night's dinner-dance at the Raffles Hotel.

After eating I folded my paper, placed it in my flying kit, and joined several others going to the drome to see what was happening. A couple of new fires pumped black smoke into the sky north of us, and the familiar smoke pall looked much heavier than before, more frightening. It was drifting right across the city, most of which was darkened by its shadow. An omen?

As I snapped a few photographs, a standard formation of twenty-seven bombed the dock area just a couple of miles away, so that the staccato booming of the explosions reached us, shaking the ground under our feet. A couple of good-sized fires got going there within a few minutes, putting up a lot of black smoke. Later Air Headquarters informed Denny, "You're to take the two other most experienced pilots with you and fly the three Hurricanes down to Palembang." Our part in the battle for Singapore was over!

Denny selected Brownie and me to go with him. We drove to the hotel, parked the car close to our rooms, and began loading our bags into it. I still had Bruce's bag which I was keeping to send to his folks. Back at the drome within the hour, we found Tom Watson looking excited. He'd managed to get a Brewster fighter repaired and said he was going with us. He also said that the Japanese were almost at the airfield!

We had trouble finding maps of Sumatra. Denny finally got a pretty good one, which he would use because he was leading us, and I got part of an old naval chart that showed the coast line of Sumatra and the River Moesi which ran from the coast inland to Palembang. All three of our Hurricanes were in questionable condition, having been patched up and put together hurriedly, but the hard-working New Zealand ground crews were doing all they could for them. Whatever we accomplished in those last few days of operating at Kallang, we owed largely to those men.

Each of us picked a machine and began carrying our bags to it. Ted was helping us get our things unloaded from the car. He and the rest of the fellows were going to try to find a ship on which they could travel to Palembang. All at once we heard a sharp explosion from a grove just northeast of us, and then an answering burst overhead. Looking up we saw a round black cloud, a couple of hundred feet high, over the middle of the airdrome. "Oh, oh!" I thought. "So they're almost here!"

The next several minutes were the most suspenseful of my life. I was jamming bags into cavities inside my Hurricane hoping they would ride securely and not fowl the controls, the field piece was lobbing air bursts over the drome at an increasingly frequent pace, and rifle fire broke out in a grove not more than a quarter of a mile away. Brownie had borrowed my screwdriver, so I had to run to his aircraft to retrieve it in order to button up the panels I'd removed. Meanwhile Ted had driven my car to the hangar not knowing that the last two bags were locked in its trunk. I agonized, for one of the bags was Bruce's. I hated to leave mine and couldn't leave his.

Down the field a little way, we could hear the whine of an American inertial starter speeding up. Tom was trying to get the Brewster started. Over the city a couple of enemy reconnaissance planes cruised leisurely at low altitude.

Denny, finished with his packing, stood by his airplane watching me, trying to conceal his anxiety. The cracking of rifles was growing in volume and seemed to be getting a little closer. Occasionally a bullet or two whined overhead. Finally, seeing Ted drive up to the dispersal hut, I raced over, unlocked the trunk with the duplicate set of keys, and jerked the precious bags out. Then I tore back to my machine and started stuffing them in the bottom of the fuselage. A couple of ground crew chaps, who had arrived to help, told me to get in while they put the panel back under the fuselage.

Tom had already taxied his Brewster to the end of our take-off strip, and soon Denny, Brownie, and I joined him. Fully expecting Japanese soldiers to spill out onto the field, I paused to let Denny take the lead, then shoved my throttle forward. Brownie and Tom followed. We made one circuit of the airdrome followed by Japanese anti-aircraft fire. I took two snapshots, one to my right of a fire raging in the northern part of the city and another over my tail when we were some two or three miles out. My final memory is of a bright green country, resting on the edge of the bluest sea I'd ever seen, lovely in the morning sunlight except where the tragic mantle of smoke ran across its middle covering and darkening the city on the shore. The city itself, with huge leaping red fires in its northern and southern parts, appeared to rest on the floor of a vast cavern formed by sinister curtains of black smoke which rose from beyond and towered over it, prophetically, like a great overhanging cloak of doom.

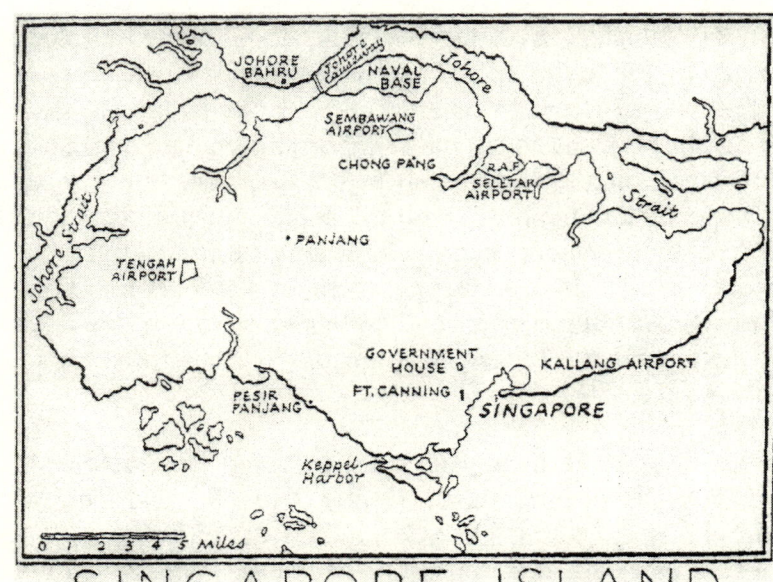

SINGAPORE ISLAND

Denny Sharp, Ted Tremlet, and Arthur "Brownie" Brown (RCAF) on "business trip" to Singapore pose for Art's camera.

240

Hurricane in brick dispersal pen, Tengah Airdrome.

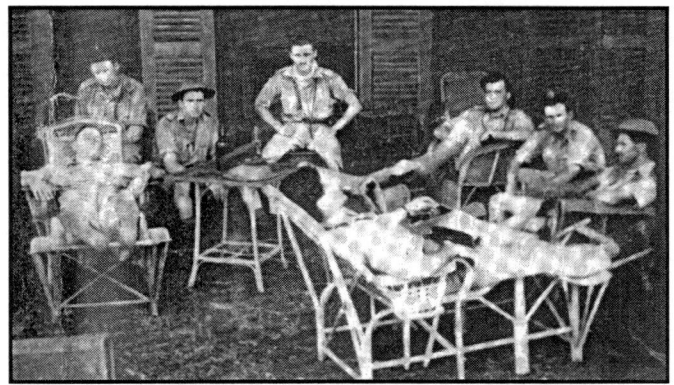

Pilots of 258 Squadron lounging on veranda overlooking Tengah Airdrome.

Dispersal hut at Kallang Airdrome.

241

Squadron billet at Sea View Hotel, Singapore.

Art "on readiness," Kallang Airdrome.

242

Shot down by enemy fighters, 232 Squadron Commander Eric "Rickey" Wright landed wheels up at Kallang. The Japanese later repaired, flew, and determined the Hurrricane's capabilities.

Singapore burning. Photo taken by Art Donahue on the last flight of British aircraft from Singapore—February, 1942.

243

Chapter Twenty

Out of the Frying Pan

The four of us in our patched-up airplanes now headed across the Strait of Malacca. When we were eight or ten miles out, I noticed that my engine seemed to be working unusually hard to keep up with the other machines. Then I realized that I hadn't retracted my wheels. I'd been so busy looking back and monkeying with my camera that I'd forgotten all about them! I raised them hurriedly, feeling embarrassed and hoping the others hadn't noticed, and my airplane speeded up at once, so that I was able to ease my engine considerably.

Sergeant Newlands had flown my Hurricane in from Seletar that morning landing with an inoperative airspeed indicator, and it continued to register zero throughout my journey. Additionally, one of my wheels wouldn't lock in the retracted position and kept dropping down. I had to raise it every couple of minutes. The position indicator light for my wheels wasn't working, so at first I could never tell for sure when this wheel was entirely up. Then, noticing a hole in the bottom of my fuselage right by the place where the wheel nested, I found I could tell by the amount of daylight coming through the hole whether the wheel was up.

On top of that, the airplane was "out of trim," so that I had to keep holding the stick to one side to keep it level. The engine purred nicely, however, and the oil pressure and radiator temperature were normal, so I didn't mind the other faults. Denny seemed to be having the same trouble with his undercarriage as I, since one of his wheels kept coming down. Tom, in his Brewster, flew for the first ten or fifteen minutes with both his wheels down, as he couldn't determine how to raise the landing gear since he'd never flown the type before. Brownie seemed to be getting along all right, although later he told me his propeller pitch control was inoperative and his engine ran at any speed it felt like.

Usually in movements involving single-engine machines flying over water, a Blenheim or Lockheed bomber led the way, but we were all alone, we lacked proper maps, and our aircraft were far from setting a standard of airworthiness. On top of our collective mechanical problems, the weather off the nose began to look ominous. Despite our own predicament, I couldn't help but think about those who'd stayed behind. Ted and the ground crew were obviously considering their options as they huddled beside my Ford when I taxied out. At least they had a chance. They had the skills needed to fight another day, and that one fact would most likely put them on the evacuation list. Those unfortunate soldiers locked in combat had but two choices: death or surrender to an enemy who held in utmost contempt those who chose the second option—and treated them accordingly.

What about dependents, civil servants, just plain civilians? How would the Japanese treat the smiling Chinese boy who'd brought my tea? Their record in Nanking, where conquering soldiers had gone on a rampage of pillage and rape resulting in the slaughter of two hundred thousand Chinese, showed little regard for the niceties of International Law. What of my squadron-mate, Stewie, who lay abandoned in Alexandra Military Hospital? What of the medical people—the nurses? The dark-haired girl with the greyhounds?

Later I learned that British subjects interned in Singapore's Changi Gaol—men, women, and children—were reasonably well off compared to members of the military. The civilians elected their own hierarchy, organized schools for the children and classes for the adults, presented plays and musicals, staffed hospitals, operated a library, printed a camp newspaper (*The Pow Wow*), and maintained order. They suffered most noticeably because of rations such as tasteless rice and water "*bubu*" porridge twice a week if lucky, bread every second day, a few sardines, and a quarter-tin of bully beef with half a dozen tins of soup for three hundred people. Prisoners also endured arbitrary punishment, segregation from family, overcrowding, hard work, disease, boredom, and fear.

God grant that the girl found herself in Changi rather than with the 65 members of the Australian Nursing Service. Those women evacuated the city aboard the steamer *Vyner Brooke* which was sunk by Japanese planes off the coast of Sumatra. A dozen died during the attack or drowned abandoning the ship. Twenty-two, along with a number of wounded men, reached Banka Island by lifeboat only to be captured. Soldiers dragged the men into the jungle and dispatched them with bayonets. Then they ordered the women to walk into the surf where they shot them. One survived by playing dead, then pulled herself into the tree line where she was found by other Japanese some days later. She told the tale but subsequently died in captivity.

After the war other accounts of appalling atrocities and ill-treatment of prisoners surfaced. The Japanese warrior's code held no compassion for those who surrendered. The western mind, more pragmatic in this respect, could show empathy with those who had exhausted all options then chose surrender over pointless sacrifice. Not so the Japanese. When negotiating the surrender of Allied forces in Java, for example, Lieutenant General Maruyama readily agreed that prisoners would have the protection of the Geneva Convention of 1929. In the event, nothing could have been further from the truth.

The Japanese used prisoners, frequently including officers, as laborers on projects such as airfield construction and the Siam-Burma "Railroad of Death." Of the 5,102 RAF men captured by the Japanese, a third—1,714 men—died in captivity. This compares to the deaths of 152 of the total 9,879 RAF people held by the Germans.

My musings evaporated some twenty minutes before our expected landfall when Denny abruptly descended toward one of the islands scattered along our route. The remaining three of us circled as he made several passes at an open field. Then he joined up on me and indicated by hand signals that I should continue on course. When he turned up some time later, he said he'd landed because fuel wouldn't feed from one of his wing tanks, so that his making Palembang was impossible. He had

248

enjoyed the hospitality of four Dutch civilians and a British civil servant until a boat could take him to Djambi on Sumatra's east coast. From there he caught a small steamer to Java.

We turned left once we crossed the coastline, searching for the mouth of the Moesi which marked our doorway to Palembang. Rather than the one river depicted on my crude chart, I discovered almost a dozen waterways inviting me to fly into oblivion. Making matters worse, thunderstorms and rain forced us to descend below a thousand feet drastically restricting our visibility. Additionally our fuel state deteriorated about as fast as the weather, so we couldn't tolerate a navigational error on my part. If I picked the wrong river, we'd run out of fuel, and I'd be responsible for putting three precious fighters into an impenetrable jungle.

After overflying several good-sized rivers, out of the mist and rain appeared one that seemed to take the right direction in from the coast, curving like the one on my map, so I turned inland, praying I wasn't making a mistake. Within a few minutes I saw a couple of steamers and, a little later, Palembang itself.

Even though the city sparkled in bright sunshine, a huge storm raged just to the north where the airdrome we called Palembang One or, more usually P.1, was located. Consulting the jiggling needles on my fuel gauges, I turned the flight southwest toward P.2, the secret jungle strip where I had landed during my trip from Java up to Singapore. As I had so often done in the States, I decided to get there by rail, so we picked up the narrow-gauge tracks running southward from the city and soon were circling to land.

Chapter Twenty-one

Into the Fire

The weather in Sumatra was hot and stifling as before, local thunderstorms occasionally broke the heat for short periods, after which the sun would come out brighter and hotter than ever, and the air would be stifling again, heavy with moisture from the steaming ground. I was anxious to rejoin 258 Squadron at P.1 where our fighters clustered along with those of our sister squadron, 232, but the weather dictated that we wait until the next morning. Rumors that the boys in 258 had suffered catastrophic losses increased my apprehension, but no one seemed to know for certain how the unit had performed.

Next morning, Thursday the twelfth of February, we made the short, twenty-mile hop north to P.1 where Squadron Leader Thomson greeted us heartily then drove us to our billets in town. Our squadron mates hadn't been wiped out by any means, but they'd lost most of their airplanes. For three days—February sixth through eighth—

the enemy sent wave after wave against P.1, sometimes catching them on the ground refueling.

A number of pilots, such as my New Zealand friend Pilot Officer Charles Campbell-White, had gone missing but survived bale outs and crash landings eventually to return. Others like my fellow American, Cardell Kleckner, had been killed outright. Both "Cam" and Kleck were members of a six-ship formation returning to land after an early patrol. They waded into fourteen Ki 43 fighters of the 59th *Sentai*, the second of two groups to attack P.1 during the morning of the sixth of February. Although we pilots had by this time realized that a Hurricane couldn't match Japanese fighters in a turning contest at low altitude, the combination of little warning and overwhelming enemy numbers seldom gave us a choice.

While dogfights swirled at fifteen hundred feet within sight of the airdrome, some of the enemy strafed the field inflicting a number of casualties including a recent posting to our squadron, Pilot Officer Keith Dawson-Scott, who was killed. Not intimidated, Red Campbell stood exposed at the end of the runway calmly firing his Smith and Wesson .38 revolver at the low-flying attackers. Many years after the fact, our squadron mate, Terence Kelly, wrote in his book *Nine Lives of a Fighter Pilot* that Red Campbell "was unquestionably the most reckless and foolhardy (as well as the bravest) man I ever met."

Once the raiders departed, the surviving Hurricanes circled for landing amidst smoldering debris that included the wreckage of two Brewster Buffaloes set alight by the enemy. Sergeant Dick Parr landed his aircraft after having taken an explosive bullet in the cockpit which severed the little finger of his left hand. Sergeant Nelson Scott, a big, husky chap from Alberta, escaped injury after a crash landing that destroyed his machine. Kleckner and Campbell-White were listed as missing. No one knows the exact circumstances of Kleck's death, but searchers later found his body still strapped in the cockpit of his aircraft. He was laid to rest in Palembang Cemetery. Cam, having crashed in deeper jungle, was rescued by natives who brought him out by boat to a place where a Dutch army vehicle picked him up.

Saturday, February seventh, can best be described using a term frequently heard: "shambles." It started with our receiving insufficient warning of a late afternoon raid that sent Hurricanes scrambling amid falling bombs delivered by Ki 48 "Lilly" light bombers and single-engine, fixed-geared Ki 30s of the 90th *Sintai*. All made it off the ground only to be swarmed upon by fifty-nine Ki 43 and six Ki 27 fighters again from the 64th and 59th *Sentais*. RAF losses on the ground were six Blenheim bombers, three Hurricanes, the flying club's Piper Cub, and a Moth trainer. A further eleven Hurricanes, a Buffalo fighter, and a Hudson bomber suffered damage.

In the air, Pilot Officer Doug Nicholls riddled a bomber but got hammered and baled out thirty miles west of Palembang. A search party of Indonesian and Dutch soldiers brought him back a week later! Pilot Officer Micky Nash and Sergeant Roy Keedwell each landed his perforated machine on the airdrome; Nash's wheels-up arrival was his second such experience in a week. Sergeant Artie Sheerin helped drag Roy clear of his blazing Hurricane, and the badly burned pilot was rushed to the Dutch hospital in Palembang.

Trading his revolver for a Hurricane, Red Campbell shot down a Ki 43 on the eighth (the day before the Japanese forced the Johore Strait), and Pilot Officer Ambrose Milnes claimed one fighter shot down and one damaged. Sergeant Nelson Scott claimed another damaged. As that battle raged, an unsuspecting pair of 258 Squadron Hurricanes returning from convoy patrol fell at the hands of a dozen Ki 43s. Sergeant Ken Glynn was killed; Pilot Officer Jock McCulloch crash-landed and later returned to duty with a wonderful story about being rescued by natives, put up in first-class style, and treated to the finest imported European foods.

Such unremitting attrition had relegated 258 Squadron to a non-operational status by the time I got there, but Thomson expected to get back in the air as soon as Engineering Officer Tudor Jones could patch up his unserviceable machines (including the two we delivered) and replacement fighters arrived from Java. *HMS Athene*, the seaplane tender in which we had sailed from Scotland so long ago, had finally docked on the third of February at Batavia with our sorely missed support personnel and thirty-six crated Hurricanes. Air Headquarters dispatched seven pilots to Tjililitan airdrome aboard a twin-engine Dutch Lockheed Lodestar to ferry machines back to P.1 as soon as they were assembled.

On the tenth of February, two days before I rejoined the boys, headquarters staff and ground maintenance personnel belonging to ours and two other squadrons finally arrived after crossing to Sumatra by boat from Batavia, taking the train to Palembang, and riding trucks to the airdrome. This was the same route traveled by some forty replacement Hurricane pilots, most of whom were just out of training and completely inexperienced in the fighter

254

pilot's trade. Wing Commander Harold J. Maguire, a Battle of Britain veteran, commanded these men who had traveled aboard *City of Canterbury* in the same convoy as *Athene*. With its only military facility being a single, Dutch-manned operations room boasting just one telephone line, P.1 was rapidly being inundated by people, many of whom were but a drag on the grossly deficient supply lines.

It's relatively easy in hindsight to organize in one's mind the events that led from *HMS Indomitable* to Singapore to Palembang, but it's difficult—sometimes impossible—to put a human face on a long list of casualties. Vic de la Perelle, Roy Keedwell's flight commander, did it about as well as could be done when, over coffee at Palembang's Luxor Hotel the night I arrived, he described Roy's last hours. I remember him speaking slowly and haltingly, pausing occasionally to get control, eyes blinking and watching the ceiling, avoiding mine. For Roy was a wonderful lad and Vic had been his close friend.

He told me that Roy had been wounded in the leg and his airplane shot up badly, but he managed to get back and land. Then, while he taxied across the field, his machine caught fire. The gas tank must have been holed, for the Hurricane was all ablaze in an instant; and because of his wounded leg, Roy had trouble getting out. By the time he scrambled clear, he was badly burned about the face, legs, and arms.

In hospital he seemed to do all right for the first twenty-four hours. Then shock set in and he started weakening. Vic went to see him as often as he could get time. He visited about eight o'clock in the morning of the third day, promising to be back again at four that afternoon. As he departed, however, he realized that all was not well, for the doctors were letting Roy have morphine to ease the pain, something they had refused him before.

Extremely busy all that day, Vic didn't return until a few minutes past four. There he found, to his grief, that his friend had just passed away.

The sisters told him that Roy held on desperately until four, because he wanted so badly for Vic to be with him when he died. But when Vic didn't arrive on time, his strength gave out. Just before he died, he looked around at the sisters and begged, "Someone please hold my hand and call me 'Roy' before I die!" One of the nurses took his hand and called him "Roy," and that was how he died, halfway around the world from his home in Toronto.

Friday, the thirteenth of February, Brownie and I made our way to the drome even though we weren't flying. The early patrol, about a dozen Hurricanes, had gone out at dawn looking for flying boats reported on the water near the northeast coast of Banka Island. At about the same time in Java, Wing Commander Maguire, leading the pilots sent to ferry back our reinforcement Hurricanes, departed for Palembang. After a lengthy and fruitless search, and running low on fuel, our patrol returned to find the drome under attack by twenty-nine Ki 43s escorting seven Ki 48 light bombers.

At this precise moment, Maguire appeared over the station with seven brand-new Hurricanes, each also flying "on the fumes." Five had no alternative but to land; however Maguire and Sergeant Henry Nicholls of 232 Squadron slammed into the enemy's fighter escort. Maguire later said, "I claimed one 'Zero' although I'm pretty sure he was first damaged by his own number two, possibly over-excited." Nicholls claimed two destroyed and one damaged before he was hit and baled out at 600 feet. Natives picked him up and delivered him to a missionary who arranged for transportation to Oosthaven, on the southern tip of Sumatra.

On final approach to landing, Sergeant Nelson Scott found two Ki 43s latched onto the tail of his new Hurricane. One opened fire slightly wounding Scott and destroying his engine. Zooming to 700 feet, Scotty hit the silk while the Japanese pilot, Lt. Masabumi Kunii, snapped off his wings as he pulled abruptly away. "Ting" Macnamara was in the pattern behind Scott but managed to avoid the enemy and landed safely as did the other four machines.

While this melee was going on, three 232 Squadron Hurricanes scrambled followed by Squadron Leader Brooker and several others. Sandy Allen claimed two fighters destroyed and one bomber probably destroyed. Brooker claimed a second bomber and Sergeant Ken Holmes a probable. Several Ki 43s chased Pilot Officer Leslie Emmerton just above the treetops until they killed him. Pilot Officer Tom Watson launched in an unserviceable Hurricane to prevent its being strafed, but the enemy pounced and shot him to pieces. He dead-sticked onto the drome and was able to walk away from an aircraft that had to be written off the books.

Returning to their bases, the Japanese claimed three Hurricanes destroyed, two more as probables, and four "large aircraft" destroyed on the ground. They recorded the loss of three aircraft, including two Ki 48 bombers.

Brownie and I volunteered to pull readiness for a couple of boys who had been flying, and we launched about midmorning but accomplished nothing. After landing others took our places, and I spent the afternoon in town doing some shopping, cabling my folks that I was safely out of Singapore, and getting some items to fix up my quarters. Although we took our meals in the Luxor Hotel, we slept across the street. In my book, *Last Flight from Singapore*, I referred to our billets as having been "a sort of rooming house." Actually, as Terence Kelly confessed in one of his books, it was a former brothel. The girls had been packed off elsewhere, along with all the furniture, so we had to arrange for our own accouterments.

Reporting early on the morning of February fourteenth, I wondered what kinds of Japanese Valentines we could expect. The mood wasn't hearts and flowers but rather increasing tension and anticipation as we generated a maximum effort to counter an invasion fleet approaching the mouth of the Moesi River. Including replacement aircraft from Java, we now had twenty Hurricanes, fifteen of which stood ready to escort our attacking bombers.

About mid-morning Squadron Leader Thomson led pilots of both squadrons to rendezvous with Blenheims launched from P.2. Six arrived fifteen minutes late, and our fuel state demanded we depart without the nine others expected from 84 Squadron. Unbeknownst to us fighter pilots, sixteen Hudson bombers flying in three separate raids had already "had a go" at a fleet composed of twenty-five to thirty transports escorted by twelve or so warships including the carrier *Ryujo*.

Attempting to take off before dawn, the lead aircraft of the first bomber wave had flown through treetops necessitating a crash landing at P.1 without loss of life. The remaining four encountered no enemy fighters but also scored no hits. The second attack force of six used cloud cover to evade fighters, lost one bomber to anti-aircraft fire, and reported multiple hits by four crews. Navy Zeros jumped the third wave, shooting down four of five Hudsons with only two crewmen surviving. One crew returned to claim hits.

Our formation encountered heavy clouds enroute to the target but no opposition, so our Blenheims bombed from 8,000 feet sinking the 989-ton *Inabasan Maru* and damaging several others. Nine stragglers from 84 Squadron arrived, bombed unopposed from 6,000 feet, but observed no damage.

Returning to P.1 with fuel gauges indicating uncomfortably close to empty, we blundered into what we later learned was a parachute assault on Palembang. Preceded by hordes of strafing Ki 43 fighters and Ki 21 medium bombers dropping anti-personnel bombs, 270 Japanese paratroopers leaped from forty-one transports into two drop zones—one in scrub brush between the air base and the city to its south and the other west of the Pladjoe oil refineries. Despite repeated warnings from P.1, many of us with inoperative radio receivers remained unaware of the gravity of the situation.

Nevertheless, some of us who heard the warnings strafed the landing zones as fuel would allow, and others tore into a passel of what we took to be Navy Zeros. At the "Tally Ho!" my number two, whose job it was to stick with me and protect my backside, dived away chasing something more interesting. A few seconds later, I looked back to see a fighter diving on me, his stubby round nose and silver-colored propeller spinner identifying him as an enemy at quite a distance. Another followed him. Opening my throttle I swung around to face the leader in a head-on show, both of us coming straight at each other shooting, seeing who would give way first before we collided; but he didn't seem to want that now that he'd lost his chance for surprise. With the advantage of height and speed, the pair had no difficulty zooming up and away from me.

Pilot Officer Bill Lockwood and his number two, Sergeant Ian Fairbairn, slashed through a formation of bombers most probably destroying Lieutenant Naohiko Sudoh's Ki 21 which didn't return to its base. Pulling out of their dive at treetop level, they penetrated a tropical downpour, spotted the Moesi River, and found P.1 where they observed a red signal that diverted them south to P.2.

Three pilots, all with faulty radios and more pressing challenges, eventually landed at a "queerly deserted" P.1. Ting Macnamara had harassed several bombers, got hammered dreadfully by their escort, but managed to crash-land on the air field. Chased at low altitude "all over southern Sumatra," Terence Kelly lost his pursuer, and then shot down a fighter before landing with almost empty tanks. Bertie Lambert, similarly deaf and low on fuel, landed right behind him. P.1's Duty Pilot, our squadron-mate Micky Nash, explained that he expected parachutists to appear at any moment, so Kelly and Lambert risked making the short flight to P.2 with what fuel their tanks contained. Now without a mount, Macnamara knew he had to find other means of rejoining his mates.

Minutes later four Hurricanes, the survivors of a nine-ship formation ferrying replacements from Java, landed wondering what the hubbub was all about. As their fuel state was perilous, Micky called for a petrol tanker, arranged for Ivan Julian to rendezvous over the drome as their guide to P.2, and saw the last of his charges on their way.

By this time I was safely down at P.2. Towards noon I volunteered to do a reconnaissance between the two airdromes. Scouting the road all the way, flying just above the treetops and getting lost once or twice in the rain, I didn't see anything that looked like military traffic. At Palembang itself the Dutch had set fire to some of their oil storage tanks. The frightening red flames with angry black smoke pumping skyward would have awed me if I hadn't come so recently from Singapore.

Once I had given my report, I rang up our quarters in Palembang City hoping someone would be able to rescue the small traveling bag into which I had packed nearly all the films I had taken in Singapore. None other than Red Campbell answered the phone. Good old Red! He said he'd gather up my things, as well as valuables belonging to the others, and head for the western coast where he'd have a chance to commandeer a boat.

Our new operating location, amazingly still unknown to the enemy, had served as our primary bomber base in Sumatra although it was equipped neither to support bombers nor fighters in anything but an emergency. Little had changed since I'd first visited some two weeks previously on my way to Singapore except that some 1,500 men struggled to exist in sparse accommodations designed for 250. Distances of two to three miles separated crew quarters, operations room, and jungle dispersal areas where our airplanes were hidden. No vehicles existed for crew transportation, and forty-gallon drums provided the only means for fueling. The un-paved ground was soft and deeply rutted from the weight of taxiing bombers, primarily the American B-17 "Flying Fortresses" that passed through on occasion. These ruts posed extreme hazards for aircraft, especially fighters, during take-offs or landings. In addition, no electronic navigational aids existed to help aircrews find their way at night or make instrument approaches in bad weather.

Despite these and untold other deficiencies, throughout the afternoon groups of Blenheim and Lockheed bombers had been going out as often as they could return and load up. The parachute landings, as anyone could see, were a prelude to invasion on a scale vastly larger than our small forces in Sumatra could hope to withstand, but we believed we could upset the enemy's timetable and make them pay a substantial price.

Our C.O. attended a conference in the operations room until late that evening. When he came back, he told me I was to lead the six airplanes left in our squadron on an operation at dawn and then reconnoiter Palembang before landing.

I had a rather bad night of it, as I usually did when I had a particular operation planned for the following morning, because I couldn't keep it out of my mind, and so I would go to sleep thinking about it. Then after I'd been asleep awhile, at the time when one's normal defenses were down and nerves and feelings bare and sensitive, the dread would set in and all the dangers would seem vivid and terrifying. After Singapore my nerves weren't at their best anyway.

Chapter Twenty-two

Last Flight from Sumatra

It was still pitch-dark when the phone rang. Five o'clock, time to go down to the field and get our airplanes ready. I roused the boys who were to accompany me, and we stumbled sleepily out of the Mess and trudged along the damp, sticky roads to the drome. The rain was over, the sky just beginning to grey in the east, so that we could discern the ghostly outlines of our machines. An odd bird or two occasionally called back and forth in the jungle. I felt relieved at being in motion at last, with the knowledge that it would be over soon and then I could relax.

Arriving at the watch office, I found that the telephone line to bomber headquarters in Palembang had been disrupted thereby causing our station commander, Group Captain McCauley, to inherit control of the remaining bombers and fighters in Sumatra. Based upon a reconnaissance report, he ordered attacks on troop transports and landing barges seen in the estuaries of the Moesi and adjacent rivers leading toward Palembang.

Three Hudson bombers flown by Australian crews prepared to launch at half past six to be followed by three Blenheims. Our half-dozen Hurricanes would provide escort and cover within the target area. Watching the Hudsons trundle past, I had no premonition of meeting the crew of the third machine under unusually stressful circumstances later in the day. As we taxied out, I noticed little wisps of fog among the treetops just outside the airdrome, but I didn't think much about it. There were usually isolated patches of fog around the countryside on early mornings. The thick trees on each side of the runway made our position like that of being down in a canyon, unable to see outside.

Turning at the far end of the runway I gave my engine the gun to take off without waiting for the others to get in formation with me because I wanted them to take off one at a time. After I left the ground, my attention was occupied for a moment by the mechanics of raising my wheels and changing my throttle and propeller pitch settings, so it was not until I was up perhaps a hundred feet that I looked around and then realized we were in a terrible jam. A carpet of fog lay all about and was quickly closing the hole which happened to open over the airdrome!

Hoping desperately that at least part of my formation might still be on the ground, I switched on the transmitter and called, "Don't take off! Do not take off!" But when I looked back, I saw it was too late. Hurricanes were rising from the grey blanket that covered the earth in all directions. The airdrome had disappeared completely, and no other alternate landing fields existed within our range of action.

At the same time I turned, dropped my wheels, and throttled back my engine, making for a slight depression in the fog which I hoped marked the airdrome. I was lucky. I broke through the bottom of the grey mist right over the runway, and I got down O.K. Sergeant Bertie Lambert had also recognized the situation and dropped back onto the field.

Then began a nerve-racking half-hour, trying to get the others down. The fog was thin enough so that pilots could spot the drome when they passed directly overhead, but they lost sight of it as they maneuvered to make an approach. I borrowed a Very pistol and all the available green cartridges from the watch office and ran out to the middle of the runway. Then every time I heard an airplane approaching the field, I'd shoot a cartridge straight up, the little ball of green fire rising and arcing over just at the top of the fog, to spot the field for him.

That helped, and soon one of the Hurricanes managed to break into sight more or less over the edge of the field, and by means of a hair-raising vertical turn close to the ground in order to get in line with the runway, and some violent fishtailing to kill his speed, the pilot made it. He came taxiing back, and I saw it was Kelly. He grinned at me and made a motion as if wiping sweat from his forehead. I held up clasped hands in congratulation.

The other three were still droning around up there: first one, then another throttling down and gliding into the fog at the point where he hoped the airdrome was, the sound of his engine breaking out again at full throttle as he zoomed back up after finding he was wrong.

Finally all of my pilots were able to grope their way to a landing. One Hurricane, flown by RCAF Sergeant John Fleming, tipped over on its back after hitting a soft spot in the turf. A group of us raised one wing enough to prop it on the bed of a truck, and John emerged bruised and dirtied, but uninjured.

Meanwhile the intrepid bomber crews sortied without escort, knowing they had the range to land elsewhere if necessary. Intercepted by Japanese fighters, the Hudsons used the fog for cover and two of the three bombed ships of the invading fleet clustered in the Bangka Strait. The Blenheims also encountered fighters but evaded, attacked landing barges, and claimed five or six sunk. All bombers returned safely under cover of fog and smoke from oil tanks burning near Palembang.

About nine o'clock the fog dissipated and a second raid by six Hudsons of the RAF and the RAAF roared off. Their escort was provided by pilots of 232 Squadron who launched in eight of the depleted pool of Hurricanes our two squadrons shared. They returned after an hour or so, all the pilots in great spirits, having had a wonderful show. They had caught the unprotected boats and barges, each crammed with enemy soldiers. It had been a massacre, and they estimated they had killed hundreds. Some light anti-aircraft fire had come from the boats, apparently from machine guns, but only one airplane was hit and that by a single bullet.

We of 258 squadron had grabbed a bite to eat while our friends were in the air and were waiting to swap airplanes when they returned. The airdrome swarmed with men and machines coming and going in an almost steady stream. Nine Blenheims of 84 Squadron, launched against

266

the shipping in the Moesi estuary, bombed and claimed as sunk a medium-size transport then strafed the traffic headed up-river. Although all returned safely, not one of the bombers escaped damage from the fire thrown up by the ships and barges.

Six more Blenheims of 211 Squadron plunged into the fray against the same targets. From reports of returning aircrews, we realized that the strafing on the Moesi was turning into what we Americans would call a "turkey shoot." The most glaring deficiency was that our aircraft were using Dutch 250-pound bombs whose casings were larger than British models thereby forcing the Blenheims to fly with their bomb bay doors partially open. Rather than being fused for low-altitude, delayed-action delivery, the bombs were set to explode on contact (thereby endangering any aircraft releasing below a thousand feet). The Dutch ordnance also tended to hang in the bays rather than release as our crews expected.

Again all six bombers returned although three suffered damage caused by small-arms fire and by dropping their bombs too low—in one case fifty to a hundred feet! The final bomber sorties were flown in early afternoon by two Hudsons that made runs on transports and destroyers in the estuary then strafed barge traffic on the homeward leg. Eight Hurricanes, once again in the hands of pilots of 232 Squadron, protected the bombers from three defending Ki 27 fighters, damaging two that subsequently crash-landed on their base at the occupied P.1 airfield. One of two attacking Mitsubishi F1M floatplanes was shot down in the target area by Flying Officer Richards' bomber crew. The second, however, seriously damaged the Hudson and wounded Squadron Leader Garrard who, while "along for the ride," had manned one of the side guns and shot down the first F1M.

Again the 232 boys returned without loss and wheeled in for refueling and rearming. In a short time pilots from 258 Squadron were all set, and we started up and taxied to the end of the runway, where we got into squadron formation before taking off. Two more machines had been made fit, so for this sortie Squadron Leader Thomson launched at the head of ten Hurricanes! It was the first time we'd taken off in squadron formation since we came to the Far East. Our objective was a hundred miles or so away, and we pulled up to three or four thousand feet, just under a gloomy overcast of heavy cloud. It was a dull murky sky with local rainstorms sitting around the countryside like great white pillars rising from the jungle up to the clouds, so that we appeared to cruise on and on through a great pillared hall—its floor the flat jungle-covered land below, and its ceiling the heavy flat clouds above.

Finally the dull blue-grey water of the Bangka Strait appeared ahead, and as we neared the coast, we swung northward until the River Moesi appeared ahead of us, winding snake-like through the dark carpet of jungle. Somewhere up its course, we should find our enemies. We were in battle formation, well spread out to guard each other's tails.

On the way up-river, we strafed a few boats parked close to one bank. I fired but a brief burst anticipating bigger game ahead. We re-formed and continued some fifteen or twenty miles till we discovered scores of boats in a long silent line, perhaps two miles from end to end, strung out parallel to the south bank of the river and a hundred yards or so away from it. This was one of the moments for which we had been sent halfway around the world!

This seemed to be such a wonderful opportunity that I wanted to make the most of it, so I circled a moment studying the line of boats and planning my approach. Soon I could see the other Hurricanes far below, like tiny moths floating over the jungle. Then one of them approached the line of boats from one side; as he drew near, his set of delicate white tracers appeared in front of him as if by magic, reaching out ahead and touching one of the boats like a wand, and a cloud of white spray almost completely enveloped it. I had seen twenty or thirty men killed in a twinkling!

Other airplanes followed with their attacks, each in turn approaching one of the boats and raising a mountain of spray around it with his bullets. Now I could see light blue smoke floating away from some of the boats, and I presumed it was from the anti-aircraft fire which the boys of 232 had reported.

My own plans made, I flew eastward until I was a mile or so east of the rearmost; I took a careful look all around for enemy fighters noting that Kelly had stuck with me and was positioned to follow me in. Then I turned downward into my dive, arcing around back towards them, tensing myself for the bath of anti-aircraft fire as one does when going under an icy shower. I was planning to attack lengthwise, down the line of them, and I leveled out perhaps a hundred feet above the water and about a mile behind them; I took a last glance all around for Navy Zeros, then concentrated on aiming. I was coming fast after my dive, the trees on my left streaking past in a blur.

I held my aim on the first boat as I neared it, waiting for it to grow large enough in my sights. Almost close enough; aim a little high at first to allow for bullet drop: now! There's nothing to it, really. You just press with your thumb. There was the abrupt shattering roar from the guns in my wings and then the eight ghostly white tracers snaking out ahead eagerly toward the boat and its helpless passengers. They would know nothing more.

Wanting to make the most of my ammunition, I broke off after a short burst, not even waiting to see the first bullets strike, then turned and fired at another boat. Not so good; I was turning when I fired and the first bullets threw up their shower of spray to one side of it. I stopped turning and held the nose up in a sideslip to get the sights centered better, and the shower moved over to encompass the boat just as I broke off.

I snapped short bursts into two or three others at close range, just a second or so into each. They loomed in front of me faster than I could possibly shoot at them all.

I had dropped down too low now, so I nosed up and passed over a few to take good aim at one boatload farther on. I could see the men looking at me as I fired—twenty or thirty of them, riding backwards—and then my tracers smacking right into the middle of the close-packed bunch of faces, and for some reason I just held the sights on them, still firing right up to point-blank. I zoomed a little then, turning to aim at another boat, and then—WHAM!

It's hard to recall all of what followed, and in what succession. I was conscious of having been hit harder than I had ever been hit in my life—a quick, cruel blow in the calf of my left leg; I had a momentary glimpse through a big rent in my trousers of two holes in the side of my leg, one small and round, the other a gaping sort of thing an inch wide by a couple of inches long, with raw red and blue flesh and muscle laid open, before the blood welled up and started streaming out.

I was banking hard to the left to flee out over the jungle, more by instinct than plan probably, I was so stunned. Then my mind seemed to start working, and the first thing it told me was that I was in one of the worst jams of my life, for I was nearly a hundred miles from the airdrome, and a weakness of mine is that I tend to faint when I'm hurt and bleeding—and I had never been hurt like this before, had never bled like this before!

I'd grabbed my torn trouser leg above the wound with my left hand, remembering what I'd heard about tourniquets, and twisted on it frantically, trying to stop the blood, but the flow was still running fast, down my trouser leg, sock, and shoe, and dribbling off to form a sickening bright red puddle in the heel rest, a sort of flat metal trough below the rudder pedal.

At this low altitude it would be all over if I fainted for even a few seconds, and now the sight of the blood had made me worse. I looked straight ahead trying to keep my mind off it, but there were blood and bits of flesh spattered over my instrument panel and windshield. My ears were beginning to ring and bright specks floated around the cockpit.

I'd had sense enough to lean back, relaxing what I could and drawing deep breaths. Then I thought of my oxygen supply and let go of the stick long enough to twist the regulator valve on my instrument panel, opening it until

I was getting enough oxygen to fly at forty thousand feet. I looked down again to check, and the blood was still running. I let go the hold I had on my trouser leg above the wound, grabbed up the torn cloth right over it, twisted it, and then jammed my gloved fist, knuckles first, as deep as I could into the large hole, and held it that way.

I had another sinking spell, probably the worst of the lot, but managed to draw my mind away from thinking of my wound and put it to work getting me back to the drome. I checked my engine instruments and fuel gauges and saw that all was normal. I was still a stricken bird, the kind the enemy dreamed about, so I settled into a regular sequence of checking for enemy fighters. When I summoned up enough courage, I looked at the wound again to find that I had stanched the flow of blood. The pain, which never had been agonizing, had settled to a heavy ache as from a badly bruised muscle. My hopes of making it really soared.

Reducing throttle to ease the strain on the engine, I occupied myself with looking for fighters, altering heading around rain showers in order not to over-fly the railroad out of Palembang, and talking to myself to keep my mind off the wound. Spotting the rail line, I swung left and scooted along over the treetops beside the tracks. "Only ten minutes more now, old boy, and you're all O.K. You'll sleep in bed tonight, too, and have breakfast in bed tomorrow morning!" That sort of chatter and lots of other silly things, anything to keep my mind away from the wound and how I felt. I thought of friends I'd write to in the hospital and what I'd tell them, and of all kinds of things like that, while the trees streaked by beneath my wings and the long curving miles of railway track unwound out of the distance ahead and spun past and reeled away behind, until all at once the jungle was broken ahead and there was the airdrome!

Getting down was somewhat of a problem, because there are lots of gadgets to work in landing a Hurricane, and I didn't dare to take my left hand out of the wound, for fear my glove should be stuck in it and cause a spasm of pain and bleeding. I decided to try to make it with one hand, cursing the unconventional type of control stick we had on RAF fighters, which you can't handle with your knees like ordinary control sticks.

I managed to overfly the field rocking my wings to signal I was in trouble, and then concentrated on lowering my wheels and flying a decent circuit. On final approach I throttled back, shoved the hydraulic control into the "Flaps Down" position, and sideslipped to line up with the runway. I bounced my faithful machine onto the ground and felt almost boisterous as I taxied up to the watch office.

American volunteer, "Larger Than Life" John A. "Red" Campbell, and fellow Hurricane pilots. Location unknown. Perhaps "P1," Palembang's Municipal Airport.

Maintenance men struggle to repair Hurricane at P-2, "secret" jungle landing strip.

Camouflaged Hurricane probably at P-2, 50 miles southwest of Palembang.

P2 Air Strip. Primitive facilities, unpaved "runway," never discovered by the enemy.

258 Squadron Leader James A. (Jim) Thomson dismounts after battle.

Unidentified "Happy Warrior" of 258 Squadron.

275

Art's "snaps" of unidentified pilots of 258 Squadron. Precise locations unknown, but most probably Singapore or Sumatra.

Chapter Twenty-three

Million-dollar Wound

Some of the boys lifted me out of the cockpit and applied a field dressing on the wound. Then they packed me off in an ambulance to the dressing station, and my spirit waned as I realized I'd be placed in a hospital in imminent danger of being overrun by the enemy. Instead, once the wound was properly dressed, I was bundled into the ambulance and hustled back to the airfield where Squadron Leader Thomson had found space for me on a Java-bound Hudson bomber belonging to Number 1 RAAF Squadron. Inexplicably, orders had arrived at P. 2 before noon that all operationally unserviceable Hudsons (those that could get off the ground but not fly in combat) were to evacuate to Java. Five did so. Then, a few hours later, and certainly before reports of our amazingly successful bombing and strafing operations had moved up the command chain, all remaining aircraft of all types were ordered to Java "on completion of allotted tasks."

Writing of this incident in *Hurricane over the Jungle*, Terence Kelly states, "There were many things about the war . . . I never understood but of them all perhaps the most incomprehensible was the fact that we were not ordered to repeat the attacks on the barges . . . It is not at all impossible that a couple more strikes would have stopped them in their tracks."

Squadron Leader Thomson and I had none of this on our minds as he supervised my loading on the aircraft. We had only a moment of farewell, two old friends each realizing he might never see the other again, one going to what appeared to be safety if not salvation, the other staying to face an implacable enemy and an uncertain future. As we shook hands, each of us knew what the other was thinking, and our forced smiles were wistful. I was to see him in life just once more.

Once airborne our pilot, Flying Officer Gibbes who had flown this same aircraft in the formation I was to escort at daybreak, kept us at about two thousand feet, staying below the overcast and depending upon the rain showers, the camouflage paint on our machine, and the dark backdrop of the jungle to mask our flight from prowling enemy fighters. My companions in the cabin were Air Commodore Hunter, Air Officer Commanding 225 Bomber Group, sitting on a couple of suitcases across the aisle from me and a Flying Officer sitting behind him on a box of some sort. I was sitting up, facing backwards, on a green leather cot which had been placed on the left side of the cabin. My wound did not hurt to any unusual extent, most probably because the doctor at the dressing station had given me a light dose of morphine.

The interior of the bomber was painted dark green, the left side of the aircraft housed six windows, whereas the right side contained seven, exactly like passenger versions of this model. The fifth window on each side contained a hole through which the barrel of a machine gun protruded. The rear part of the cabin was littered with suitcases, cans, flying kit (including my own), and drums of machine gun ammunition. Looking directly aft I could just see the rear gunner's legs and bottom of his trousers through the opening in the turret. I remember these details because I scribbled them in my pocket notebook as a way of keeping my mind off my wound. When I wasn't writing, I pondered how I might parlay my situation into a brief trip home!

Two hours later I was safely in bed, three hundred miles from the fighting zone, in the Dutch Military Hospital of Bandoeng, a beautiful city in the mountains of west central Java. I had all that I'd promised myself: a bed to sleep in, with clean sheets, and the prospect of breakfast in bed in the morning! In addition I had a pretty nurse to look after me.

I had been hit by a half-inch machine-gun bullet. The bullet must have struck some part of the airplane first, so that it was tumbling over and over when it hit me. It hadn't touched the bone, however, so only flesh and muscle were damaged. I could hobble around a little at the end of four days.

The morning after my arrival, I heard the nurses talking in the hallway. Singapore had been surrendered the previous day, the fifteenth of February, 1942, the same day I was wounded. Even though I had known when I left that only a miracle could ever save the city, the final news overwhelmed me. Now the war would last much longer, and many, many more lives would have to be sacrificed to win it. The thought of thousands of those filthy people swarming over the beautiful island and city was almost too much. One of them no doubt would be driving my Ford; too bad I hadn't set fire to it.

I thought too of the exotic dark-haired girl we'd watched on the lawn of the Sea View that last morning, and wondered again what might have become of her and all the other civilians who were still there when I left.

The dominoes continued to tumble. Palembang fell the day I learned of Singapore's fate. No one doubted that Sumatra itself would be rolled up quickly and that Java stood next in line. Within a few days, the Japanese bombed the airfield on the outskirts of Bandoeng as Dutch Brewster Buffaloes engaged Japanese fighters in a dogfight within view of those of us in the hospital. The whole scenario reminded me of watching German raiders flying over my hospital near Maidstone during the Battle of Britain.

After that the raids were virtually a daily affair, and we knew that the invasion of Java would be only a matter of time. One morning we British patients were told our passage was booked on a hospital ship leaving from Batavia and that we must leave immediately on the 120-mile drive. I felt miserable as I went around shaking hands and saying good-bye to my friends among the doctors, nurses, and Dutch patients. They knew as well as I what they were being left to. They only smiled, bravely if wistfully, and wished me luck. I left my wings with Ann, the little nurse who first took care of me.

Our send-off from Batavia was a thirty-minute air raid on the city and harbor about an hour before we sailed.

All afternoon our little hospital ship cruised westward from Batavia, the northwest coast of Java an irregular green panorama bounding the warm blue sea on our left. The pleasing sight, together with the feel of soft tropical sea breezes soothed my discouraged heart and aching wound.

After supper I made my way up to the top deck. It was nearly dark, and the ship's lights were on, the first time I had ever traveled on a lighted ship. Spotlights illuminated the red crosses on its deck, sides, and funnel. The sky was clear and most of the stars were already out. There are medium-sized mountains near this part of the coasts of both Java and Sumatra, and I could see both from where I sat: those of dark Sumatra on our right, already conquered and occupied by the enemy, and those of beautiful Java on our left, doomed to a similar fate in a few more days. They were great dark silhouettes against the stars, looking, I thought, sad and brooding. I felt sad, too, and spiritually tired.

There's no need denying that I was terribly disillusioned by much of what I had seen and experienced, things that I passed over in my second book because I thought that it wasn't in my province as a member of the forces to speak of them. The enemy didn't advertise their failings either. I had seen many things that were bad. The humiliating memories of those incidents and the overwhelming realization of the great defeat we had suffered with the consequent imperiling of our entire cause—after all the bright hopes I'd had—combined to make me more discouraged and heartsick than I had ever been before.

Of the forty-eight beautiful new Hurricanes we had flown to Singapore, scarcely a dozen were left the day I

281

was wounded. No doubt they were all gone at this time. A few more than half the pilots were alive, and we had little to show. We had stopped our enemies nowhere.

As I reviewed the past and the shambles that remained of a great nation's power, I began to question whether we would prevail. Were these, I wondered, perhaps the last days of our civilization? Surely I had seen most of the weaknesses that had proceeded the fall of other great civilizations: the softness and decadence that came from easy living, the lack of appreciation for the good things of life that came from the too easy attainment of them, the failure to appreciate freedom that came from taking it for granted too long.

It was only a mood, a discouraged, dismayed sort of mood, that came from the too recent, too vivid, memories of all these "things that were bad," which tended to push older memories of bigger and better and much more important things out of my perspective and give me a distorted view, as an ant in a burning bush might think the world was on fire.

I began to realize this, as I sat there letting the cool night breeze and the soothing, endless throb of the engines comfort and reassure me, and gradually my view of it all seemed to broaden. Although we were beaten in this theater of the war, it was only an outpost of the British Empire, garrisoned by a fraction of Britain's strength, which had been overwhelmed by almost the full strength of another great nation while Britain herself was engaged in a death struggle with Germany and Italy, almost half-way around the world.

The "things that were bad" were not typically British, for I had served more than a year in England, where the universal fighting spirit and loyalty had made me feel inferior. The people there were anything but decadent, and the miserable creatures who had let down their King and country so woefully in the Far East were no more true British than the fifth columnists and saboteurs in my own country were true Americans. I began seeing things in a better light, a light which seemed to show the Rising Sun very near its zenith.

Chapter Twenty-four

Passage to India

As our ship cleared the southern tip of Sumatra and began rolling to the rhythms of the Indian Ocean, the captain altered heading west-northwest. None of us knew our destination, nor cared as long as Southeast Asia continued to grow smaller off our stern. For me a sense not unlike shame settled over my spirit as I contemplated the fate of my friends. I had received the "million-dollar" wound: one that merited evacuation but was not life threatening. In fact, before my final sortie, I had joked with Kelly and the others saying that such a "nick" was all I needed to guarantee a leave back in Minnesota and an eventual transfer into the American air force.

In the austere cabin of that bomber fleeing to Java, a feeling—much later named "survivor's syndrome"—intensified the depression that had hounded me since taking leave of Squadron Leader Thomson. What about Kelly, and Red Campbell, and Denny Sharp, and all the others? How would they get away? Where would they go? Was there a plan? How silly of me to even think of such a thing; with no plan for resistance in Singapore, Sumatra, or Java, surely nothing existed to give our boys a chance of escaping capture or evading death. They were on their own, and even their great courage and resourcefulness wouldn't be enough to carry them across the broad expanse of ocean separating them from India or Australia.

But courage and resourcefulness did get them from Sumatra to Java. Kelly, Lambert, and Sheerin found Hurricanes abandoned at P.2 as being unserviceable and flew them to Tjililitan. A party under Ting Macnamara composed of engineering officer Tudor Jones, A1C Peter Lamont, Red Campbell, Jock McCulloch, and R. L. Cicurel evacuated Palembang City by motor launch, truck, and canoe before walking the final twenty miles to Matapoera where they caught rides to Oosthaven and boarded a ferry to Batavia.

In view of the twenty-five or so Hurricanes available, only limited numbers of pilots were needed to fill the ranks of two re-constituted squadrons. Harry Dobbyn was assigned as a flight commander and two Americans, Campbell and Cicurel, volunteered to stay. The others drew cards to decide their fate, with Sergeants Kelly, Lambert, and Healy drawing low. As those drawing high prepared to depart on *Kota Gede* bound for Columbo, Ceylon, Sergeant J. G. Vibert, a young New Zealander, gave his slot to Nicholls saying that since he'd trained for the job, he might as well stay where the action was sure to be.

Those staying behind joined 605 Squadron as its "B" Flight. In action against navy Zero fighters on the eighteenth of February, Dobbyn was killed and Campbell shot down just after destroying one of the enemy.

286

Subsequently Campbell, Cicurel, Healy, Kelly, Lambert, and Vibert became prisoners of the Japanese, ultimately to be liberated at war's end.

Sad as I felt, I wasn't without friends aboard ship. Two former squadron mates—John "Stewie" Stewart and Michael "Micky" Nash—greeted me, and numerous other comrades-in-arms from all services and nations allowed me to make their acquaintance. I hadn't seen Stewie since the previous Sunday, when he and I scrambled with six others from Kallang Airdrome against incoming raiders.

A rough-running engine had caused him to drop out of formation at about twenty thousand feet. Whereas we never made contact, he blundered into the bombers, whipped through a torrent of tracers, and sent one machine down in flames. Turning his attention to a second, a sudden explosion perforated his left leg and filled his cockpit with oil, steam, and glycol fluid. Rolling into a dive for Kallang, he knew he was committed to landing on its pock-marked runway despite his wound and a windshield obscured by congealed engine oil. Choosing to land wheels up, he slid to a stop amid the bomb craters and subsequently explained to the duty officer and crash crew, "Sorry, boys, they got me!"

Alexandra Military Hospital was no place for a quip even though his wound caused him little discomfort. One day after his incident, the Japanese landed on Singapore Island, and he knew that he was in a tight spot. Three days later, the day of my last flight from Singapore, Stewie heard rifle and machine-gun fire just outside and determined to shoot himself when the Japanese burst in. Before he had to face that sobering event, a doctor entered the ward and invited all who were able to join him in a run for the harbor. Being the only person capable of leaving his bed, Stewie used a broomstick to steady himself and hobbled after the physician and three other men previously recruited. He told me that he would never forget "the look of utter despair" in the eyes of his bedridden ward mates as he left them.

Shortly after the party's departure, troops of the Imperial Guards Division committed one of the most savage atrocities of the war against helpless patients and hospital staff whose dress included red-cross brassards. The first soldier to enter bayoneted to death a medical officer standing at the rear doorway holding a white flag. Japanese pushed into an operating theater bayoneting the medical team standing with raised hands and killing the patient on the table. They forced medical officers and ambulatory patients from the wards, packed them into rooms without space to sit, and allowed the effects of thirst and stifling heat to take their toll over night. Periodically they removed small groups and bayoneted them to death.

The number killed reached 323 including 230 patients. The many wounded were never calculated. Forty-seven percent of the medical staff was killed along with fifty-five percent of the officers assigned to the hospital. The morning following the massacre, General Yamashita visited the hospital to apologize for the conduct of his troops and to pass out to survivors tins of peaches that he opened with the blade of a bayonet. The fruit, no doubt, came from "Mr. Churchill's supplies," since Japanese quartermasters had depended upon such booty for their entire supply of fuel and food since their battles around Kota Bharu.

Yamashita's gesture was a departure from his strict *samurai* code. A complex, religious man of integrity, he believed death was the honorable punishment for those who had failed to carry out their mission or had otherwise dishonored themselves. That belief most probably allowed him to accept stoically the sentence of an American court-martial that he should hang for atrocities against Allied prisoners of war committed by Japanese sailors during the defense of Manila. As the involved men were under naval command, this marked the first time an enemy general was tried not only for actions taken, but also for those not taken during war, and it set the pattern for all future trials of suspected war criminals.

Unaware of the fate they had escaped and surviving a bombing raid en route, Stewie's group made its way to the docks in an ambulance riddled with shrapnel holes, walked a half-mile to the 12,656-ton *Empire Star*, and squeezed aboard. In convoy with six or seven other ships, and escorted by an armed merchantman and the cruiser *HMS Danae, Empire Star* sailed with some 2,500 evacuees at first light the next morning. Still in the channel where zigzagging was impossible, she suffered three direct hits from dive-bombers which killed eighteen people and started two small fires. Later in open water, sixty-seven bombers attacked in successive waves, but the captain's skillful maneuvering saved his ship from further damage. *Empire Star* docked in Batavia, Java, where an army doctor directed Stewie to board the waiting hospital ship.

I'd last seen Micky Nash on Saint Valentine's Day when he was Duty Officer at P.1. An air of optimism had infected pilots of both squadrons that day because for once we were almost up to strength in aircraft, and everyone was primed to stop the approaching invasion fleet. But that was also the day of the Japanese parachute assault, and Micky had his hands full. After seeing that his duties were complete, he joined those evacuating to Palembang city by hitching a ride in an automobile driven by a doctor. Proceeding a bit ahead of the main convoy, they ran into a roadblock where a grenade's shrapnel punctured Micky's throat. Both men scrambled into a roadside ditch.

"I thought I was dying," he told me. "The blood in my throat made a rattling sound when I breathed. The doc must have thought so, too, for he kept reaching over and feeling my pulse." They spent an anxious two hours expecting each moment to be discovered and killed as were many others who blundered into the trap after them. A mixed bag of Dutch soldiers and RAF ratings at the head of a long column of lorries and cars cleared the road and rescued them, but still the group had to fight its way through numerous ambushes. Once in Palembang, Micky encountered a gigantic traffic snarl as vehicles jockeyed to board the single ferry that was their ticket south to temporary sanctuary. He had his wound dressed, got across the river, and tapped into the evacuation route leading to Java and a hospital ship bound for India. Unfortunately he was fated not to survive the war, as a flying accident in Burma later claimed his life.

Ever since finishing the manuscript of *Tally Ho!*, I had been thinking of what kind of writing project would hold anyone's interest. Being on shipboard offered me the opportunity to think, interview my friends, and write in my journal. I transcribed my notes into a more permanent form and read them to Stewie and to Micky to see if I had the facts straight. Both agreed that I did, and with that was born the idea of doing a book on the Singapore experience. I realized that I had participated in two pivotal operations—

the Battle of Britain and the debacle in Singapore and Sumatra—and that I had a duty to write my first-hand impressions. Not only that, but writing had become a way of life for me as something to fill time that would be otherwise wasted. Additionally, the success of *Tally Ho!* almost guaranteed that Macmillan would publish a second manuscript.

So within a few days of leaving Java, I began scribbling away in pencil, filling the pages of an old, ruled exercise book. My working title was "Last Days of Singapore," which Bob later changed to *Last Flight from Singapore*. I had been comparing Singapore's catastrophe to that which had befallen ancient Pompeii, but Bob saw the value of connecting my title with the genre of popular aviation.

Because of the heat, many of us "walking wounded" slept at night on mattresses spread on deck. One of my new friends, John Hewitt, and I spent much time getting to know each other, recounting our most recent adventures, and planning for the future. John was a naval officer who had suffered extensive wounds during the sinking of his ship. Indeed, he was the sole survivor of an action which left him with a concussion, a useless left eye, and temporary paralysis of the left arm and left leg. Yet he realized that he was "one of the lucky ones in this war!" John minced no words when talking about the Japanese. "Personally," he once said, "I hope that there won't be a live Jap after the war to sign a Peace Treaty!" His wife and two small children were living in Penang, Malaya, and he was at sea "when Tojo attacked." Fortunately she evacuated south, crossed onto Singapore Island, and eventually found passage on a ship departing for Australia. John wanted to go back to Malaya "when the Japs have been cleaned up."

I told him I was itching to get back into a cockpit and do what I had hired-on to do. I was really beginning to think about getting back to Britain, perhaps back into 91 Squadron as I had enjoyed the audacity of its reconnaissance mission. Once the Japanese momentum dissipated, I could see the Pacific and Indian Ocean theaters staying for some time in a defensive mode as the Allies stockpiled material. Europe would be the action point, the place where a pilot could settle old scores as our forces went on the offensive.

Chapter Twenty-five

Respite

Passing abeam Columbo, and emerging from the ocean's swell pattern, our ship stopped the continuous rolling which had been the most unpleasant feature of the journey, and we sailed quite placidly to Bombay. Lorries and ambulances transported us patients to the military hospital at Poona where I was housed with numerous friends including Stewie, Micky, John Hewitt, and Squadron Leader T.P.M. "Mike" Cooper-Slipper (a Battle of Britain veteran) who had seen heavy action in Singapore and was suffering from an ulcerated stomach. I spent a great deal of time stretched out on my bed finishing my manuscript.

Much was happening in the world as I lay on the sidelines. On the first of March, the day we sailed from Batavia, the Japanese had invaded Java on both its eastern and western coasts. Two days later their carrier-based bombers attacked flying boats anchored in Broome harbor,

Australia. Java surrendered on the eighteenth, the same day Rangoon fell. Japanese air elements subsequently then went wild in Burma crippling allied air power in raids on Magwe, Akyab and Mandalay. This meant that control of the Bay of Bengal and that portion of the Indian Ocean east of India and Ceylon had shifted to the Japanese. The focus of future action, however, seemed to me to be Burma and the Philippines rather than India or Ceylon, so I felt comfortable in asking for convalescence leave in the United States. My request was tentatively approved, and I wired Bob to send me a thousand dollars from the proceeds of *Tally Ho!* in the event that I would have to pay some of the air travel fare.

About this time we in the ward began to question John Hewitt and our other "expert," Royal Navy Lieutenant J. Shorten, about the possibility of an attack on Ceylon or India. They reminded us that the Japanese surface fleet, augmented by its superbly trained naval aircrews and protected in many places by land-based bombers, had complete mastery of whatever area in which it chose to operate. I began to realize that trying to get back to see the folks wasn't a good idea considering that my leg was almost healed and that experienced fighter pilots were in short supply.

Our speculation over the enemy's intentions ended Easter morning, the fifth of April, when a task force of five carriers under Vice-Admiral Nagumo launched 127 naval aircraft—fifty-three B5N torpedo bombers loaded with bombs, thirty-eight D3A dive bombers, and thirty-six A6M "Zero" fighters against Columbo, Ceylon, which lacked control and warning radar equipment. Having gained warning of the fleet's approach from a sacrificial PBY "Catalina" reconnaissance patrol the previous day, some forty-eight ships scattered from Columbo and Trincomalee on the opposite side of the island. Circumstances prevented twenty-four merchantmen and Royal Navy ships from departing Columbo immediately, so they were fated to ride out what everyone believed would be the first strike of an invasion.

Crossing Ceylon's eastern coast at about seven thirty in the morning, the leading Zeros encountered a flight of "sitting ducks"—six bi-winged Fairey "Swordfish" torpedo-bombers in-bound for landing at Ratmalana airdrome. Within minutes the Japanese had shot down all six, machine-gunned one crewman in his 'chute, and strafed others who'd crash-landed. Simultaneously twenty-one Hurricanes of Number 30 Squadron scrambled from Ratmalana, four being caught taxiing by diving D3As. Strafing Zeros swarmed all over the rising Hurricanes and the six navy Fairey Fulmars that followed them. They bagged some before their wheels had lifted into their wells.

Joining into formation proved impossible, so our boys found themselves in the most untenable of positions— mixing it with Zeros at low altitude and slow speed. Meanwhile, getting airborne from nearby Racecourse airstrip, Hurricanes of 258 Squadron—reconstituted with inexperienced pilots and a small cadre of its veterans who'd evacuated Java on *Kota Gede*—managed to form up and gain some altitude before throwing themselves upon a bunch of dive bombers. They did so knowing the top cover would not let them go unpunished.

And punished they were. Of 258's fourteen machines, the Japanese shot down nine killing five pilots including my close friend and fellow American, Don Geffene, whose aircraft dived straight into the jungle drilling itself deeply into the earth. As was often the case under such circumstances, the site was not excavated but rather smoothed over so that it became Don's final resting place. Later a white cross bearing his name, rank, and date of death was erected and a memorial service held.

As usual both sides overestimated the number of aircraft destroyed or damaged. Japanese fighter pilots claimed thirty-three of our machines along with eleven probables. Dive bomber crews claimed six more shot down. We actually lost twenty-one Hurricanes—two of which force-landed and were later repaired. Several others received battle damage. The six obsolescent Swordfish and four of the outclassed Fulmars swelled the enemy's tally to thirty-one. Our boys claimed 16 shot down, eight probables, and nine damaged in air-to-air action. Anti-aircraft crews put in for five more. Post-war Japanese records listed only three dive bombers and one Zero destroyed, along with seven dive bombers, three Zeros, and five torpedo bombers damaged.

Harbor facilities and shops suffered moderate bomb damage, an armed merchant ship and a destroyer were sunk, and a submarine depot ship and a merchantman received damage. Without doubt our beleaguered defenders had disrupted the enemy's aim, thereby preventing further loss of life, ships, and material. The marauders departed about half-past nine, heading back to their carriers lying some 120 miles off-shore and leaving only twelve Hurricanes available to protect the base from follow-on attacks.

Stung by having found the harbor almost empty of ships, Nagumo had no intention of returning to Columbo. Instead he ordered his scouts to scour the waters south of

Ceylon. In short order that morning, they found two cruisers, *HMS Dorsetshire* and *HMS Cornwall.* Attesting to Japanese bombing skill when not opposed, fifty-three D3As dived on the two ships that afternoon; and within fifteen minutes both had gone to the bottom. Thirty hours after the disaster, three Australian warships arrived to pull 1,222 men from the shark-infested water. Four hundred twenty-four men had lost their lives.

As Nagumo cruised south of Ceylon, Vice-Admiral Ozawa's "Malaya Force," consisting of a light carrier, five heavy cruisers, one light cruiser, and four destroyers roamed the Bay of Bengal wreaking havoc on Allied shipping. Between the fifth and the ninth of April, the Japanese sank twenty-three ships; Ozawa could claim most of them.

On April ninth the Trincomalee naval base on Ceylon's eastern coast felt the wrath of Nagumo's naval air power when the enemy hit shore installations, bombed ships remaining in harbor, and worked over the airstrip at China Bay. Alerted by a report transmitted from a Catalina flying boat that subsequently fell to Zeros with no survivors, the defenses awaited a radar contact. It came when the fleet had approached to within a hundred miles.

Vectored to intercept an inbound formation of ninety-one B5N torpedo bombers loaded with bombs and forty-one A6M Zeros, a dawn patrol of three Hurricanes dropped on the escort from twenty-two thousand feet. Two of the "Navy Naughts" spun into the ocean as the escort, in turn, enveloped our boys sending one of them down trailing black smoke. Fighting "in the vertical," the Hurricane leader used the last of his ammunition to blast a third Zero. As this tense and uneven dog fight progressed, twelve

Hurricanes scrambled to do what they could against the Japanese armada then expected to arrive over the harbor at about half-past seven. Having been delayed, their squadron commander—a Battle of Britain veteran—launched in the midst of the attack, was set alight by Zeros just after clearing the field's boundaries, and survived a low altitude bail-out. The untried pilots of Number 261 Squadron attacked with abandon, doing a commendable job considering the odds and the fact that their adversaries were probably the best trained, most experienced fighter pilots in the business. In the process, they lost half of their aircraft with two pilots killed and five wounded.

As at Columbo, both sides over estimated their successes. The Japanese claimed fifty-one of the sixteen defenders, whereas our boys logged eight destroyed, four probables, and four damaged. Surviving Japanese naval archives list only three Zeros and two bombers destroyed and three bombers damaged.

Despite having withheld most of his dive bombers so as to be able to react to a possible challenge by Allied naval units, Nagumo's strike did considerable damage to harbor facilities, ships, and people. Even more devastated was the air base at China Bay where hangar number two lay in ruins, buildings burned, and numerous aircraft had been transformed into molten metal. Again, however, the admiral realized that the capital ships he prized had dispersed into the open sea and only the sharp eyes aboard his scout planes could offer him the chance of gaining a significant victory.

Shortly before eight o'clock, reports of sighting a carrier and three escorting destroyers south of Ceylon caused Nagumo to unleash the dive bombers he'd held in reserve. Within the next three hours, eighty-five D3As escorted by nine Zeros launched, found *HMS Hermes* and the Australian destroyer *HMAS Vampire*, and sank them both. Minutes later the dive bombers sank a corvette, *HMS Hollyhock,* and a fleet auxiliary vessel. Eighteen bombers of the total force—those belonging to the carrier *Soryu*—arrived too late to engage *Hermes* but discovered a hospital ship and two merchantmen north of the scene. Sparing the non-combatant, they made short shrift of the others.

Over engrossed in their work, four of these bombers fell to the guns of eight navy Fulmars, the only aircraft available to answer *Hermes'* distress call. The Fulmars lost two of their number but also succeeded in damaging an additional five D5As. Fortunately no Zeros intervened, or the accomplishments of the obsolescent Fulmars would have been much less sparkling.

When I learned of this turn of events, my thoughts of course reverted back to the good times I'd had with Don Geffene aboard *Athene* and later bumming around Gibraltar, and I mused a bit about his escape from custody after he'd forced landed his Hurricane in Spanish territory. Don had wanted so badly to do his bit against the enemies of freedom. Having flown with two of the three Eagle Squadrons before his posting to 258, he was a seasoned pilot. He had also been a good and trusted friend.

I felt more than a bit nostalgic about the loss of *Hermes* also, as she had proved a faithful guardian to all of us when our convoy moved from Scotland to Gibraltar. She had been the oldest carrier still in front-line service, and she'd been caught at a disadvantage having no fighters of her own for protection and not being able to get air cover in a timely manner. Like *Repulse* and *Prince of Wales*, she'd been overwhelmed by the sheer numbers of superbly trained aircrews who conducted their attack like a text-book drill.

Hermes also had a connection with a fellow Minnesotan who happened to be one of my heroes, Charles Lindbergh! In September of 1931, just as I was beginning my training with Max Conrad, he and his young wife, Anne Morrow Lindbergh, found themselves in China after having flown from New York over the pole in their Lockheed *Sirius*—an adventure recounted by Anne in *North to the Orient.* Finding that the Yangtze had flooded some fifty million people out of their homes, Lindbergh volunteered to survey the extent of the flood and, by so doing, give officials up-to-date planning data otherwise unobtainable.

Nearing the most northern part of their project, the Lindberghs landed their float-plane next to *Hermes*, which lay at anchor on the swift-flowing river at Hankow. They accepted the offer to have *Sirius* hoisted aboard and to make *Hermes* their temporary base. An accident caused by the current as their plane was being lowered to the water on the last day of their survey damaged the craft enough to require repairs. *Hermes* provided transportation to Shanghai.

HMS Hermes deserved better. With only one surface escort and eight late-arriving Fulmars against almost a hundred enemy machines, she was a sitting duck. A courageous Fulmar pilot later wrote "*Hermes* was not on fire but seemed to be very full of holes." In fifteen minutes she began her long plunge to the bottom taking her captain, who'd been killed by the bombing, and 306 officers and men. They all deserved better.

Attempting to put a bright face on the action, British sources stressed that Nagumo's raid on Columbo and Trincomalee accomplished less than the figures suggested. *Dorsetshire* and *Cornwall* were described as "elderly," *Hermes* was the "smallest and oldest" carrier, and damage could be "fairly easily repaired." As the pipeline could be depended upon to supply increasing numbers of Hurricanes and pilots to fly them, they judged that Ceylon's air defense would quickly become adequate. They also prophesied that America's production capacity would soon deliver long range bombers and an expanded Pacific fleet that would seek out and destroy the enemy.

From my bed at Poona, however, things looked grim immediately after the Columbo raid; so I started badgering my doctors to declare me medically fit for assignment back to the cockpit. Even though I was suspicious of Ceylon's being the target of invasion since the initial assault hadn't been followed up, I still knew I'd feel better being back at the sharp end again. Marshaling my arguments, I persuaded a medical board to assign me back to flying duty on Tuesday, April seventh. The following Saturday, in light of news of the Trincomalee action, I learned that the trip to Minnesota was not possible and that I was to travel by rail to rejoin 258 Squadron at Royal Air Force Station, Ceylon. On what turned out to be a tremendously educational as well as dirty and uncomfortable journey by rail, I managed a detour to Agra to see, marvel at, and photograph the Taj Mahal. That exquisite, white marble mausoleum with its towering minarets and reflecting pool had lodged itself in my imagination since school days in St. Charles. I left it with an appreciation of beauty personified and a satisfaction gained from having accomplished another of my life's goals.

Finally reaching Ceylon on the eighteenth of April, the same day sixteen American B-25 medium bombers launched from the carrier *USS Hornet* to strike Tokyo and four other Japanese cities in the United States' first offensive air action, I walked into a tumultuous welcome at the squadron's mess. No one knew I was coming, so we had a marvelous time exchanging stories. My joy was tempered, however, by the absence of many familiar faces. Of the pilots who had left Scotland with 258 Squadron, only nine were still with the unit. Eleven of the balance were dead, missing, or presumed to be prisoners of war.

One of nine 258 Squadron pilots killed by overwhelming Japanese fighters during an Easter morning, 1942, attack on Columbo, Ceylon; Don Geffene's remains rest with his Hurricane. "Red" Campbell stands at left during a post-war memorial service.

Chapter Twenty-six

Once More Again to England

That evening a cable arrived from Bob congratulating me for being listed as the recipient of the Distinguished Flying Cross, the RAF's third-highest decoration and a tremendously wonderful surprise. He also informed me that the last letter received from me had a Sudan postmark despite my having written from Singapore, Sumatra, and Java. As far as mail from home, none had reached me since Gibraltar. Bob's cable also informed me that *Tally Ho!* was in its fifth printing and that a separate edition was being published in England. That news caused me to intensify my search for a new typewriter on which to do the final version of my hand-written "Singapore" manuscript.

In a letter home, part of which subsequently appeared in *Last Flight from Singapore,* I told the folks that I was still dithering about transferring into the air force of the United States. A number of my American colleagues were processing the necessary paperwork, and I had been offered the opportunity. I explained that the salary increase would be nice, but I didn't look forward to learning the ropes in a new service.

In a personal letter to Bob discussing mostly the financial matters of publication, I told him frankly that I'd decided to stick with the RAF for a time and not to apply for a job in Canada or the States (although I felt sure I could get one) because I believed that events in the Far East were at a critical stage, and I felt I should stay for awhile until things stabilized. I told him that I would apply for leave state-side in the fall or winter. Secretly I was beginning to line up my ducks to get a visit over Christmas. All of the dust, heat, and humidity made me yearn for a big pile of clean Minnesota snow!

On the ninth of May, we got news of the two-day air and naval engagement in the Coral Sea, the initial carrier-against-carrier battle in history and the first without an exchange of shots by surface ships. The Americans turned back a Japanese invasion force headed for Port Moresby on New Guinea's southern coast, sinking an escort carrier the first day and damaging a fleet carrier on the second. The Japanese damaged the American carriers *Yorktown* and *Lexington* (the latter so badly she had to be sunk). Most important, against eighty-one United States aircraft destroyed, the Japanese lost a hundred and five along with their irreplaceable crews. Additionally, the Battle of the Coral Sea marked the first time since hostilities began that a Japanese threat had been thwarted. It seemed that my prediction that the Rising Sun had almost reached its zenith was beginning to come true.

Early in May when nothing was happening, and it became evident that the carrier strike on Columbo had been a raid rather than the beginning of a thrust toward India, I started lobbying the RAF to post me back to England, specifically to 91 Squadron. Summarily I was informed that all of us who had congregated in India had incurred a three-year tour of duty in Southeast Asia. My reply was short and somewhat uncharacteristic. I simply told them that I would immediately transfer to the American Air Force. As if by magic, orders came through instructing me to proceed by rail to Bombay for subsequent sea transportation to England.

I truly hated to leave my associates, especially Jim Thomson who had befriended me during the Battle of Britain, recruited me for our most recent adventure, and arranged my evacuation from Sumatra. He'd been promoted Wing Commander and placed in charge of Racecourse airfield. As we stood together, each gripped by a tangible sadness as he tried to express his feelings, I slipped from my wrist the watch presented to me at the testimonial dinner back home and extended it to him.

"I can't accept this," he said pointing to the inscription which read: "Presented by the citizens of St. Charles, Minnesota."

"That's why I want you to have it," I said, "so you'll know just how I feel."

I did a lot of thinking on the train to Bombay. I realized how fortunate I was to have been able to exert my will on what for so many others was inexorable, blind fate. Rebuffed by our own Air Corps in 1939 because I'd not attended college, I had chosen to throw in my lot with the Royal Air Force, and they had granted my wish to pilot a Spitfire at the sharp end of the battle. When circumstances thrust me into the Eagle Squadron long before it would see action, I had successfully protested. Later I had chosen to accept Thomson's invitation to join 258 in a move toward overseas action. And just now I had played my ace to get back to where the war was an everyday challenge and where momentous events would soon be taking place. I was living white-hot history. What a story I'd have to tell!

Having shot another dozen or so rolls of snaps of every kind of people and every phase of life as well as landscapes, temples, and anything looking promising (totaling well over two hundred counting those taken on the journey, around the Taj Mahal, and down to Ceylon), I finally arrived in Bombay to find it no cleaner or better in any other way than before. In a long letter to Bob, I told him I'd soon be in England where I would look into publishing the Singapore story in a periodical such as *Colliers, Saturday Evening Post,* or *Life* before offering it to Macmillan for a book.

Looking in the largest bookstore in town, I bought the last of a dozen copies of *Tally Ho!* they had received from America. They were expecting copies of the British edition at any time. I was more than pleased with the job Macmillan had done and with the way Bob had added the official British communiqués that corresponded with certain points in the narrative. Otherwise the text was just as I had submitted it, unblemished by the kind of blatant editing that had ruined the *Post* article for my taste.

As quickly as I had read the book, I packed it off to John Hewitt who was still hospitalized in Poona. Unfortunately time didn't permit my visiting him, but we had swapped several letters. Meanwhile I continued to putter with the Singapore manuscript, so that it would be ready for the censor's review once I was in England.

Back at Ceylon I had asked several of my squadron mates to criticize "Last Days of Singapore," which was then about 43,000 words. They said it was "better than *Tally Ho!* by quite a ways." That was nice to hear especially as it agreed with my own appraisal. One thing that concerned me was the material at the beginning of the new book about my hush-hush activities with 91 Squadron before transferring to accompany Jim Thomson. Rather than become embroiled in controversy with the censor, I decided to finesse the whole thing by giving a page and a half of action from one patrol and then moving directly into the genesis of my association with 258 Squadron.

In Bombay I was fortunate to run into Cooper-Slipper and Stead, both newly released from hospital, and to travel with them by boat to England with a stop-over at Durban, on the east coast of South Africa on the second of July, and arrival in the British Isles in early August. The crossing was the usual wartime convoy featuring endless days of monotony, complete blackout at night, and frequent zigzagging, but it allowed me to do a great deal of work on the book.

Once in London, I spent a couple of days at the Air Ministry to get my posting settled. They allowed me seven days to take care of personal affairs, so I spent some time shopping and doing some chasing around in connection with my new book and then took a quick trip to Hawkinge to check on my old friends. I stayed over one night and went back to London the next day, but that visit caused the C.O. to ask that I be assigned to his squadron. Even though I had requested posting to 91 Squadron and was qualified beyond question, still the C.O.'s recommendation was needed to cement the deal.

On Friday of that week I had quite a big day. To begin with, I was invited, along with three other RAF boys (Americans) to have coffee with Ben Lyon and Bebe Daniels at their home, where we worked out the script for a radio interview subsequently beamed to the United States. That was in the morning, and about noon we went over to Broadcasting House and made the recordings. Afterwards we had Bebe autograph copies of our scripts. She and Ben Lyon were, I suppose, a rather unusual pair in that they were actors who actually married, made a go of it, and were still together after the end of their careers in the movies. They seemed much attached to each other, lived quietly in a nice house just outside the main part of town, and devoted their time to radio work, mainly for the forces.

In the afternoon I attended an open-house tea given for Americans by Noel Coward, the internationally famous actor and playwright. Probably twenty or more Americans, members of the RAF, US Army, and US Navy were there, but the famous man managed to circulate among all of us.

After that some of my new American friends invited me to an informal party with four London girls. Soon I found myself paired off with a pretty but aloof-appearing brunette, who looked so cold and formal that I began to regret having come. I rather expected her to ignore my attempt at small talk, but her reserve evaporated, so that in a few minutes we were in deep conversation. Before the evening was out, we were the best of pals, although I suspected it wouldn't go any further than that. She was an "extra" in one of the English film companies, of foreign parentage (Spanish and Russian), quite spoiled by having had too much money most of the time, but a lot of fun nevertheless. Her name was Odette Sese. The last name is Spanish, and the first is French because she was born in France. She answered to the name "Curly."

Next day I met Charles Collingwood, the CBS radio correspondent in London. He'd invited me to have lunch with him, as he wanted to talk about a possible broadcast. We met just before noon, and I accompanied him to the studio where he would transmit his news report to the United States. We arrived ahead of time, as the technicians tested the clarity of their contact with New York. Then they left the transmitters on until actual time for the broadcast. Collingwood talked back and forth with New York as easily as if they were phoning from the next room. Their replies came to us through a loudspeaker in the studio. We could hear the fellows in the New York office chatting back and forth, walking about, opening and shutting the door. If anything ever tended to make me homesick, that certainly did—actually to hear those things going on in America!

That evening Jim Dittus (another American in the RAF) and I took Curly and a friend of hers to the Hungaria Restaurant, which along with such other places as the Savoy, Piccadilly, Hatchets, and the Café Royal, was one of the classier places (and most expensive). This all led to the "holiday in Bournemouth."

Bournemouth, located on the channel southwest of Southampton, was probably the most famous resort in England. Curly was to spend a week there with a sister, and she invited me to come down. My leave was up in two more days, and I had been tearing around for the entire week, so I decided to take time off and relax.

At that time of year, the amusement parks and most of the beaches were closed, but the scenery was still there. The countryside was even greener than Kent and the climate more stable because it wasn't affected by the cold sea currents that come through the Strait of Dover and produce so much fog and chilly weather. Our sole diversion during the two days I was there, barring one night when we went out to dinner, was bicycling and walking around heavily wooded lanes and parks, or along the cliffs overlooking the sea, picnicking, and being thoroughly lazy. It was an even nicer and more relaxing time than I had in Ireland with Paddy the previous year, though unfortunately shorter. I really felt one-hundred percent when I got back to London.

Art's date and companion, Odette "Curly" Sese, at seashore just before he went missing in action.

Chapter Twenty-seven

Goodbye to All That

Returning to the Air Ministry on Wednesday, the nineteenth of August, I found orders reassigning me to 91 Squadron. Once again events seemed to be falling into place. Because of my rank and experience, my old friend Squadron Leader Jean Demozay named me commander of "B" flight, one of whose members was "Bud" Young, the American from Ohio whom I knew from my previous stint with the squadron. Within a week of my arrival, the C.O. appointed me acting squadron leader during his absence on temporary duty.

The job started quietly with nothing for me to do except sit in the office and try to look intelligent, but then some troubles came up, and I got busy as the dickens. Running the show cramped my style because I couldn't fly as much as I wanted, but I enjoyed exercising the commander's prerogative of choosing for himself the most desirable missions and the best machines from our stable of Spitfires.

Heavy taskings from Fighter Command during all of July and especially the last of August when the squadron labored to protect the Dieppe raid had cost it five pilots killed or missing and six Spitfires destroyed. Dieppe had been designed as an invasion rehearsal to test the Allies' ability to land on the enemy's coast and maintain the beachhead against air and naval counterattacks. Of the 6,100 Canadian, British, and American troops involved, only 2,500 returned. The others suffered death or capture.

Many tongues lashed the Prime Minister, but overall I believed the very fact that we had mounted a "miniature invasion" bucked up the spirits of most people, and I must add that it did the same for mine. I never before dreamed that we could make a landing and hold it with so small a force, especially at that place.

As my job settled into a routine with lots of paper to shuffle, I still managed to log one or two patrols in the face of high seas and lowering clouds that promised to make our life miserable for the next several days. Since I'd taken Bud under my wing when he first joined the squadron, it was natural for that relationship to continue. Bud appreciated my interest and even wrote my sister, Blanche, that I was like his "big brother." Actually I was only repaying in kind what MacDonell had done for me. We more experienced pilots had an obligation to shepherd the younger chaps who had so much to learn.

That was particularly true in a unit such as ours which carried out a demanding, repetitive, and predictable mission. Hurtling across the channel at zero feet to escape radar detection, on occasion a pilot simply "went missing"—a term that most often was monument to a flyer's momentary inattention that caused his Spitfire to

312

knife into the water and sink without leaving a trace. Such was probably the fate of Pilot Officer Tonge, who didn't return on the twenty-fifth, and Pilot Officer Demoleshes, missing two days later.

When I took over the squadron on the twenty-ninth, the thought crossed my mind that bad things often happened in threes. I resolved to increase our commitment to blind flying practice in the instrument trainer. But after eleven months of squadron service, Bud Young needed little in the way of instruction. We did the Dieppe reconnaissance together on the thirtieth in foul weather then climbed to 28,000 feet and played around until, just for fun, we bounced two unwary Spits returning fat, dumb, and happy from France. I felt completely at ease in the Spitfire's cockpit once again; and as we taxied to our dispersal pens, I realized that I was at the pinnacle of my profession. I was a veteran fighter pilot. Not only that, but I was leading one of the most distinguished squadrons in the Royal Air Force. I felt equal to the task. I could not only write about it, but I could do it. I could teach, I could lead, and, when necessary, I could kill.

On Wednesday, the ninth of September, Bud pulled what he admitted was a "prize boner," a gaffe that set in train a series of unanticipated events. Inexplicably he flew the Ostende reconnaissance (southbound track along the French coast and into the harbors) instead of its opposite number, the Dieppe track (northbound) for which he had been briefed. Realizing his mistake after landing, he refueled and returned to fly the correct route. We had a lot of fun at his expense at the mess that night, but we reigned in our mirth when the unit's radar controller informed us that he had plotted a German night fighter, most probably a modified Ju 88, stalking Bud on his southward leg.

As the next day's schedule was already laid on, we decided that on the eleventh Bud and I would launch together, and I would fly the Ostende route and attempt to entice the Hun into a trap. Bud would fly the normal Dieppe track with the assurance that, if I was unsuccessful, he would have a crack at the assassin the following day.

So that's how I found myself near Ostende with the smell of gunpowder in my nostrils, a wildly gyrating Ju 88 filling my windscreen, and the realization that my own aircraft had been damaged—perhaps critically. Fire now streamed behind my adversary's port engine; the rear machine gun pointed straight upward; and the frantic pilot struggled to control his machine.

Instinctively retarding the throttle, I banked thirty degrees right to a heading of 260 degrees which should have split the white cliffs at Dover. Even at a lower power setting, I could feel flutters of vibration deep within the engine cavity. Reacting to a slight tick of the coolant temperature needle, I opened fully the radiator flap and further eased the throttle. The stench of battle in my nostrils evaporated in the presence of a sour, astringent, unmistakable smell of engine glycol.

"May Day, May Day, May Day!" I transmitted to my controller. "Abeam Ostende. I've taken a hit up front; engine hot and running rough. Just now flamed an eighty-eight."

"We have your May Day call. Say your intentions."

Intentions? What are my intentions? I'd clarified those in a letter to Bob back when MacDonell was captured. Eight miles to France, give or take a few. Thirty or so to Dover. Two minutes and three or four years behind barbed wire versus eight minutes to a hot breakfast and clean sheets tonight. How long will she run?

My nose informed me before my eyes confirmed the answer, and my throat had begun to choke from the noxious smell that became taste as I clipped on my oxygen mask. *Serious leak. Coolant and oil temperatures pegged. She's about to seize.*

"Hello control, I'm eight miles west of Gravelines. I'll put her on the water. Too low for bale out."

Concentrating on picking up the channel's swell pattern, I squinted to make out the water, fearful of seeing nothing but the raging whitecaps I knew were there. The engine seized with a deafening thunderclap and violent wrenching of the fuselage. My gloved hands darted about the cockpit: ignition switch off, petrol off, radiator flap closed, canopy open, goggles down, maximum oxygen pressure, harness locked. *Nothing but haze. Windscreen wet. Drizzle or spray?*

Turn her into the wind, laddie. Dump flaps, trim off the pressure, gliding nicely at one-twenty, prop frozen, one blade vertical like the gun that caused this. Raise the nose, bleed airspeed back to ninety, just like Lake Winona that year it was frozen.

"Well, Art," I said aloud to break the tension, "this is what you asked for. How do you like it?"

My body yielded to the water and my soul joined the spiritual realm as had so many of my friends.

Epilogue

Bud Young suspected something was wrong when he landed and found my dispersal pen empty. After ordering his machine refueled, he called our operations center and found that I was down in the channel. Knowing the odds against a Spitfire's successful ditching, still he grabbed Pilot Officer Eddy and both took off to search for an hour and ten minutes in what amounted to a "white out" composed of haze and brilliant sunlight. Reluctantly they relinquished their duties to another pair of Spits and returned empty-handed to Hawkinge.

There Bud learned that our listening stations had monitored my victim's distress call reporting his gunner's death and fire in the aircraft's left engine. Two minutes later the pilot announced he was abandoning the aircraft. That was all intelligence needed to credit me with its destruction.

Based upon Bud's description of the quite impossible weather and the meteorologists' forecast for no change, group headquarters canceled flying for the afternoon. As they frequently did in similar circumstances,

Fighter Command transmitted my last known position to the Germans asking them to help find me.

Braving the same miserable conditions of low cloud and restricted visibility at dawn the next day, Bud went out but found nothing. Again group operations suspended flying. Fighter Command abandoned the search on the third day.

Fortunately no one sacrificed his life in a vain attempt to find me. Even in clear weather and calm seas, my chances of surviving the impact, extracting myself from the cockpit, and clambering into a dinghy were dubious. I had known the odds as I set up my ditching pattern, but one must try. Fate had decreed that the Spitfire's fabulous Merlin engine, my savior so many times before, had this day twice failed me. Its damaged coolant system put me in the water, and its massive weight instantly dragged the aircraft under. No wreckage, not even an oil slick, marked my passage.

Bob received the telegram from the British Embassy in Washington on Sunday afternoon, the thirteenth of September: "REGRET INFORM YOU . . . YOUR BROTHER FLYING OFFICER ARTHUR GERALD DONAHUE DFC . . . MISSING FROM SEPTEMBER 11TH ASSURE YOU OF SYMPATHY IN YOUR ANXIETY . . . LETTER FOLLOWS."

Since enlisting I had lived with the dread that my misfortune would put the folks through a wringer. Now my fears came to pass as my family dissolved in grief. Initially they held to the possibility that I was indeed only "missing." My brother, who knew about such things, realized after a few days that little hope existed. Determined to stay optimistic, however, he wrote me a long

318

letter on the supposition that I had been captured. He reminded me that we'd come through some narrow scrapes so far, and that we'd survive this latest setback.

Group Captain F.W. Trott mailed follow-on letters to Blanche in Robbinsdale and to Bob in Lowell the same day he transmitted the telegram. Three days later Bob read that I'd been posted missing from 6:30 on the morning of the eleventh after failing to return from an operational flight. Trott mentioned that letters from my squadron mates would arrive giving other details as they became available.

The newspapers picked up the story and reporters crowded around the farm much as they had done when I was home on leave some eighteen months previously. Mother replied to their questions by saying, "Why should we expect to be spared what millions of others have experienced?"

A letter from the squadron arrived on the second of October saying that I had signaled that I was about to "bale out" and that search planes had no success other than observing a pilot's survival dinghy floating unoccupied some twenty-five miles off the Hook of Holland. Shortly afterwards a friend's letter related that I'd just damaged a German bomber before encountering trouble myself.

Despite managing to keep up appearances, individual family members were hard hit even as they tried to shield the others. I had addressed this contingency months previously when I wrote special letters for Mom and Dad, Blanche, and Bob as *Indomitable* approached the point of our launching into the mouth of the tiger. These letters were to be forwarded to the addressees in the event of my death.

For my parents I tried to combat the feeling which I thought they had of sympathy or even pity toward me for my nomadic life as an aviator and hand-to-mouth existence before going off to war. I assured them I'd been happy and had got more out of life than anyone I knew.

For Bob I felt free to lay the cards on the table because I believed he understood my attitude better. He knew I loved the freedom of knocking about on my own, the pleasure of looking on the sunny side of things, and the capacity to ignore the inevitable financial losses and frustrations which come as part of life.

I told him I wrote to leave "a few thoughts and sentiments with you to partially fill the gap" if we would not see each other again. After giving some specific financial instructions, I asked that remaining money go toward treatments that would allow Mother to hear voices and music again. I wrote that I had enjoyed my life tremendously; and if it proved to be short, I was sure its width would compensate. "I'll have no kicks," I continued, "so please don't ever feel sorry for me; it would be a most wasted sentiment."

I wished him a long and happy life, which—by God's Grace—he's had, and closed by expressing my love "until we meet again on the other side."

My niece said many years later that, despite my entreaties, the family seemed to shut down; she said that for years no one talked about my death as if by not doing so, they could deny it.

They couldn't deny the brief letter that arrived some ten months later in which the Air Ministry "regretfully" concluded "that he has lost his life . . . ." A card from Buckingham Palace followed expressing "the Empire's gratitude for a life so nobly given . . . ." It did "bring some measure of consolation" expressed by the King—a small measure. Mary concluded that my death "wiped out the family." Some fifty years afterwards, Bob agreed that my death "destroyed" my mother and father: "they were never the same afterwards."

My most recent letters assessing my chances of getting home on Christmas leave as "probably one in four" had inadvertently compounded the family's grief. At the time of writing, I had felt so confident of making it: confident of getting home, of transferring as a major into the U. S. Army Air Corps, confident even of surviving until final victory.

In addition, everything had been working so well as far as my literary and journalistic projects were concerned. The censor had cleared my second manuscript which was on its way to Macmillan for publication, *Tally Ho!* had become a "best seller," and I was establishing contacts with well-known personages: Ben Lyon and Bebe Daniels, Charles Collingwood, and even Noel Coward. Ben and Bebe had hosted me and several other Americans on a British Broadcasting Company radio interview beamed to the United States, and Charles was planning another. Even as I stayed focused on my duties with the squadron, my peripheral vision couldn't help but see a number of fascinating post-war opportunities.

It's not that the potential for making money intrigued me. After returning from India, I had written Bob that I saw little to recommend that one have a surplus of money. Flying in general and the war in particular, had allowed me to achieve my father's ideal of traveling, of meeting all sorts of people, and of making somewhat of a name for myself.

In any case, those opportunities were closed; the war and your world went on without me. By this time the United States had allied itself solidly with the British, the white cliffs of Dover no longer marked the forward edge of the battle zone in Europe, the Rising Sun was in free fall in Southeast Asia, and final victory lay on the planning boards. My life had indeed been short, but its length was far out-weighed by its width which had been and continues to be broad and cherished.

Fourteen months after my disappearance, Squadron Leader A.W. Fagan, my old friend from 64 Squadron, posted a brief eulogy in *The London Times* marking my transition from the "missing" category to "presumed killed in action." His words were more than kind, and I recall them only because I believe they could apply to many who responded to the need as I had attempted to do. "He had joined the RAF . . . not from any wish for adventure or personal advancement, but rather in the spirit of a crusader who had no illusions about what lay before him, and had counted the cost. He had vision and he had courage in abundant measure." He went on to say, "I hope and believe that his short life among us was happy. On behalf of myself and of many others who may not now be able to do so for themselves, I wish to pay this small tribute to the memory of a good friend and a very gallant gentleman, and to offer our deep sympathy to his family and to his friends in America."

Earlier I had written home that getting the Distinguished Flying Cross presented formally would most likely take a long time. I was right, but the presentation wasn't to me at Buckingham Palace as I had assumed but to my mother at the British Embassy in Washington on Friday, the tenth of October, 1944.

By that time Russian troops had the Germans reeling back from the Ukraine, Italy had concluded an armistice with the Allies who held a significant portion of the country including Naples, and Americans had liberated Guam and Saipan from the Japanese in our "island-hopping" offensive. Against this backdrop, my father and mother journeyed to Washington.

The event, at which eight Americans were honored, received a great deal of newspaper publicity. *The New York Times,* for example, published a long article on page five. *The Washington Times-Herald,* printed an article on page eight along with a picture of Lord Halifax pinning the medal on mother's breast. *The St. Paul Pioneer Press* used a different picture of the same event to head a front-page article.

But Robert R. Mullen, a columnist for *The Christian Scientist Monitor,* best captured the spirit of the ceremony. Beginning by observing that the overall atmosphere in wartime Washington was one of gaiety, he went on to say that "things constantly occur to keep it from getting out of bounds, to put a lump in the city's throat." After setting the scene, "all is opulence in the lush but restrained tradition of his Britannic majesty," and describing the relaxed social skills that "have won Lord Halifax a place in Washington's esteem," Mr. Mullen continued:

All is jolly. Everybody smiles, a mellow glow settles over the room . . . . An RAF officer in his sky-blue uniform arranges the decorations on a table and places them one by one on a crimson pillow that he holds before Lord Halifax. The first two presentations go off very cheerfully.

Then is intoned the name of Flight Lieutenant Arthur G. Donahue, an American serving with the RAF. The solemn Oxonian voice of an Embassy assistant reads, "This officer carried out many low level reconnaissance sorties. On one occasion, while carrying out an attack against enemy troops attempting a landing . . ." And as he speaks a little white-haired woman in a crisp new light-blue dress, Mrs. Frank Donahue of Minneapolis, walks toward Lord Halifax, who gives her a prolonged supporting smile of one himself not unacquainted with grief. It is clear to all that Flight Lieutenant Donahue did not return from his sortie and that his Distinguished Flying Cross is to be accepted by his mother.

There is an indescribable tightening in the room, the lump. In the midst of a tea party, the war . . . it is with us.

If reports of the ceremony illustrated the human cost of war to readers in the United States who had been previously oblivious, then my passing accomplished more than just the destruction of a powerful raider that threatened our reconnaissance operations. If this book has shed some light upon events so long ago, if my words have caused you even momentarily to reflect on the sacrifice millions of others have made over the years for the preservation of liberty, then my death has achieved a meaning that transcends its poignancy.

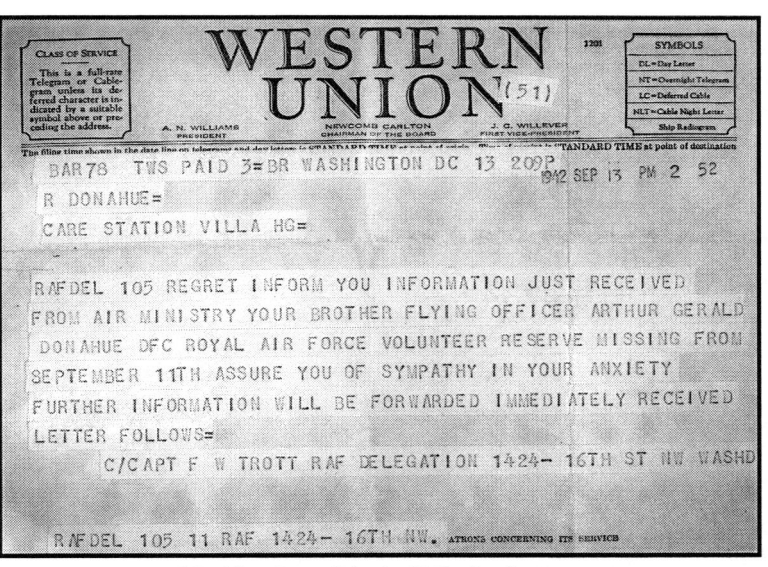

Notification of Art's "Missing" status.

R. 2017

TELEPHONE HOBART 9000

BOX 772
BENJAMIN FRANKLIN STATION
WASHINGTON, D. C.

ROYAL AIR FORCE DELEGATION

YOUR REF:

OUR REF: A.20,829/42

October 5, 1942

Mr. R. Donahue
C/o Station Villa
LOWELL, Mass.

Dear *Mr. Donahue*

    In my letter to you of September 13, I promised that
I would at once let you know when I received any further information
from Air Ministry regarding your brother, Flying Officer Arthur Gerald
Donahue, D.F.C.

    Late yesterday a signal was received from Air Ministry
which throws some light on the circumstances which surrounded their
previous report. I am only so sorry that the information received is not
more encouraging.

    Air Ministry state that on September 11 No. 91 Squadron,
of which your brother was a member, set out for a dawn patrol over the
Channel in the Ostend area.

    At 6:30 a.m. a signal was received from Flying Officer
Donahue that he was about to bale out.

    Searches were instituted but failed to trace either
the pilot or his aircraft. Late in the forenoon a dinghy was sighted 25
miles west of the Hook of Holland. Further search unhappily proved
fruitless.

    I understand that these details are being sent to Miss
Donahue in a letter from Air Ministry dated October 2, 1942.

    There is, I fear, nothing left for me to say other than
to assure you of the sympathy of all the officers at this Delegation at
this distressing time, and to invite you again to call upon us if there
is any way in which we can help you.

    Yours very sincerely

F.W. TROTT
Group Captain
Personnel Staff

JM

Condolence letter confirming Art's status of "Killed in Action."

Campaign Medals awarded posthumously by the RAF to Flight Lieutenant Arthur G. Donahue, D.F.C.

1939-45 Star, with Battle of Britain Clasp
Aircrew Europe Star
Burma Star
War Medal 1939-45

The RAF Distinguished Flying Cross was presented to Mrs. Donahue by Lord Halifax at the British Embassy in Washington on Friday, 10 October, 1944. He solemnly pinned the medal on Art's Mother's breast as she stood composed and proud.

Cover of Last Flight from Singapore, published in 1943 by the
Macmillan Company, New York.

High Flight

Oh! I have slipped the surly bonds of earth
And danced the skies on laughter-silvered wings;
Sunward I've climbed, and joined the tumbling mirth
Of sun-split clouds—and done a hundred things
You have not dreamed of—wheeled and soared and swung
High in the sunlit silence. Hov'ring there,
I've chased the shouting wind along, and flung
My eager craft through footless halls of air.
Up, up the long delirious, burning blue,
I've topped the windswept heights with easy grace
Where never lark, or even eagle flew.
And, while with silent, lifting mind I've trod
The high untrespassed sanctity of space,
Put out my hand, and touched the face of God.

Pilot Officer John Gillespie Magee, Jr.
No 412 Squadron, Royal Canadian Air Force
Killed 11 December 1941

Air Order of Battle

British Aircraft

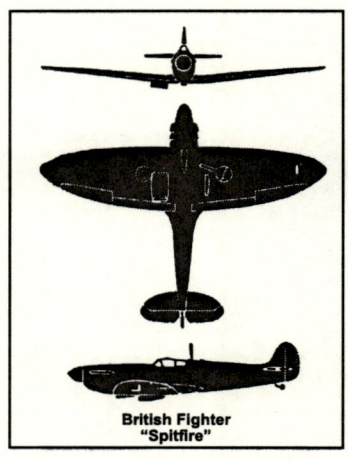

British Fighter
"Spitfire"

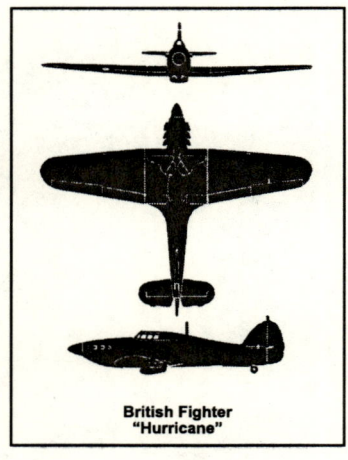

British Fighter
"Hurricane"

British Bomber
Hudson
(U.S. A-29)

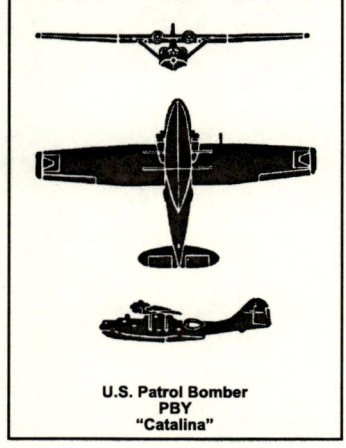

U.S. Patrol Bomber
PBY
"Catalina"

German Aircraft

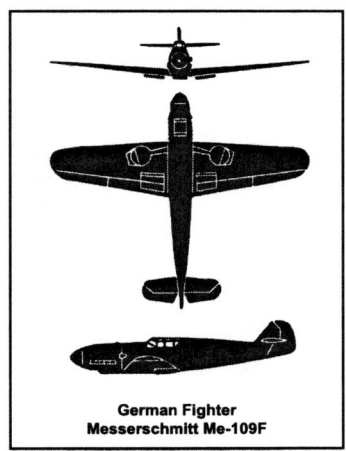

**German Fighter
Messerschmitt Me-109F**

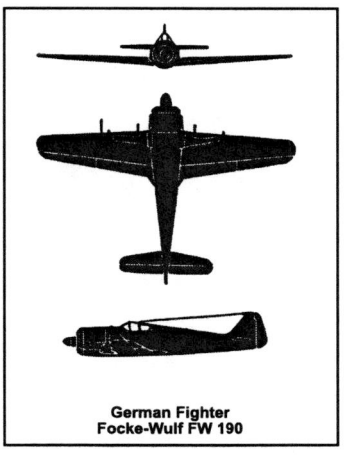

**German Fighter
Focke-Wulf FW 190**

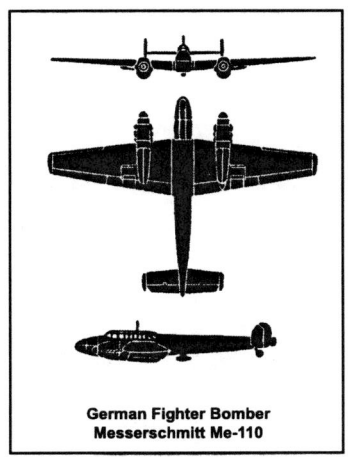

**German Fighter Bomber
Messerschmitt Me-110**

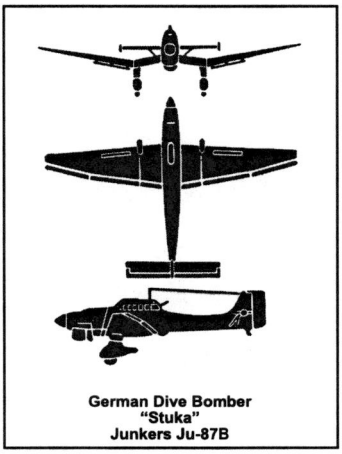

**German Dive Bomber
"Stuka"
Junkers Ju-87B**

German Aircraft *(continued)*

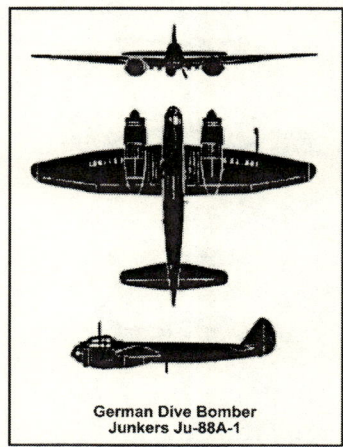

**German Dive Bomber
Junkers Ju-88A-1**

**German Bomber
Heinkel He-111K**

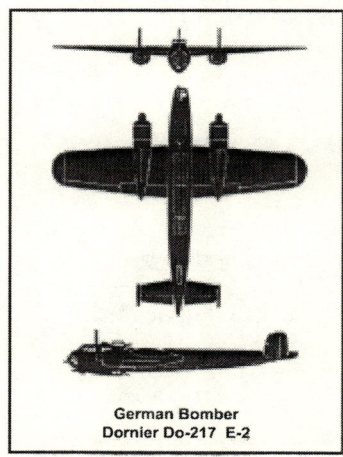

**German Bomber
Dornier Do-217 E-2**

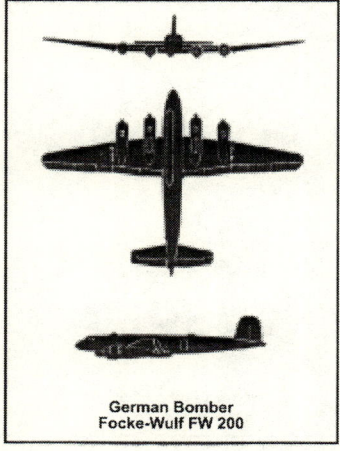

**German Bomber
Focke-Wulf FW 200**

Japanese Aircraft

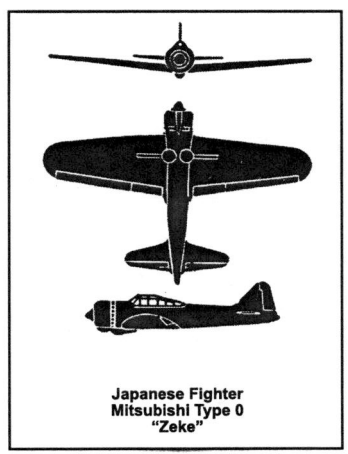

**Japanese Fighter
Mitsubishi Type 0
"Zeke"**

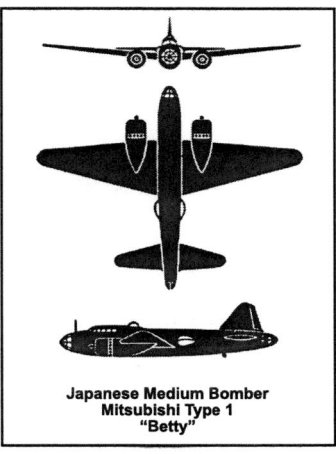

**Japanese Medium Bomber
Mitsubishi Type 1
"Betty"**

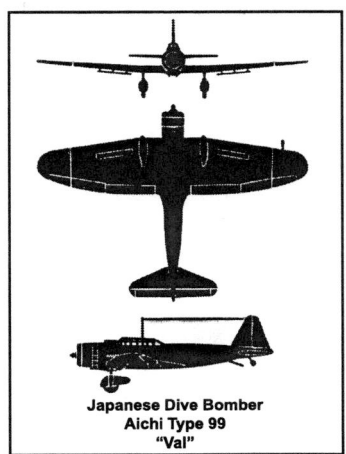

**Japanese Dive Bomber
Aichi Type 99
"Val"**

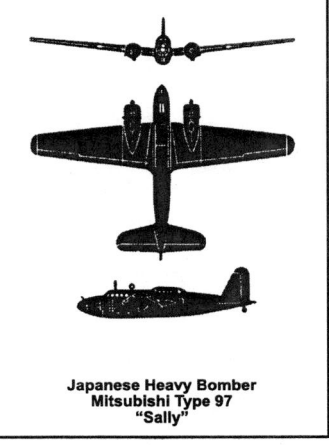

**Japanese Heavy Bomber
Mitsubishi Type 97
"Sally"**

337

Japanese Aircraft *(continued)*

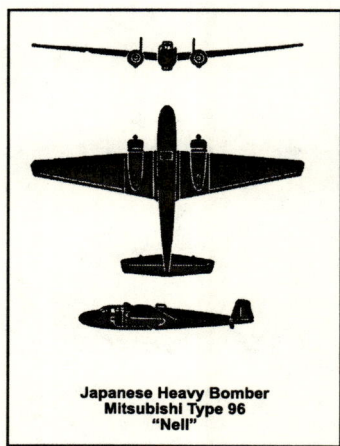

**Japanese Heavy Bomber
Mitsubishi Type 96
"Nell"**

**Japanese Flying Boat
Kawanishi Type 97
"Mavis"**

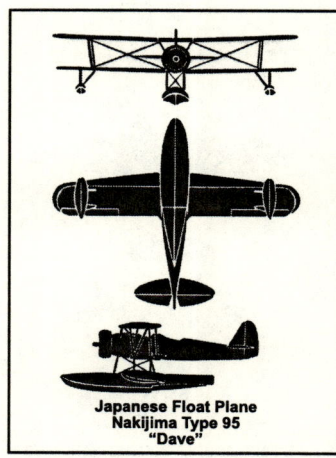

**Japanese Float Plane
Nakijima Type 95
"Dave"**

**Japanese Torpedo Bomber
Mitsubishi Type 97
"Kate"**

CPSIA information can be obtained
at www.ICGtesting.com
Printed in the USA
LVOW12*0502251117

557520LV00006B/20/P